JOHN BRAINE
and
JOHN WAIN

a reference guide

A
Reference
Publication
in
Literature

Ronald Gottesman
Editor

JOHN BRAINE
and
JOHN WAIN

a reference guide

DALE SALWAK

G.K. HALL &CO.

70 LINCOLN STREET, BOSTON, MASS.

Library of Congress Cataloging in Publication Data

Salwak, Dale.
   John Braine and John Wain.

   (A Reference guide in literature)
   Includes indexes.
   1.   English literature—20th century—Bibliography.
2.   Braine, John—Bibliography.   3.   Wain, John—
Bibliography.   I.   Title.   II.   Series: Reference guide
in literature.
Z2013.3.S24   [PR471]   823'.03   79-19290
ISBN 0-8161-8232-9

This publication is printed on permanent/durable acid-free paper
MANUFACTURED IN THE UNITED STATES OF AMERICA

for
my grandparents

Contents

Introduction

John Braine and John Wain have attracted much critical attention ever since the publication of their first novels in the 1950s. Together with Kingsley Amis, Alan Sillitoe, John Osborne, and other contemporaries, Braine and Wain ushered in a new generation of writers whose central thematic concerns and stylistic vigor altered the traditions and practices of prewar British fiction. They turned away from technical innovations, complexity, and the sensitive, introspective protagonist to concentrate on concrete problems of current society, in its cultural and social aspects. These concerns led commentators to identify the writers as "Angry Young Men"--an epithet suggesting writers of social protest or critics of man's plight in the modern world. Their works share a commonality of theme and style: a realistic portrayal of working-class or lower-middle-class life in England, a preference for provincial backgrounds, an anti-hero who directs his protests against the class structure and the Welfare State, and an unadorned use of everyday language.

Although their popularity fluctuated in the early years of their careers, both Braine and Wain are recognized as important voices in the contemporary literary world. Academic essays and journal reviews of their works appear regularly, and a substantial body of criticism now exists. The approach to the work of these writers has varied according to the critical focus of the reviewer. For instance, some reviewers present surveys. Many emphasize the writer's craft in an attempt to see the whole of each work, while others set forth conclusions which try to draw together the various threads running throughout their writings. Therefore, this reference guide should be most useful to the student or scholar who desires to see how two literary careers developed and were received by the scholar-critic and the contemporary reviewer.

John Braine's reputation is that of a serious, tough-minded novelist writing from an Irish Catholic, lower-middle-class background. His experiences in urban, industrialized Bradford and in the rural areas of West Riding also figure prominently in his novels. Often in their reviews, critics identify some of the major themes in Braine's work, including the following: (1) the sacrifice of integrity as a price of success in society; (2) the emptiness of life at the top of

one's career; (3) the problem of religious commitment and its inher-
ent conflicts; and (4) the disagreements between people in marriage
and friendship. Braine's often vitriolic criticism of English society and the frequently harsh reality of his style have had a marked
influence on contemporary British fiction.

This influence began in 1957 when Room at the Top, his first
novel, became an instant success and gave him international recognition. Praised for its vitality, humor, honesty, and realism and
criticized for its sentimentality and weak construction, it represented the paradoxical reception generated by the works of "the Angry
Young Men." This reception was perhaps most sensitively documented
by G. S. Fraser in "Many Worlds" (1957.B9), by J. D. Scott in "Britain's Angry Young Men" (1957.B18), by Hilary Corke in "Getting to the
Bottom of the Top" (1962.B14), and by J. W. Lee, whose John Braine
remains the only booklength study devoted exclusively to Braine
(1967.A1). On the basis of Room at the Top, these critics and others
considered Braine to be one of the most promising of the postwar novelists. Had his book appeared before Lucky Jim and Look Back in
Anger, Braine's name might well be better known today than those of
Kingsley Amis and John Osborne (1957.B20).

However, there were critics who were less enthusiastic about the
works and the promise of this new writer, and they surfaced to review
his next two novels. Neither his sequel, Life at the Top (1962), nor
the intervening novel, The Vodi (1959, published as From the Hand of
the Hunter, 1960) enjoyed the popularity and prestige of Room at the
Top. In considering the former, for instance, both A. Alvarez
(1962.B2) and Mordecai Richler (1962.B34) felt that Braine was
merely capitalizing on the success of his first novel. As for the
latter, John Coleman (1959.B6) and Arthur Mizener (1960.B10) were
among those critics who felt that Braine's skillful storytelling and
compassionate insights into human suffering failed to compensate for
such technical defects as disparity of tone, obscure details, uneven
pace, and lack of climactic power. Ultimately, the book succeeded
"not where it [tried] to be new but where it [did again] what was
well done in Room at the Top" (1959.B2).

Admirers of Braine were relieved to find that his succeeding novels were not imitations of anything he had written before. For example, Bernard Bergonzi (1965.B7), Peter Buitenhuis (1965.B9), and
J. W. Lee (1967.A1) viewed The Jealous God (1965) as an important
turning point in Braine's career. His control of characters, refined style, exploration of serious themes, and command of point of
view and focus dispelled fears that he was a one-novel writer. The
Crying Game (1968), on the other hand, was praised as an exposé of
the decadent urban life but criticized for weak conflicts and insufficient distance between author and hero. On this disappointing
novel with virtually no story, Anthony Burgess commented, "the hedo-
nism is too often self-conscious, . . . and the narrative style gives
off the stale apple smell of old popular magazines" (1968.B4).

Furthermore, Ray Gosling (1968.B7), David Haworth (1968.B9), and
Katherine Gauss Jackson (1968.B11) found it to be hastily written and
unpleasant in its characterization.

Since then, Braine has written four more novels, all of which
have met with varying critical success. As an analysis of marital
discord, Stay with Me Till Morning (1970, published as The View from
Tower Hill, 1971) was deemed repetitious and ambiguous. Was it a
morality tale? A documentary? An indictment? These questions per-
plexed Christopher Derrick (1969.B7), Frederick P. W. McDowell
(1969.B13), and Felicia Lamport (1971.B7). Equally perplexing was
The Queen of a Distant Country (1972). Both Auberon Waugh in "Celebrating the Bourgeois" (1972.B9) and Ronald deFeo in "Voice from a
Distant Country" (1973.B7) found the conversations about writers and
the writer's world to be authentic, while other commentators felt
that this was an extremely pompous and self-indulgent book about
Braine himself. His next novel, The Pious Agent (1975), was judged
to be a routinely competent caricature of a spy story with few surprises. Budd Arthur (1976.B3) and Judson LaHaye (1976.B7), among
others, felt that it was saved only by Braine's characterization and
smooth, sophisticated writing style. Most recently, Waiting for
Sheila (1976) was seen as a working model for Braine's own novelistic
methods. Ferdinand Mount in "The Durable Consumer" (1976.B8) praised
the plotting, characterization, and celebration of sex as being of
"sound quality," but wished that Braine would allow himself to be
carried away in a longer, in-depth study of decadent London.

If he has never been short of detractors, Braine has had his de-
fenders, too. Over the past twenty-three years his reputation has
grown as a middlebrow writer who pays steady attention to the basics
of writing. Few writers today have a firmer sense of milieu. His
ear for dialogue is accurate, and his grasp of narrative technique is
impressive. Readers interested in an overview of Braine's development as a novelist should consult Frederick R. Karl's "The Angries:
Is There a Protestant in the House?" (1962.B22), Anthony Burgess' "A
Sort of Rebels" (1967.B3), J. W. Lee's John Braine (1967.A1), and
Claude Alayrac's "Inside John Braine's Outsider" (1971.B1). As far
back as 1967, one writer suggested that with his talent, his tolerance of human foibles, and his total commitment to writing, Braine
might well become a major figure in modern English fiction (1967.A1).
"His chief danger is a certain over-facility, which, at times, de-
generates into the slickness of a strip-cartoon; at his best, however, he is an honest and intelligent observer of the social scene"
(1959.B2).

The second subject of this reference guide is John Wain. Whereas
Braine is viewed as a tough-minded realist, Wain is considered a
scholarly and poignant observer of the human scene. Totally dedi-
cated to the writer's craft, with an unfailingly serious attitude to
literature, his is, as one reviewer remarked, a "painfully honest"
personality (1965.B21). Because of this honesty, some critics

consider him to be one of the most interesting and gifted of contemporary authors on the English scene. Unlike Braine, however, he did
not become widely known outside England until 1975 when his biography
of Samuel Johnson became a bestseller. By then, Wain had distinguished himself not only as a novelist, but also as a poet, editor,
essayist, reviewer, biographer, and lecturer--indeed, as a modern
man of letters.

As a scholar-writer, Wain has the seriocomic touch. His fic-
tional themes of the dignity of the human being, the difficulty of
survival in the modern world, and the perils of success have estab-
lished him as a moralist principally concerned with ethical issues.
In this context, Wain's developing moral vision was traced carefully
by James Gindin in "The Moral Center of John Wain's Fiction"
(1962.B10) and by Elgin W. Mellown in "Steps Toward Vision: The
Development of Technique in John Wain's First Seven Novels"
(1969.B7). Moreover, Wain has been moderately successful in blending
comedy with seriousness, farce with realism. Hurry on Down (1953,
published as Born in Captivity, 1954), for example, captured the mood
of the 1950s but failed to attract the attention given to Room at the
Top or Lucky Jim. The English reviews were mixed; a few were hos-
tile, and it took several years for it to sell ten thousand copies.
The vast number of early reviews are represented by key essays such
as those of Walter Allen (1953.B1), R. D. Charques (1953.B3), Edmund
Fuller (1954.B7), and Dan Wickendon (1954.B13). To Anthony Burgess,
Hurry on Down was an ill-constructed novel written in an "indifferent
style." He recommended that Wain give up writing novels and con-
tinue producing short stories, in which he demonstrated a more consistent control (1967.B8).

Wain's next several novels did little to advance his reputation.
Living in the Present (1955) was neither an artistic nor a financial
success; The Contenders (1958) was recognized as a technical and
thematic advance over his earlier work but was criticized for its
ambiguous moral center; and A Traveling Woman (1959), The Young Visitors (1965), and The Smaller Sky (1967) were felt to be inconclusive.
Some commentators pointed out that too often the subjects in these
novels were not big enough for the extended treatment; others felt
that perhaps Wain's actual understanding of his subjects is inadequate. This phase of Wain's career was reliably assessed by William
Van O'Connor in "John Wain: The Will to Write" (1960.B11), by Rayner
Heppenstall in "They Like It Here" (1961.B15), by P. Yvard in "Literature and Society in the Fifties in Great Britain" (1973.B20), and
by James Gindin in "John Wain" (1972.B14).

In 1970, however, Wain replaced his earlier extravagances of
humor and ambiguous intentions with philosophical depth--in a novel
entitled A Winter in the Hills. Some writers noted that this novel
went farther in defining and developing Wain's basic concerns as a
writer than did most of his earlier works. The value of tradition,
the notion of human understanding, the ability to love and suffer are

the chief moral values which critics found in this novel. "Observing social situations, catching hints of character and motive in conversational habits, contriving elaborate and efficient plots"--these are Wain's strengths as a novelist (1970.B5).

As prolific as he has been, however, Wain's abilities as a novelist have been overshadowed by his success as a literary critic and poet. Both Preliminary Essays (1957) and Essays on Literature and Ideas (1963) were noted for their clarity of expression, wit, and profusion of ideas. The later publication of Samuel Johnson (1974) made him an international celebrity. For it, he received the James Tait' Black Memorial Book Prize and the Whitbread Award. It was a featured selection of the Book-of-the-Month Club, and both Donald Greene (1974.B14) and Angus Wilson (1974.B30) praised it highly. Samuel Johnson is fully discussed by Martin Green in "Biography and Culture" (1975.B29), by John W. Morris in "John Wain's Samuel Johnson" (1975.B36), and by Christopher Ricks in "John Wain's Life of Samuel Johnson" (1975.B46). These critics discovered that the biography was both an account of Johnson--his life, times, and works--and an implicit statement of Wain's own views on the state of twentieth-century England. It became clear to them that Wain sees the eighteenth-century provincial life as a time of dignity, pride, and self-sufficiency lacking in the twentieth century. Like Johnson, Wain defends the value of reason, moderation, common sense, moral courage, and intellectual self-respect.

Furthermore, in his verse Wain offers moral statements consistent with the views set forth in his fiction and essays. Upon publication of Mixed Feelings (1951), Wain was identified as a "member" of the poetic "Movement" of the 1950s. Philip Larkin (1964.B15), John Press (1969.B8), and Ian Hamilton (1971.B8) explained that this new generation of poets--including Kingsley Amis, Robert Conquest, and Philip Larkin--preferred the tight, if sometimes elaborate, forms of William Empson to the lax rhythms and indulgent rhetoric of much of the 1940s poetry. Wain's early verse is typically casual in approach. It is technically traditional, literate, witty, and candid. Some reviewers found the verse patterns rigid, as if a formula had taken the place of inspiration. However, with each succeeding volume, critics perceived an advance in Wain's range and technique without a sacrifice in honesty. Weep Before God (1961), for example, was looser, more declamatory than his earlier verse. The Shape of Feng (1972), on the other hand, displayed stylistic variety and was taken as evidence that Wain was one of the leading poets of contemporary England (in 1973 he had been elected Professor of Poetry at Oxford). Moreover, he has developed powerfully in the direction of politics and social commentary. Lawrence R. Ries offered an interesting examination of Wain's role as a spokesman for the neohumanistic position (1977.B7), while other critics found that under the influence of D. H. Lawrence, Wain widened his scope and made his form freer.

In retrospect, both as a literary critic and as a poet, though rather less as a novelist, Wain's development since 1953 has been remarkable. His continuing impact on the literary scene is attested to by extensive publications of both hardcover re-editions and original works. Although he continues to show much promise as a writer, many scholars feel he has fallen short of expectations. Those who dislike his work find him to be repetitious, hasty, and sentimental; whereas those who praise him, do so for his elaborate plotting, sincerity, and wit. Some commentators conclude that Wain takes his critical writings too seriously and his novel writing not seriously enough. In spite of this judgment, his principal strength continues to be his engagement with serious, important ideas. In all three genres his vigor and his sincerity mark him as a member of the distinguished company of scholar-artists.

Although no bibliography of this kind is ever complete, every attempt has been made to make as comprehensive a listing of the criticism as possible. The annotations are descriptive, not evaluative. In the abstracts of interviews, bibliographies, and biographical notes, I have emphasized scope except in the case of very brief items. Thus, it is hoped that this reference guide will provide the interested scholar with a useful research tool and that continued interest in Braine and Wain will lead to additional studies of their works, their impact on the literary scene, and finally their significance as artists who hold "the mirror up to nature" and reveal to us "the very age and body of the time."

This reference guide is divided into two sections, one on each writer. Arrangement is by date of publication of writings. Each year is divided into two sections. The first section, "A", lists full-length books and dissertations devoted exclusively to the respective writer. The second section, "B", lists all articles and reviews as well as books only partially devoted to the author. Names of periodicals and newspapers are given as they appear on the title page of the issues in which the articles appeared. The works cited for any given year are listed alphabetically in the "A" or "B" section. An article cited as "1975.B3" would be the third article in the "B" section for 1975. This code is employed within the text to refer to reprints and scholarly replies; it is also used in the index at the back of the guide. The index is inclusive, with authors, titles, and subjects interfiled.

This project could not have hoped for success without the cooperation and interest of those who aided me. I am particularly indebted to Professor L. David Sundstrand at Citrus College, Professor Ronald Gottesman at the University of Southern California, and my mother, Frances H. Salwak, for their detailed corrections and suggestions; and to Cheryl and Garth Epler, who performed the tedious task of compiling both indexes. I should also like to thank Dorothy Warriner and Lois Bond of the Hayden Memorial Library at Citrus College for their help in locating and obtaining material through interlibrary loan.

JOHN BRAINE

Writings by John Braine
1951-1976

The Desert in the Mirror (1951)

Room at the Top (1957)

The Vodi (1959; as From the Hand of the Hunter, 1960)

Life at the Top (1962)

The Jealous God (1965)

The Crying Game (1968)

Man at the Top (1970, 1972)

Stay with Me Till Morning (1970; as The View from Tower Hill, 1971)

The Queen of a Distant Country (1972)

Writing a Novel (1974)

The Pious Agent (1975)

Waiting for Sheila (1976)

Writings about John Braine
1957-1977

1957 A BOOKS - NONE

1957 B SHORTER WRITINGS

1   ANON. "New Fiction." London <u>Times</u> (14 March), p. 13.
        Review of <u>Room at the Top</u>. In this "able and striking"
first novel, Lampton is "an amoral sensualist with a con-
veniently adjustable idealistic streak in him." Praises
the north country humors (realistic), Lampton's emotional
encounters (faithfully observed), and the characters and
dialogue (authentic northern tang), but finds the construction to be weak.

2   ANON. "Uphill Fight." <u>Times Literary Supplement</u> (5 April),
      p. 205.
        Review of <u>Room at the Top</u>. A novel of "bounding vitali-
ty and talent." Braine's observations are acute and exact.

3   ANON. "Lucky Jim and His Pals." <u>Time</u>, 69 (27 May), 106.
        Review of <u>Room at the Top</u>. Lampton is an intellectual
ruthlessly making his luck. Discusses the Angry Young Men
with emphasis given to Amis, Osborne, and Braine.

4   ANON. "Fiction." <u>Kirkus Reviews</u>, 25 (15 August), 598.
        Review of <u>Room at the Top</u>. A serious novel of the
"'beat generation.'" Those who enjoy Amis will like this
novel because both novelists write for the same audience.

5   ANON. "Fiction." <u>Booklist</u>, 54 (1 December), 199.
        Review of <u>Room at the Top</u>. A realistic portrayal of
class-consciousness in England today, written for sophisticated readers.

1957

6   BALLIETT, WHITNEY. "Books: The Successful Zombie and the
    Grade Two Girl." New Yorker, 33 (2 November), 186.
        Review of Room at the Top. Lampton fits into the tradi-
    tion of the great English social novels in this "brilliant-
    ly sustained tragicomedy." He appeals to the reader in the
    way that Holden Caufield did in The Catcher in the Rye; his
    affair with Abigail is handled "with delicate and touching
    realism." Like Forster and unlike Dickens, Braine avoids
    sentimentality and regards his generation with "a buoyant
    detachment." Also praises the dominant tone ("a loping
    nuttiness"), the background of major figures (carefully
    filled in), and the last chapter ("a masterpiece of night-
    marish horror").

7   DEASY, PHILIP. "A Man Whom Nobody Blamed." Commonweal, 67
    (27 December), 340.
        Review of Room at the Top. Lampton, who "whines, moans,
    purrs," is hardly an heroic figure. He is almost totally
    devoid of potential for growth; he lacks any inner life or
    spiritual stature; he is cheap and childish, motivated by
    "calculated self-interest"; and he is "the perfect antith-
    esis of the committed, the engaged, the Outsider." How-
    ever, moments of honesty save him from coming across as
    wholly despicable. When he agonizes over Alice's suicide,
    for example, the reader sees his latent decency in what is
    "the most vivid and intensely moving" section of the novel.
    Perhaps Lampton's ultimate value will be as "another socio-
    logical case history of postwar welfare statism." Although
    Braine has the creative power, he requires something to
    write about "commensurate with his gifts."

8   DORN, N. K. Review of Room at the Top. San Francisco Chron-
    icle (27 October), p. 36.
        Brief mention with plot summary.

9   FRASER, G. S. "Many Worlds." New Statesman and Nation, 53
    (16 March), 358.
        Review of Room at the Top. A striking first novel which
    gets "very vigorously into the thick of life." Lampton has
    something of "the ruthlessness, the awkwardness, and the
    shocking youthful vulnerability of Julien Sorel." Con-
    cludes that the slick writing may reflect both Lampton's
    and Braine's values.

10   GORER, GEOFFREY. "The Perils of Hypergamy." <u>New Statesman</u>
     <u>and Nation</u>, 53 (4 May), 566-67.
         Review of <u>Room at the Top</u>. Braine's novel confirms what
     has long been suspected ever since the appearance of <u>Lucky</u>
     <u>Jim</u> and <u>Look Back in Anger</u>--that men of working-class ori-
     gin are being ruined by "male hypergamy." That these
     cross-class unions do not succeed is shown with "humor and
     anger and passion and sentimentality."

11   GRAY, JAMES. "Young Arriviste." <u>Saturday Review</u>, 40
     (19 October), 20.
         Review of <u>Room at the Top</u>. Almost anything can be made
     of Braine's material, from a study of greed and missed love
     (as in Flaubert's <u>Madame Bovary</u>) to comedy (as in Bennett's
     <u>Denry, the Audacious</u>) to spitefulness (as in O'Hara's <u>Pal</u>
     <u>Joey</u>). But Braine offers little that is new to the game of
     seduction, human relations, or human society. Hardly an
     angry writer, he lacks both a "maturity of insight and the
     flair for style." The story is told in "the idiom of the
     little theatre rehearsal room." Considers it a mistake to
     have written the novel from the first-person point of view.
     Concludes that Braine may have tried to write a novel too
     soon. The final pages, for example, have a kind of "woeful
     authenticity" and could stand alone as a short story.

12   HARRINGTON, ALAN. "A Question of Price." <u>Nation</u>, 185
     (7 December), 438.
         Review of <u>Room at the Top</u>. Braine is a powerful and
     honest writer. Lampton is a memorable young man whose
     goals are somewhat reminiscent of Clyde's in <u>An American</u>
     <u>Tragedy</u>. Hardly an angry book, Braine's novel is "a novel
     of recognition--that the cramping system of class distinc-
     tion in England has had it, and can, will and must be
     beaten by such as Joe Lampton." It is also a sardonic and
     sad novel in which the author regrets that a man "should be
     forced to such extremes of maneuvering in order to rise out
     of his class."

13   JOHNSON, VERNON. "New Fiction." <u>Manchester Guardian</u>
     (19 March), p. 4.
         Brief mention of <u>Room at the Top</u>.

14   PRITCHETT, V. S. "These Writers Couldn't Care Less." <u>New</u>
     <u>York Times Book Review</u> (28 April), pp. 1, 38-39.
         General discussion of Braine, Amis, Wain, Thomas Hinde,
     and Peter Towry as Angry Young Men.

1957

15 QUINTON, ANTHONY. "The Post-Freudian Hero." London Magazine,
      4 (July), 59–60.
          Review of Room at the Top. A timely novel, which ac-
      counts for its success. As a 1957 version of This Side of
      Paradise, it is a "romantic and sentimental work, a richly
      unrealistic epic of social mobility, full of the most ex-
      traordinary assumptions about life and human motives but
      carried along by the vigour, freshness and enthusiasms with
      which it is written."

16 ROLO, CHARLES. "Reader's Choice: Upstart and Downstart."
      Atlantic Monthly, 200 (November), 247–49.
          Review of Room at the Top. Compared to Amis, Wain, and
      others, Braine is unique because he is the first writer to
      deal with the price paid for opportunism. "Braine has
      gifts which could carry him far--humor and vitality, an
      unsmutty forthrightness in the handling of erotic love, and
      a capacity to project with passionate sharpness the hungers
      of youth."

17 RUGOFF, MILTON. "Yorkshire Man on the Way Up." New York
      Herald Tribune Book Review (13 October), p. 8.
          Review of Room at the Top. Readers are attracted by
      Braine's "penetrating and sometimes cynical presentation
      of life on the middle and upper levels of Yorkshire so-
      ciety." Finds appealing Lampton's hunger for women.
      Braine's scenes are handled with "economy and a fine sense
      of the dramatic," but his greatest achievement is "the
      genuinely feral quality" that marks Lampton. However, the
      deus ex machina resolution evades the issue of whether
      class distinctions would have defeated Lampton. Also, the
      dialogue occasionally "strains to be smart."

18 SCOTT, J. D. "Britain's Angry Young Men." Saturday Review,
      40 (27 July), 10.
          Lampton's story in Room at the Top differs from that of
      other Angry Young Men. He doesn't come from a provincial
      university, but is a qualified accountant on the edge of a
      middle-class milieu. Hence, Lampton uses culture--as well
      as his sexual attractiveness--to get ahead. The life he
      yearns for bears some "dim provincial relationship to the
      Somerset Maugham life." To many readers, Lampton seems to
      represent "the angry young man turned conformist, and this
      has brought something like a sigh of relief and floods of
      praise for Mr. Braine."

19   SNOW, C. P. "The English Realistic Novel, 1957." Moderna
        Språk, 51 (Spring), 265-70.
            Braine, Wain, Amis and others represent not merely a
        change of direction in writing realistic novels, but a re-
        newed interest in the "individual condition" as well as
        "the social condition."

20   STERN, JAMES. "Out for All He Could Get." New York Times
        Book Review (13 October), pp. 5, 36.
            Review of Room at the Top. This is a first novel of
        "quite exceptional power and maturity," greeted with praise
        by every reputable critic in England and weakened only by
        too many misprints. Lampton is not an Angry Young Man.
        Rather, he is an opportunist, driven by envy, and a thor-
        oughly sympathetic human being who never commits an offense
        against good taste. The love scene between Lampton and
        Alice is "one of the most moving episodes of its kind in
        modern fiction." Their "hate" scene two chapters later is
        brilliant in "its illumination of character and the stand-
        ards of class." Concludes that the novel's strengths are
        humor, wisdom, shrewdness, narrative point of view, eye for
        significant detail, and economical and unaffected prose.

21   WATERMAN, ROLLENE. "A Gallery of Lucky Jims." Saturday Re-
        view, 40 (27 July), 9.
            Brief biographical mention. Unlike Wain's Charles
        Lumley (in Hurry on Down), Braine's hero--Lampton--knows
        exactly where he is going. Like Wain, Braine is quite
        angry.

1958 A BOOKS - NONE

1958 B SHORTER WRITINGS

1   ALLSOP, KENNETH. "The Neutralists," in his The Angry Decade:
        A Survey of the Cultural Revolt of the Nineteen-Fifties.
        London: Peter Owen, pp. 78-85.
            Examines the origins of the Angry Young Men's social and
        intellectual attitudes and the reception of their books.
        Focuses on Room at the Top.

2   ANON. "Look Back in Anger." London Times (28 June), p. 10.
            News release that Room at the Top will be adapted to
        the screen. The filming will take place at Bradford and
        the Shepperton Studios. The movie, adapted by Neil Peter-
        son and directed by Jack Clayton, will be true to the
        novel.

1958

3   BAILHACHE, JEAN. "Angry Young Men." <u>Les Langues Modernes</u>, 52 (March–April), 31–46.
        A study of Braine, Amis, Wain, and Osborne. Questions whether their success and anger will last. Concludes that the writers will be remembered for their new hero--the anti-snob rebel.

4   BRINNIN, JOHN MALCOLM. "Young But Not Angry." <u>Mademoiselle</u>, 46 (April), 151.
        Brief mention of "the private anarchies and small laughter" of the heroes of Braine, Wain, and Amis. For these writers, the Angry Young Man designation may to some degree accommodate their views.

5   COOPER, LETTICE. "The New Novelists: An Enquiry." <u>London Magazine</u>, 5 (November), 18.
        In <u>Room at the Top</u>, Braine turns to "straightforward story telling that keeps the reader guessing up to the end."

6   COUGHLAND, ROBERT. "Why Britain's Angry Young Men Boil over: Most Talked about Writers of To-Day Reflect Frustration of Declining England." <u>Life</u>, 44 (26 May), 141.
        Brief mention with biographical details of the Angry Young Men phenomenon. Notes that Braine still lives in "the grimy, unutterably depressing Yorkshire industrial town of Bradford."

7   ESTY, WILLIAM. "The Old in Heart." <u>Nation</u>, 186 (26 April), 373–76.
        The Angry Young Men are less effective than the myth of youth created by Huxley and Waugh. They are not angry, but confused, and this "confusion makes for poor novels."

8   GINDIN, JAMES. "The Reassertion of the Personal." <u>Texas Quarterly</u>, 4 (Fall), 133.
        Review of <u>Room at the Top</u>. This work is an example of how much "flavor and force" a contemporary British novel loses when it is not comic. Told in "deadly earnest," the story is about a hero quite different from "the sensitive, aware, often silly, always self-conscious heroes of Amis, Wain, Wilson, and the others."

9   HARKNESS, BRUCE. "The Lucky Crowd--Contemporary British Fiction." <u>English Journal</u>, 47 (October), 395–96.
        All of the Angry Young Men novels, including <u>Room at the Top</u>, suffer from three defects. These are: (1) adaptation of old themes; (2) improbable solutions to the plot, and

(3) "a dangerous tendency toward letting the hero's spon-
taneity fall into a pose."

10   HARVEY, W. T. "Have You Anything to Declare? or, Angry Young
      Men: Facts and Fiction," in International Literary Annual,
      No. 1. Edited by John Wain. London: John Calder, p. 53.
           Disagrees with Doris Lessing when she compares Room at
      the Top to Stendhal's novels to illustrate that British
      literature is provincial (see Lessing, 1958.B14). Rather,
      one should say that Room at the Top is "a skilful but es-
      sentially synthetic piece of work with the right doses of
      sex and violence injected into the story at the appropriate
      points; put thus, the moral limitations of the work have
      nothing at all to do with the issue of provincialism."

11   HILTON, FRANK. "Britain's New Class." Encounter, 10
      (February), 62-63.
           The fictional characters in the early writings of
      Braine, Amis, and Osborne are examples of "the declassed
      intelligent underdog." Sees Lampton as the "nastiest" of
      the heroes. Because he is from a provincial town--instead
      of a metropolis--Lampton typically is unable to forget his
      power and inferiority. Because of his sensitivity, he uses
      force and guile to do something about his low status.
      Whereas Dixon (in Lucky Jim) allows circumstances to impose
      situations upon him, Lampton makes things happen by being
      ruthless and violent. But Lampton's behavior is an
      anachronism. His situation is not unlike that of Rastignac
      one hundred years ago. Apparently there are thousands of
      working class young Britons who promise themselves a better
      life someday.

12   HUGHES, RILEY. "Books." Catholic World, 186 (January),
      310-11.
           Review of Room at the Top. Lampton fits into the "Lucky
      Jim" character type, a fresh phenomenon in English novels.
      This type is "the snarling young man on the make who breaks
      through the class barrier." Says Lampton's love affair is
      "clinically described."

13   HURRELL, JOHN D. "Class and Conscience in John Braine and
      Kingsley Amis." Critique, 2 (Spring-Summer), 40-42.
           Finds similarities between the heroes of Wain, Braine,
      Amis, and Osborne. Says Lampton's climb to social success
      results in a loss of moral and emotional integrity--a fa-
      miliar tragic pattern in modern fiction. Braine implies
      that Lampton typifies many in present-day England. Unlike
      Osborne's characters, who scream against a class barrier

still unbroken, Braine's hero crashes the barrier but suffers wounds that may be spiritually fatal. "Osborne re-
gards his characters with pity, Braine with a deeper
compassion." Concludes that the "desire to compromise, to
lower moral or intellectual standards in a search for social or professional success, continually forces a crisis
of conscience on the young man." Amis treats this crisis
comically, Braine tragically.

14   LESSING, DORIS. "The Small Personal Voice," in Declaration.
     Edited by Tom Maschler. New York: E. P. Dutton, p. 197.
         Compares Room at the Top to Stendhal's writings to il-
     lustrate her definition of provincial literature; that is,
     the writers' "horizons are banded by their immediate expe-
     rience of British life and standards." Unlike Stendhal's
     heroes, Lampton "does not see himself in relation to any
     larger vision. Therefore, he remains petty." Replied to
     in 1958.B10.

15   MACKWORTH, CECILY. "Le Roman anglais d'aujourd'hui."
     Critique: Studies in Modern Fiction, 14 (Spring), 32.
         Brief mention of Braine and Room at the Top. (In
     French.)

16   STANFORD, DEREK. "Beatniks and Angry Young Men." Meanjin, 17
     (December), 417-18.
         Both Braine and Wain are possessed by the theme of
     "careerism." Lampton's sentiment for other's success looks
     like "rationalised envy." Concludes that Room at the Top
     reminds one of Maupassant's Bel Ami.

17   TYNAN, KENNETH. "Men of Anger." Holiday, 23 (April), 92-93.
         Survey of the Angry Young Men phenomenon. Says all of
     the writers hate the establishment, are bored, and believe
     that Art is an "influence on life."

18   WEAVER, ROBERT. "England's Angry Young Men." Queen's Quar-
     terly, 65 (Summer), 183-94.
         Survey of the Angry Young Men. Distinguishes between
     Colin Wilson (as Mystic), Amis, Wain, and Braine (as Pro-
     vincials), and Osborne (as Radical). Finds in their work
     a reflection of "the drabness and frustrations of postwar
     England."

1959 A BOOKS - NONE

1959 B SHORTER WRITINGS

1   ANON. "New Fiction." London Times (19 November), p. 15.
         Review of The Vodi. Discusses both the strengths (rapid
    narrative pace, crisp dialogue, "stark emotion," and at-
    mosphere) and the weaknesses (flashbacks, kids talking like
    adults, weak fantasy element, and unclear moral) in this
    novel. Although The Vodi may not win the acclaim of Room
    at the Top, "its enterprise increases [Braine's] stature."

2   ANON. "Combating Malevolence." Times Literary Supplement
    (20 November), p. 673.
         Review of The Vodi. Braine shares some of the concerns
    of the other Angry Young Men, but his technique differs.
    To some critics, the works of Amis and Wain seem "marred by
    an inability (or unwillingness?) to maintain a consistent
    narrative style: these writers tend to lapse, suddenly
    and without warning--or any apparent justification--from
    flat naturalism into the crudest melodrama." In contrast,
    Braine seems "agreeably old-fashioned." Praises Room at
    the Top as "a sustained and most competent piece of story-
    telling, all-of-a-piece and written in a consistent and
    compelling style wholly suited to its subject." The ending
    to The Vodi, on the other hand, seems "contrived and per-
    functory." Braine is better at social observation than
    fantasy, for this novel lacks "the drive and confidence"
    of Room at the Top. "His chief danger is a certain over-
    facility, which, at times, degenerates into the slickness
    of a strip-cartoon; at his best, however, he is an honest
    and intelligent observer of the social scene."

3   ANON. "The Arts: Films of the Year." London Times
    (24 December), p. 2.
         Names the film version of Room at the Top second-best
    foreign film of the year.

4   BALAKIAN, NONA. "The Flight from Innocence: England's Newest
    Literary Generation." Books Abroad, 33 (Summer), 267.
         Review of Room at the Top. Braine writes with a mixture
    of naiveté and hard-headed realism, a slick magazine fa-
    cileness and bright originality of phrasing." In one re-
    spect, Room at the Top is an old-fashioned tale: it is an
    "explicitly moralizing one." Finds Lampton more cunning
    than Wain's Joe Shaw (in The Contenders). In spite of the

1959

pathos of the ending, the prevailing mood in Braine's novel
is "good-humored satire"; therefore, the violent sex scenes
are never obscene.

5   BUTCHER, MARYVONNE. "A Film in Context." Commonweal, 70
    (3 July), 346–48.
        Review of the film version of Room at the Top. "It is
    almost unique . . . in being an adaptation of a novel which
    is wholly true to its original or, when it diverges, im-
    proves." Comments on the casting (excellent), acting ("ex-
    ceedingly good"), script ("sustained"), and dialogue
    ("lively").

6   COLEMAN, JOHN. "Sick and Tired." Spectator, 204
    (20 November), 730.
        Review of The Vodi. Because the Vodi eventually drop
    out to leave the reader with Corvey's drab story, the title
    is illicit. The construction is "slapdash," and Corvey's
    bitterness is "too quirky and pathological, his nascent
    ambitions too restricted, to engage sympathy."

7   MERTNER, EDGAR. "Der Roman der jungen Generation in England."
    Sprache und Literatur, 3 (Winter), 101–23.
        Detailed study of Braine, Amis, and Wain as members of
    the so-called Angry Young Man movement. Studies the socio-
    logical implications of Room at the Top and The Vodi. (In
    German.)

8   PEARSON, GABRIEL. "Hard Luck Story." New Statesman, 58
    (21 November), 718.
        Review of The Vodi. Belongs to the tradition of Ben-
    nett, Wells, and Orwell. "This tradition is sub-
    Dickensian." Like Dickens, Braine's concern is with "the
    bizarre surface of the contemporary world." Corvey's
    gradual decline is reminiscent of the old Clayhanger in
    Bennett's novel. Yet, The Vodi is "curiously aimless in
    its direction and lax in its structure." This is because
    Braine does not want to construct "a drama to expose a
    conflict of values, as in The Room at the Top; but rather,
    to reveal a state of mind." As a novel about bad luck,
    The Vodi is filled with "masochistic imagery" and "an
    ambiguity towards success." However, "certain passages do
    show a compassionate insight into human suffering, and
    promise better things to come."

9   VAN DER VEEN, ADRIAAN. "Boze Jongelieden in een Zich Ver-
     nieuwend Engeland." Vlaamse Gids, 43 (April), 232-36.
         Studies the disillusion with the Welfare State as ex-
     pressed in the works of Braine, Amis, Wain, and Osborne.
     These writers express no desire to make a better world.
     (In Flemish.)

10 WEINMANN, ROBERT. "Die Literatur der Angry Young Men. Ein
     Beitrag zur Deutung englischer Gegenwartsliteratur." Zeit-
     schrift für Anglistik und Amerikanistik, 7 (Fall), 117-89.
         Analyzes the political, social, and educational back-
     ground of postwar England. Comments frequently on Room at
     the Top. (In German.)

11 WHANNEL, PADDY. "Room at the Top." Universities and Left Re-
     view, 6 (Spring), 21-24.
         Says the film version of Room at the Top may herald the
     "revival of the British cinema." Those critics who re-
     sponded unfavorably to the movie are "unwilling to break
     out of the 'nice' circle" of their experience to explore
     "the hidden recesses of postwar Britain."

12 WILSON, COLIN. "The Writer and Publicity: A Reply to
     Critics." Encounter, 13 (November), 10-11.
         Discusses the public's response to new writers. Says
     that Room at the Top sold 40,000 copies in hardcover and
     another 500,000 copies in paperback. Because the royalties
     on these books and subsequent film rights were low,
     Braine's artistic success was by no means a financial
     success. With the release of The Vodi, it wouldn't be
     surprising if the public reacts with resentment towards a
     writer who is too continuously successful.

1960 A BOOKS - NONE

1960 B SHORTER WRITINGS

1   ANON. "Fiction." Kirkus Reviews, 28 (15 January), 63.
         Review of From the Hand of the Hunter. Weaker than Room
     at the Top because of Braine's sentimentality, seen in Cor-
     vey's redemption through love. Praises the fantasy element
     and satire, the description of youth at work in industrial
     Britain, the pubs, and the description of Corvey himself.

1960

2   ANON. "Fiction." Booklist, 56 (1 April), 477.
         Brief mention of From the Hand of the Hunter. Calls
     this a "sympathetically related story." Unlike Lampton,
     Corvey is "a diffident, unambitious young man."

3   ANON. "Room at the Bottom." Time, 75 (4 April), 98.
         Review of From the Hand of the Hunter. Only Braine's
     sure knowledge of his characters saves this "grey, de-
     pressing tale." Calls Braine "unpitying."

4   ANON. "New Fiction." London Times (6 April), p. 15.
         Brief mention of From the Hand of the Hunter.

5   BECK, WARREN. Review of From the Hand of the Hunter. Chicago
     Sunday Tribune (3 April), p. 6.
         This is a novel symbolic of "a commonplace, poignant
     human situation." Finds no "inflated scenes of high pas-
     sion or crude violence," but a sense of strain for the
     invalids and younger generation. Braine holds despair at
     a distance by "extravagant, faltering hopes."

6   BLEHL, VINCENT F. "Look Back at Anger." America, 103
     (16 April), 65.
         General study of the Angry Young Men. In spite of rave
     reviews, Room at the Top "betrayed all the symptoms of a
     second-rate novel." Perhaps Braine's obsession with ex-
     cessive sex distracted him "from the rich social theme
     which lay buried underneath the surface sensuality." How-
     ever, the characterization, settings, and moral perspective
     are noteworthy. As for The Vodi, this is a "thinly dis-
     guised variation" of Room at the Top's theme.

7   GERARD, ALBERT. "Les Jeunes Hommes Furieux." Revue Générale
     Belge, 60 (February), 21-30.
         Survey and discussion of the Angry Young Man movement,
     focusing on Braine, Amis, and Wain. (In French.)

8   GREEN, MARTIN. "New British Novels: Room at the Middle."
     Commonweal, 72 (8 April), 38.
         Room at the Top is "a solidly constructed realistic
     novel" whose hero is to be disapproved of but not disliked.

9   MANN, C. W. "Fiction." Library Journal, 85 (15 February),
     776.
         Review of From the Hand of the Hunter. Braine's obser-
     vations are sharp but perhaps a little "overrefined." Some
     of the details are obscure, though worked in with great
     care. The Vodi remind one too much of science fiction.
     "As a storyteller, Mr. Braine rates very high."

1960

10   MIZENER, ARTHUR. "Another Dubious Battle." New York Times
        Book Review (20 March), pp. 4, 22.
            Review of From the Hand of the Hunter. Like Amis and
        Waterhouse, Braine has focused on the British lower middle-
        class, turning away from "custom and ceremony" and reject-
        ing the arty novel. In this novel there is a certain
        amount of "sprawling and floundering." The shifts in point
        of view are distracting, and many scenes are devoted to in-
        significant minor characters. But Braine's gifts as a
        novelist make up for any weaknesses. The reader is able to
        see the characters and places, and Braine has an accurate
        ear for dialogue. "Above all, he has an instinct for
        bringing the particulars of his book under the organizing
        control of conflicting views of experience." This conflict
        is between Corvey's impulse to die and to love life.
        Braine's successful handling of this conflict makes evident
        the limited conception of experience in the book. But
        there are signs that he will not remain in this simplified
        view of experience.

11   GRANSDEN, K. W. "New Novels." Encounter, 14 (May), 78.
            Review of The Vodi. Although not as "sensational" as
        Room at the Top, Braine's new novel is "readable, profes-
        sional, and reasonably entertaining." However, the story-
        telling is vague, as if Braine himself is not really inter-
        ested in failure stories. "Mr. Braine has tried to breathe
        a soul into a neat piece of engineering; I do not think he
        quite succeeds."

12   MONAGHAN, CHARLES. "Dog-Eat-Dog in Yorkshire." New York
        Herald Tribune Book Review (10 July), p. 8.
            Review of From the Hand of the Hunter. Braine gives a
        different perspective on the "dog-eat-dog world" of Room at
        the Top. Lampton lived with zest; Corvey lacks a will to
        live. The scene shifts are handled skillfully, and the
        first half of the novel is a technical advance over his
        first novel. The second half is less successful, however,
        because it is "less technically adventurous" and because
        emphasis is shifted from Corvey onto other characters.
        This causes a "disparity of tone" between the two halves.
        Moreover, the single focus is lost and with it the tight-
        ness. Concludes that Braine's vision is proletarian. Be-
        cause it is unusual, the novel is given "a distinctive
        energy that makes it--despite its defects--a vigorous and
        readable novel."

1960

13   PESCHMANN, HERMANN. "The Nonconformists: Angry Young Men,
     'Lucky Jims,' and 'Outsiders.'" English (London), 13
     (Winter), 16.
          Although Lampton in Room at the Top is an Outsider, he
     is one of a totally different kind from Colin Wilson's be-
     cause he desperately tries to become an Insider. He
     attains this goal but loses real happiness and his soul in
     the process. Hence, Room at the Top is a "powerful but
     ultimately unsatisfactory novel."

14   PRICE, MARTIN. "Deeps and Shallows: Some Recent Fiction."
     Yale Review, NS 49 (March), 444-45.
          Review of From the Hand of the Hunter. This novel suf-
     fers from "a loss of satiric dimension." It is repeti-
     tious, the movement is suspended, the later parts suffer
     from "limpness." Moreover, as a study of the awakening of
     a man's ego and the creation of his will by the desires of
     others, it is "a slower, less brilliant book" than Room at
     the Top. The finest scenes occur when Dick and Tom take a
     short-cut to school. Also finds impressive the "solidity
     of scene and character" and Braine's "sense of milieu."

15   QUINTON, ANTHONY. "Masculine, Feminine and Neuter, or Three
     Kinds of the Contemporary Novel." London Magazine, 7
     (April), 66.
          Review of The Vodi. "Mr. Braine has moved a long way
     from the melodrama and sentimentality of Room at the Top
     without losing that book's admirable enthusiasm for the
     concrete, empirical world." Finds that Braine's moral pur-
     pose rests somewhere between Baden-Powell and Schopenhauer.
     Admires the "excellent vitality" of the description of
     Northern small-town life.

16   ROSS, T. J. "They're Killing Each Other." New Republic, 142
     (28 March), 18-19.
          Review of From the Hand of the Hunter. The anecdote to
     the British edition bridges from Braine's first to second
     novel, for in his second novel he "continues to render his
     sense of how contemporary experience is 'killing' in the
     terms established by his first." Finds that Room at the
     Top is distinguished by a balance between facts of plot and
     "sweetness of tone" (comparable to the balance in the best
     films of Griffith or King Vidor and in Fitzgerald's The
     Great Gatsby), rapid narrative, well-made plot, and fantasy
     elements. In From the Hand of the Hunter, however, there
     is an uneven pace and a "lack of climactic power" resulting
     from an uncontrolled use of flashbacks. Its strengths lie
     in an "integral emotional drive" and a fantasy which

"struck home to living concerns." Compared to Room at the Top, Braine's latest novel is more realistic and "'textured' by a fund of details . . . and by references symbolical of popular moods over the past fifteen years, all woven into rapidly sketched views of sundae-filled schooldays and of familial patterns, both solacing and tragic. Yet these elements fail to come together."

17 SWADOS, HARVEY. "By an Act of Will, a Life Reborn." Saturday Review, 43 (26 March), 27.
    Review of From the Hand of the Hunter. Corvey's situation is all too recognizable in this terribly disappointing novel. Braine's concerns are "no longer compelling to sophisticated readers."

18 WEEKS, EDWARD. "The Atlantic Bookshelf: The Moods of Fiction." Atlantic Monthly, 205 (April), 110.
    Recalls that when Braine was 21, he was hospitalized with tuberculosis. While there he made notes for Room at the Top and began writing poetry. Calls From the Hand of the Hunter "a sublimation of this early experience." The novel holds "pathos and power," and Corvey's reverie and recovery are of "rising interest."

1961 A BOOKS - NONE

1961 B SHORTER WRITINGS

1 BRYDEN, RONALD. "British Fiction, 1959-1960." International Literary Annual, No. 3. Edited by Arthur Boyars and Pamela Lyon. London: John Calder, p. 43.
    For Braine in Room at the Top, England is a battleground. Technically, the novel is old-fashioned, reminiscent of 1890s naturalism in which "every detail is charged with significance." Calls The Vodi "an understanding if not tender companion-study of a provincial youth who opts out of the struggle."

2 GREEN, MARTIN. "British Comedy and the British Sense of Humour: Shaw, Waugh, and Amis." Texas Quarterly, 7 (Fall), 226.
    Brief mention. Sees Braine, Wain, and Larkin as "collaborators" with Amis.

1961

3   KETTLE, ARNOLD. "Poiski Puti: Zamyetki O Sovremennoy Anglij-
     skoj Literature." <u>Innostrannaja Literatura</u>, 8 (August),
     182–88.
          Brief examination of the contemporary novels of Braine,
     Amis, and Wain for theme, structure, and development. (In
     Russian.)

4   _____. "Quest for New Ways (Notes on Contemporary English
     Literature)." <u>Innostrannaja Literatura</u>, 7 (July), 182–88.
          Calls <u>Room at the Top</u> the best book of the Angries.
     General survey of the Angry Young Man movement. (In
     Russian.)

5   PHELPS, G. H. "The Novel Today," in <u>The Modern Age</u>. Vol. 7
     of <u>Penguin Guide to English Literature</u>. Edited by Boris
     Ford. Baltimore: Penguin, pp. 489–90.
          Examines Lampton's political disillusionment in <u>Room at
     the Top</u>. Finds that the novel is marred by "sensationalism
     and sentimentality, and by frequent descents into copy-
     writer's English." Braine fails to assess fully the "'shiny
     barbarism'" of the times.

6   SCOTT-KILVERT, IAN. "English Fiction 1958–60, II." <u>British
     Book News: A Guide to Book Selections</u>, No. 247 (March),
     237–44.
          Discussion of Braine, Amis, Wain, and others. All of
     these novelists denounced "a whole complex of literary con-
     ventions, . . . political and ideological commitments,
     romantic or grandiose modes of writing, and . . . attacked
     their immediate predecessors."

1962 A BOOKS – NONE

1962 B SHORTER WRITINGS

1   ALLEN, WALTER. "A Self-Made Prisoner of Success and Safety."
     <u>New York Times Book Review</u> (7 October), p. 5.
          Review of <u>Life at the Top</u>. Braine's first novel was a
     success because as in Bennett's works, the reader could
     feel the place, the milieu was fascinating, and Lampton was
     not unattractive in spite of his ruthlessness. <u>Life at the
     Top</u> is not as good, however. Although Lampton's vulnera-
     bility and helplessness are "true and touching," and al-
     though he remains an attractive figure because of his
     honesty with himself, the novel lacks "the sense of the
     actuality of a community that made the earlier book so ex-
     citing." Braine deals with a narrower segment of society--

the expense-account society--which is difficult to respond
to with interest. The most that can be said about Lampton
is that in the end he recognizes he is a prisoner in a
self-made prison, and that in this prison "lies whatever
safety he will ever know."

2   ALVAREZ, A. "Braine at the Top." New Statesman, 64
    (5 October), 458.
        When Room at the Top was published, Braine was fashion-
    able because it was easy to identify with his hero; Lampton
    was "a grimmer, more single-minded, less imaginative fig-
    ure" than Dixon or Porter; and the book was convincing be-
    cause "Braine himself seemed convinced. He had created a
    moral crook who had the courage of his crookedness." Also,
    the novel was timely because the plot was "a kind of Tory
    fairy tale" with a mixture of "coy old-chappery and rather
    chill self-righteousness." Although Lampton lusts after
    riches and success, he hates himself for doing so, and this,
    too, appealed to the readers. This split in Lampton's feel-
    ings produced a tension in the writing.
        The Vodi, on the other hand, was a more complex, imag-
    inative work lacking in assurance. Braine shows the same
    "quirky, more artistic impulse" which controlled Room at
    the Top, but the novel failed. Readers and critics had al-
    ready pigeonholed Braine. In Life at the Top, Braine tries
    to recoup his losses by writing a moral tale with "the ac-
    ceptance of responsibility" as its theme. However, the
    mechanical plot lacks "life and substance," the characters
    are "generalized types," the dialogue is not relaxed, and
    the writing is as "vague and blank as the people." More-
    over, in Room at the Top, Lampton's drive gave him sub-
    stance. Now that he has gotten what he wanted, he has
    degenerated into a snob. "Yet the flabbier he becomes, the
    less his creator finds the heart to step back and put him
    artistically, morally, in his place."

3   ANON. "Fiction." Kirkus Reviews, 30 (1 July), 585.
        Review of Life at the Top. Lampton's "touchy resent-
    ment" in Room at the Top has changed to "a kind of rueful
    resignation." Although his anger has become subdued and
    even diminished by life, he is still "a very likable sort."

4   ANON. "Back with Ideas for Russian Novel." London Times
    (25 August), p. 8.
        Mentions Braine's return from Russia. Says he is con-
    sidering the writing of a novel portraying "the common
    likenesses between 'us and the Russians.'"

1962

5   ANON. "Books for Adults: Fiction." <u>Wisconsin Library Bulle-</u>
     <u>tin</u>, 58 (September), 345.
          Brief mention of <u>Life at the Top</u>. "The dialogue is
     candid and refreshing; the characters, human and interest-
     ing, although drinking and illicit affairs become tiresome."

6   ANON. "Fiction." <u>Booklist</u>, 59 (1 September), 28–29.
          Brief mention of <u>Life at the Top</u>. "Everything is seen
     from Lampton's point of view with a somewhat thinning ef-
     fect in presentation of characters."

7   ANON. "Near Summitry." <u>Times Literary Supplement</u> (5 October),
     p. 773.
          Review of <u>Life at the Top</u>. The first 200 pages are suc-
     cessful. As in O'Hara's <u>Appointment in Samarra</u>, the reader
     believes the "hero's honour, dignity . . . , total sense of
     what he is, will not allow him to survive." But then the
     story collapses. It is hard to believe in Lampton's re-
     conciliation. With this false turn are revealed the dis-
     appointing quality of dialogue and "the assured naiveté
     about what is materially smart." Finds that Braine has
     imposed events on characters instead of allowing them to
     develop spontaneously.

8   ANON. "New Fiction." London <u>Times</u> (5 October), p. 16.
          Review of <u>Life at the Top</u>. Braine shows that the top is
     a much drearier place than the way up. Whereas <u>Room at the</u>
     <u>Top</u> "effectively used the observed panoply of good living
     to explain, and even excuse, Joe Lampton's discontent, no
     such symbols are on hand to offset the self-contempt he
     feels."

9   ANON. "Lampton at Large." <u>Newsweek</u>, 68 (15 October), 114.
          Review of <u>Life at the Top</u>. Braine's talent is still
     expanding in this depiction of Lampton's stirring maturity.

10   ANON. "Briefly Noted: Fiction." <u>New Yorker</u>, 38 (17 Novem-
     ber), 246.
          Brief mention of <u>Life at the Top</u>. This is a predictable
     novel because Braine implied what would happen in the final
     pages of <u>Room at the Top</u>.

11   BURGESS, ANTHONY. "The Birth of a Best-Seller." <u>Observer</u>
     (7 October), p. 24.
          Brief mention of <u>Room at the Top</u>.

12 CARVER, WAYNE. Review of Life at the Top. Chicago Sunday
    Tribune (11 November), p. 4.
      Brief mention of Life at the Top with plot summary.

13 CORBETT, EDMUND P. J. "Books." America, 105 (27 October),
    961, 963.
      Review of Life at the Top. A dreary novel, lacking
    character. It is like reading "a social worker's dossier
    about a young couple who have gone out of their way to mess
    up their lives."

14 CORKE, HILARY. "Getting to the Bottom of the Top." New Re-
    public, 147 (3 November), 23-24.
      Examines the reasons behind the success of Room at the
    Top. The theme was right for the time because England is
    full of dislocated young men. Braine's book is the narra-
    tive equivalent of "the current sociological treatises upon
    'the meritocracy' or 'organization man.'" Also, the book
    was timely because it appears to cut through the hypocrisy
    over money. Moreover, the "dynamics" of the book rest upon
    two truths: (1) it is better to be rich than poor, and
    (2) one can pay too large a price for wealth. Finally, the
    sexual passages are reminiscent of early Lawrence; Braine's
    social morality, though naïve and crude, is on the right
    side. As a first novel, Room at the Top was fresh and the
    author was a nice man. Concludes that although Braine has
    an honest vision and a succinct style, he lacks "the quali-
    ty of understanding either individual motivations, or the
    way the social world is put together, or the nature of
    creative language, that would place him in any first
    class." Also, his conception of what constitutes "the top"
    is "unreal and immature." Says Life at the Top is not new;
    it is "perhaps a little better, perhaps a little worse."

15 DERRICK, CHRISTOPHER. "Not Proven." Tablet, 216 (20 October),
    988.
      Review of Life at the Top. Questions whether the reader
    is to regard Lampton as foolish or wicked. The conversion
    seems doubtful, the conclusion is suspended. Although the
    novel lacks the "tragic momentum" of Room at the Top, it
    offers "a close and harrowing analysis of contemporary
    stylings in folly and sin."

16 FIXX, JAMES F. "The Author." Saturday Review, 45 (6 October),
    20.
      Biographical background and interview with Braine.
    Covers his literary life, dress, writing habits, school
    days, the initial impact of Room at the Top, the film ver-
    sion of that novel, and his favorite authors.

1962

17   HICKS, GRANVILLE. "An Interview with Granville Hicks:
        Part I." Saturday Review, 45 (21 July), 16.
            Mentions Braine to illustrate that the English novel is
        healthy.

18   _____. "Too Much and Not Enough." Saturday Review, 45
        (6 October), 20.
            In his desire to get ahead economically and socially,
        Lampton is similar to Horatio Alger. However, whereas the
        typical Alger hero gets ahead by saving the rich man's
        daughter from some menace, Lampton does so by getting her
        pregnant. Moreover, the Alger story ends happily, but
        Lampton's story ends unhappily. In Life at the Top, the
        hero reminds one of many stock characters of contemporary
        popular fiction who are "handsomely endowed with material
        possessions" and yet unhappy. In this novel, Braine fails
        to reveal any deeper insights into Lampton. The novel
        holds some documentary value, for it shows that the con-
        fusion of values is present in England (as well as Amer-
        ica). "What is depressing is that Braine appears to
        believe that he has risen above the confusion, when he is
        as much its victim as any slick novelist you can name."

19   IVASHEVA, V. Anglijskij roman poslednego desjatiletya.
        Moscow: Sovetskij Pisatel, 45 pp., passim.
            Examines the basic tendencies in the development of the
        1950s English novel and the "imperialist reaction" against
        realism and modernism in Braine. (In Russian.)

20   JACKSON, KATHERINE GAUSS. "Books in Brief." Harper's Maga-
        zine, 225 (December), 116, 118.
            Review of Life at the Top. Although Braine demonstrates
        the same narrative skill seen in his first novel, there are
        "too many volatile and sometimes sentimental emotions, too
        many right-about-faces to make this as affecting and cred-
        ible as its predecessor."

21   JELLY, OLIVER. "Fiction and Illness." Review of English
        Literature, 3 (January), 80-89.
            Compares Mann's Magic Mountain to A. E. Ellis' The Rack
        and Braine's The Vodi to illustrate that the world's fic-
        tion is filled with sickness. Braine's and Ellis' books
        are similar in situation and theme to Mann's. Since Flau-
        bert, writers have failed to distinguish between illness
        and health.

22 KARL, FREDERICK R. "The Angries: Is There a Protestant in the House?" in his The Contemporary English Novel. New York: Farrar, Straus and Giroux, pp. 229-31.
    Room at the Top depicts the hardships involved in a slow rise to the top by a hero dissatisfied because he must immerse himself in society's nonsense while recognizing its insufficiency. Unlike Lumley in Wain's Hurry on Down, however, Lampton never confuses means and ends. Also, there is a strong resemblance between Braine and Defoe, for both allow their heroes to confuse love with money. Sees Lampton as "a Robinson Crusoe carving an empire for himself on the island of England." Although the novel is potentially good--succinctly written--the quality of content is poor and the decision between real love and fake love is a cliché. Moreover, the minor characters rarely come alive.
    The focus in The Vodi is less sharp. Corvey's internal struggles in the sanitarium are reminiscent of The Magic Mountain. Because the material is handled unimaginatively, it becomes "sodden and formless" and Corvey's adventures become "tirelessly realistic." Concludes that in both novels the problem is not in Braine's "intention but in his execution." His conception of character and situation is too limited. "The trivial details of the narrative diminish the theme and make it too commonplace to convince us."

23 KOLJEVIC, SVETOZAC. "Putevi savremenog engleskog romana." Delo za zdravje, 8 (July), 870-89.
    Studies the contemporary novel with emphasis on Braine and Angus Wilson. (In Serbo-Croatian.)

24 LERNER, LAURENCE. "New Novels." Listener, 68 (4 October), 533-34.
    Review of Life at the Top. Braine is meticulous, objective, unsentimental, honest, and "utterly unliterary." Like Room at the Top, this book is "alive from the first moment to the last."

25 McKINNEY, JOAN. Review of Life at the Top. San Francisco Chronicle (30 September), p. 32.
    Brief mention with plot summary.

26 MOON, ERIC. "Fiction." Library Journal, 87 (15 September), 3065.
    Review of Life at the Top. As in his first book, the characterization is sharp and the writing is good, but Lampton's disenchantment is diminished. Although the circumstances differ, "the plot has a certain sameness, the dramatic wallop of Room at the Top has been cushioned."

1962

27   NORDELL, RODERICK. "Angry, Beat, and Optimistic." <u>Christian
      Science Monitor</u> (4 October), p. 9.
           Examines the similarities and differences between the
      "angries" in England and the "beats" in the United States.
      Finds in <u>Life at the Top</u> a "bedeviled regard for humanity"
      and a rather hastily optimistic conclusion similar to Jack
      Kerouac's <u>Big Sur</u>. Comments on the artificiality of Lamp-
      ton's alternating lust, guilt, affection, and high-minded-
      ness. At times these alternations seem merely melodramatic.
      "The weakness is reflected in the first-person narrative,
      which recalls the coarse language of the earlier book but
      not the sharp idiomatic crackle of its best passages."

28   NORRIE, IAN. Review of <u>Life at the Top</u>. <u>London Magazine</u>,
      NS 2 (November), 86.
           This "trite, laborious and sentimental" tale lacks the
      vigor, conviction, and "crystallised attitude of mind" of
      <u>Room at the Top</u>.

29   NOTT, KATHLEEN. "Down with the Anti-Hero." <u>New Society</u>, 1
      (November), 29.
           Discusses the cult of the "little man" or anti-hero in
      the 1950s novels of Braine, Amis, Wain, Sillitoe, and
      S. Barstow.

30   O'CONNOR, WILLIAM VAN. "Two Types of Heroes in Postwar
      British Fiction." <u>Publication of the Modern Language
      Association</u>, 77 (March), 169–70.
           Notes that Braine's heroes resemble those of Arnold
      Bennett and that the setting in <u>Room at the Top</u> resembles
      the world of David Storey.

31   PENN, RICHARD. "Latest Novels." <u>Time & Tide</u>, 43 (4 October),
      24.
           Review of <u>Life at the Top</u>. Braine looks more objec-
      tively at Lampton than he did in <u>Room at the Top</u>. The
      hero is still selfish and ruthless but no longer such a
      rebel. He reaches greater depths of emotion. Concludes
      that Braine has extended his range as a novelist.

32   PRICE, MARTIN. "The Complexity of Awareness and the Aware-
      ness of Complexity: Some Recent Novels." <u>Yale Review</u>,
      NS 52 (December), 264–65.
           Review of <u>Life at the Top</u>. This novel lacks "the sharp
      curve of action" seen in <u>Room at the Top</u>. The older Lamp-
      ton is more passive, more bewildered, and the story moves
      on a series of events "too tricky or pat to carry convic-
      tion."

33 PRICE, R. G. G. "New Novels." Punch, 243 (24 October),
      611-12.
         Review of Life at the Top. "It contains all the ingre-
      dients that made the first novel a success, apart from the
      freshness, and none of the gauche experimentation that made
      The Vodi a promising flop."

34 RICHLER, MORDECAI. "Tougher at the Bottom." Spectator, 209
      (19 October), 602.
         Sees Room at the Top as reminiscent of the traditional
      American immigrant tale. Although old-fashioned, the novel
      has "drive, power," and readability. Life at the Top is a
      version of the contemporary American morality tale, "the
      novel of suburban disenchantment" and reminiscent of Sloan
      Wilson. Like John O'Hara, Braine is obsessed by brand
      names, detailed lists of possessions, and "seemingly forth-
      right sex." Additionally, the novel is weak because of
      predictable plotting and a failure in Lampton's character-
      ization. Unlike Sillitoe's flesh and blood characters,
      Lampton lacks life. He is an attitude; his dialogue is
      barely plausible. Moreover, Braine's prose lacks distinc-
      tion. The best that can be said is that it is readable,
      fast, rather sexy, and filled with realistic documentary
      detail.

35 RUGOFF, MILTON. "At the Top and in the Clover, Everything
      but Happiness." New York Herald Tribune Book Review
      (30 September), p. 4.
         The pattern in Life at the Top is familiar, but the tale
      is told with authority, sharp dialogue, and firm character-
      ization. "Despite the spiritual conditions that are left
      in a tangle, . . . it is a mature novel, called on to face,
      like Joe himself, far larger problems than Room at the Top."
      Because the meanings are left unstated, they are all the
      more intense.

1963 A BOOKS - NONE

1963 B SHORTER WRITINGS

1   EGRI, PETER. "Anger and Form." Zeitschrift für Anglistik und
      Amerikanistik, 11 (November), 270-72.
         Discussion of the "dissentience of the fifties," with
      reference to Braine, Amis, and Wain. (In German.)

1963

2 GIBBONS, JOHN. "Some Thoughts on the State of the Novel."
Quarterly Review, 301 (January), 50-52.
The situation and characters in Room at the Top were
common enough, but Braine handled them with "uncommon belief and honesty." Comments on the vitality of its regional setting, which is realized "with more affection,
more honesty, more understanding, than most of its many
regional predecessors of the first half of the century."
The novel does not quarrel with humanity nor does it offer
"doctrinaire assertions."

3 HOWE, IRVING. "Mass Society and Postmodern Fiction," in his
Decline of the New. New York: Harcourt, Brace and World,
pp. 204-205.
Although a good many Americans scorned Braine and Amis,
one can hardly deny that their early novels offer "something of the focused desire, the quick apprehension and
notation of contemporary life" rarely found in serious
American fiction. That is, faced with a predicament of
the Welfare State, these writers transformed gripes into
causes, cloaked ambitions as ideals. Their complaints were
structured through comedy.

4 JOHNSON, LUCY. "Three Novels." Progressive, 27 (January),
41.
Review of Life at the Top. Calls this "an exercise in
self-pity and little more."

5 LODGE, DAVID. "The Modern, the Contemporary, and the Importance of Being Amis." Critical Quarterly, 5 (Winter),
337-39.
Indicates the difference between modern and contemporary
writing by comparing a passage from Portrait of the Artist
as a Young Man to one from Room at the Top. Finds Braine's
writing is "looser and thinner in texture. The words do
not give and receive life and meaning to and from each
other." Moreover, the metaphors are clichés and interest
is mainly of "a factual or journalistic kind." Braine in-
vites the reader to indulge in a gratifying, but essen-
tially demoralizing emotion. "The narrator goes on to
recognize and reject his envy, but there is nothing in the
language which places, defines, and evaluates the emotion."
Reprinted: 1966.B2.

6 McDOWELL, FREDERICK P. W. "'The Devious Involutions of Human
Character and Emotions': Reflections on Some Recent British Novels." Wisconsin Studies in Contemporary Literature,
4 (Autumn), 344-46.

In Life at the Top, Braine has filled out the design es-
tablished for his work in Room at the Top—a "readable and
sometimes compelling novel." Demonstrates that Braine is
at his best when he analyzes the "individual as he is mold-
ed by, and resents, social pressures." The strength of
this novel lies in Braine's further exploration of Lampton.
The clashes between Lampton and Susan are skillfully de-
picted in chapters six and seven.

7   SCHLÜTER, KURT. "Soziale Statussymbole und ihre künstlerische
     Verwendung in John Braines Roman Room at the Top." Die
     Neueren Sprachen, 3 (March), 193-208.
          Unlike other social climbers of literature, Lampton dif-
     fers because of his awareness of the social value of mate-
     rial objects and habits. His depersonalization originates
     in his acceptance of symbols of social status. (In
     German.)

1964 A BOOKS - NONE

1964 B SHORTER WRITINGS

1   ANON. "New Fiction." London Times (26 November), p. 16.
          Review of The Jealous God. Braine should have given
     more attention to the background and less to the central
     character. When he writes of the community, the novel has
     "strength and interest." When he writes of Vincent, it is
     difficult to take the Catholicism seriously. It seems
     Braine is merely trying to endow Vincent with a sense of
     responsibility.

2   ANON. "Room for the O.P.?" Times Literary Supplement
     (26 November), p. 1053.
          Review of The Jealous God. Braine and Alexander Pope
     seem to share, within their religion, "an almost fatalistic
     reverence for the laws of human society." Because of a
     confusion between social and spiritual offenses, Braine
     seems "a pedestrian, even monotonous, novelist." His na-
     turalistic scenes and "'prop'" characters are handled
     skillfully, but he runs into trouble when he tries to im-
     bue with life Vincent and Laura's relationship. It is
     filled with clichés and echoes former novels. It is hard
     to avoid feeling that Braine, as in his earlier novels,
     secretly dislikes his hero. "However readable, however
     likely to repeat some of his former success, Mr. Braine's
     novel disappoints because not only his material but also
     his skill as a writer seem for too long to have stood
     still."

1964

3   BRAYBROOKE, NEVILLE. "Variations on a Theme." Spectator, 213
    (27 November), 753.
        Review of The Jealous God. In his first three novels,
    distinguished by a straightforward plotting and some moral
    problems, Braine was concerned with "conscience and the
    temptations of the flesh." In his latest novel, Braine
    introduces a variation on this theme, resulting in "a
    powerful moral tale and a religious tract for the times."

4   BUTCHER, MARYVONNE. "Closed Shop." Tablet, 218 (5 December),
    1377.
        Review of The Jealous God. His best novel since Room at
    the Top. The setting is vivid, the characterization is re-
    markable, and the conflicts are convincing. "This is a
    story about real people, involved in a conflict between
    flesh and spirit which is more savage than they had been
    brought up to expect. It may shock the conventional, but
    there is a good deal to be learned about faith, hope and
    charity from these pages." The reader becomes intimately
    involved with Vincent, the mother, the three brothers, and
    the grandmother.

5   FRASER, G. S. "The Novel in the 1950s," in his The Modern
    Writer and His World. Baltimore: Penguin Books, pp. 175,
    179-82.
        Unlike Amis and Wain, who dealt with lower-middle-class
    protest, Braine and Sillitoe dealt with genuine working-
    class protest. Hence, critics looked to their novels as
    social documents. In the tradition of Hoggart and Wil-
    liams, Braine focused on the formula that "for the tradi-
    tional working classes, money and power do not matter,
    happiness and group loyalty do." Braine's prose, with its
    "slick metaphors," is influenced heavily by Raymond Chand-
    ler. Room at the Top is "powerful in scheme, in plotting
    and narrative thrust, as a moral fable about ambition."
    The novel is weak because Braine is unable to detach him-
    self emotionally from Lampton and because Braine seems
    "beglamoured" by the woman Lampton marries.

6   FULLER, JOHN. "Novel of the Twenties." New Statesman, 68
    (27 November), 844.
        Review of The Jealous God. Braine works hard to put his
    material across, but the theme and characters remain "en-
    tombed at synopsis level." Finds the plot "schematic."

7   RILLIE, JOHN A. M. "The Sweet Smell of Failure." <u>Twentieth</u>
    <u>Century</u>, 172 (Spring), 96-97.
        Finds in <u>Room at the Top</u> "the contemporary version of
    the local-boy-makes-good theme." Lampton is "the working-
    class fantasy of love and status." Braine's clarity and
    honesty in the conflict ranks this novel as superior over
    most of the contemporary genre.

8   SHESTAKOV, DMITRI. "John Braine Facing His Fourth Novel."
    <u>Soviet Literature</u>, 8 (August), 178-81.
        Soviet critics agree that Braine is a severe critical
    realist; many note a connection between <u>Room at the Top</u>
    and <u>An American Tragedy</u>. Furthermore, like Defoe's or
    Balzac's heroes, Braine's central character struggles to
    obtain all of the material benefits he can. Lampton
    helped Soviet readers understand the implications of Os-
    borne's, Wain's, and Amis' anger. Calls <u>The Vodi</u> an in-
    sufficiently interesting novel about what portion of
    happiness or bad luck determines a man's destiny. <u>Life at</u>
    <u>the Top</u>, on the other hand, adds to Lampton's "self-
    exposure and sound reasoning." Concludes that most impor-
    tant in Braine's works is "the symptomatic nature of the
    problems and the social amplitude of the portraits."

9   TAYLOR, ARCHER. "John Braine's Proverbs." <u>Western Folklore</u>,
    23 (January), 42-43.
        Catalogs and discusses the proverbs and proverbial
    phrases found in <u>Room at the Top</u> and <u>The Vodi</u>.

10 WALL, STEPHEN. "With Whip and Junk." <u>Listener</u>, 72
    (3 December), 913.
        Review of <u>The Jealous God</u>. Although the narrative pace
    is similar to that in <u>Room at the Top</u>, "its force finally
    appears factitious. The situation seems set up rather than
    lived through." Moreover, the characterization is flat or
    "dangerously near compensatory fantasy" much of the time.

1965 A BOOKS - NONE

1965 B SHORTER WRITINGS

1   ANON. "Sonny and Lovers." <u>Newsweek</u>, 65 (8 March), 95.
        Review of <u>The Jealous God</u>. Braine's gifts for charac-
    terization and narrative are revealed again, but the novel
    is weakened by "a slick facility that smoothes out the ter-
    rain of a man's doubt and decision." Braine's conveyance
    of sex" is the most effective writing in the novel. As
    <u>deus ex machina</u>, Braine "finesses, fakes, and fabricates to
    engineer the destinies of his tangled characters."

1965

2   ANON. "Books." Time, 85 (26 March), 104, 106.
         Review of The Jealous God. Braine is no longer angry.
     Now he "dabbles in religious sensibility."

3   ANON. "Briefly Noted: Fiction." New Yorker, 41 (1 May),
     188-89.
         Brief mention of The Jealous God. "Mr. Braine is espe-
     cially adept at furnishing the dwellings his characters
     pass through, as if he were a retired Navy man building
     precision ship models." Calls this "a paunchy novel."

4   BARRETT, WILLIAM. "Reader's Choice: Provincial Manners."
     Atlantic Monthly, 215 (March), 195-97.
         Review of The Jealous God. Finds fascinating Braine's
     delineation of Irish immigrants in northern England. Un-
     like Lampton's conflict with society in Room at the Top,
     Vincent's conflict is with himself between his religion and
     the desires of his flesh. Finds the style is "straightfor-
     ward, bare, energetic, and nearly always to the point."
     Unfortunately, Braine begins to manipulate the action toward
     the end until it becomes "more hysterical than convincing."

5   BEMIS, R. "Books in Brief." National Review, 17 (18 May),
     432-33.
         Review of The Jealous God. Calls this "pale melodrama."
     In the tradition of Ford Madox Ford and Graham Greene,
     Braine explores the complexities of sex and religion but
     adds little to the writers' perceptions. Typical of
     Braine, the novel reminds one of a television domestic se-
     rial.

6   BENTLEY, PHYLLIS. "Yorkshire and the Novelist," in Essays by
     Divers Hands, Being the Transactions of the Royal Society
     of Literature. Vol. 33. Edited by Richard Church. Lon-
     don and New York: Oxford University Press, pp. 151, 155.
         Notes that Braine, among other writers, has made full
     use of Yorkshire landscape in a number of superbly written
     passages.

7   BERGONZI, BERNARD. "New Novels." New York Review of Books
     (11 March), pp. 19-20.
         Review of The Jealous God. Whereas Life at the Top sug-
     gested Braine had fallen to self-imitation, his new novel
     puts to rest any hints of failing inventiveness. Although
     the milieu is the same, Braine has added a new dimension
     with his focus on Catholicism. Praises Braine's charac-
     terization of Vincent, finding "something Prufrockian"
     about him. Although Laura fails to come to life, his

characterization of the Dungarvan family and of the Catholic community of Charbury compensates for this. American readers may find the traditional technique to be old-fashioned, but this characteristic is typical of Braine's generation of writers.

8   BERNARD, J. F. "Fiction." Bestsellers, 24 (15 March), 480.
        Review of The Jealous God. On the surface, the book is a disaster because it is tedious and pretentious. Its dialogue is "ghastly" and its speculations on metaphysics are "sophomoric." "Here and there we find traces of the old John Braine: the conflict between the son and the mother is grippingly real for the most part; one or two of the minor characters--the brother's wife, and the brother himself--are sketched masterfully." In spite of these strengths, however, this is Braine's "dullest book."

9   BUITENHUIS, PETER. "Vincent and Laura." New York Times Book Review (7 March), p. 4.
        Review of The Jealous God. For a time, it seemed that Braine might be a one-book novelist. His latest book puts an end to those fears, for in it he shows he is able to reach beyond his own immediate experience. Most successful is the novel's "sense of the family group." Says the influence of Henry James is apparent in Braine's use of a central consciousness to control and order his narrative and in his precise style. Wishes Braine had made Vincent less the spectator. Had he gone into his consciousness further, "his reader would at least be able to understand why Vincent is a sort of mute, inglorious Hamlet."

10   COOK, RODERICK. "Books in Brief." Harper's Magazine, 230 (April), 117.
        Review of The Jealous God. The promise noted in Room at the Top has yet to be fulfilled. It is all right to write an old-fashioned tale, but this one lacks character and never strikes "a contemporary note." The dialogue and setting lack a sense of time and place, the writing is "unspirited," and Vincent's anguish comes across as "mere religiosity."

11   CURLEY, THOMAS. "Hamlet as Irish-Catholic." Commonweal, 82 (23 April), 158-59.
        Review of The Jealous God. In this good novel all of its faults are out in the open. Braine accepts traditional Catholic morality; he has taken Vincent, an ordinary man, and imagined him according to his own standards. The ending is forced, for Robert's suicide moves Vincent out of his problem too easily.

1965

12 FRIEL, BRIAN. "Still Room at the Top." Critic, 23 (June-
    July), 69-70.
         Review of The Jealous God. Finds it hard to take this
    novel seriously because the characters' Catholicism is hard
    to believe in. It seems Braine has set up his idea the way
    Euclid sets up a theorem, and this will not work. Praises
    the atmosphere, the lucid writing, and the interesting plot,
    but as a study of the conflict between flesh and religion
    the book is "shallow and easy and untrue."

13 GARDINER, HAROLD C. "Book Reviews." America, 112 (10 April),
    494-95.
         Review of The Jealous God. An "engrossing book" in
    which it is unclear of whom or what God is jealous. Mrs.
    Dungarvan is "the most fully realized character," whereas
    Vincent is "rather bloodless." Although a good, "workman-
    like novel," it does not go very deep into the mysteries or
    meaning of Catholic life.

14 HICKS, GRANVILLE. "A Moral Sensuality." Saturday Review, 48
    (6 March), 23.
         Review of The Jealous God. This is "a subtle study of
    love and sex." Vincent's views on sex are more complicated
    than Lampton's. Because of Braine's power, the reader is
    made to feel sympathy for Vincent. He is not the typical
    ambivalent hero of modern fiction, for his aloofness is
    unique and his actions are controlled not by religious
    dogma but by temperament. He is neither a conformist nor
    a rebel; he is himself.

15 M., M. "New Fiction." Christian Science Monitor (1 April),
    p. 11.
         Calls Braine a kind of British Sinclair Lewis with his
    "knack for fresh observation of the obvious." Finds a
    similarity between Lampton (in Room at the Top) and Bab-
    bitt, for Lampton became representative of a social myth--
    the Angry Young Man. But with the publication of Life at
    the Top, what Lampton stood for seemed banal. And in The
    Jealous God, the problem stems from "a case of the deadly
    success of realism: too true to be good."

16 MONTGOMERY, JOHN. "Young? Angry? Typical?" Books and Book-
    men, 11 (December), 88-89.
         Survey of the 1950s novels and the Angry Young Men.
    Discusses the social and political influence on the writ-
    ers. Brief mention of Braine and a photograph of him.

17 MOON, ERIC. "Fiction." <u>Library Journal</u>, 90 (15 March), 1345.
      Review of <u>The Jealous God</u>. Braine's concerns turn from
   "fiscal and physical" to the soul. Finds Vincent a de-
   pressing character. Laura is a very "human characterization of a librarian." Although the novel is a little too
   predictable, tidy and pat, it does have depth and warmth
   and "reads like falling off a log." Moreover, the sex is
   neither "too frequent nor too explicit."

18 PAUL, LESLIE. "The Angry Young Men Revisited." <u>Kenyon Re-
   view</u>, 27 (Spring), 344.
      Brief mention of Braine as one of the Angry Young Men.

19 RYAN, STEPHEN P. "New Books." <u>Catholic World</u>, 202 (October),
   62.
      Review of <u>The Jealous God</u>. A "powerfully moving" novel
   in spite of its somewhat contrived ending. Praises
   Braine's sense of time and place and portrayal of Dungarvan. This novel may serve as a prototype of future
   "Catholic" novels.

20 SHEED, WILFRID. "Pomp and Passion before Prayer." <u>Book Week</u>
   (21 March), pp. 4, 14.
      Review of <u>The Jealous God</u>. This "quiet, low-pitched,
   reasonable story" is better than <u>Room at the Top</u>. It is a
   class-novel, but of "a non-hysterical, non-fingerwagging
   type." Braine's writing is distinguished by his unself-
   conscious attitude about regional limitations, with social
   conditioning the most interesting character in the book.
   Contrasts Braine's Catholic world to Greene's.

21 SPENDER, STEPHEN. "Literature," in <u>The Great Ideas Today</u>.
   Edited by Robert B. Hutchins and Mortimer J. Adler. Chicago and London: Encyclopedia Britannica, pp. 176-93.
      General discussion review of contemporary English nov-
   elists, including the Angry Young Men.

<u>1966 A BOOKS - NONE</u>

<u>1966 B SHORTER WRITINGS</u>

 1 LOCKWOOD, BERNARD. "Four Contemporary British Working-Class
   Novelists: A Thematic and Critical Approach to the Fiction
   of Raymond Williams, John Braine, David Storey and Alan
   Sillitoe. Dissertation. University of Wisconsin.
      Analyzes Braine's themes while paying particular atten-
   tion to his working-class attitudes. Calls <u>Room at the Top</u>

1966

a "savagely satiric indictment of a class-divided, money-oriented society." The narrator is endowed with a "mordantly ironic sense of humor." His subsequent novels are not artistically satisfying, however, because of a basic weakness in characterization and plot and a loss in "satiric dimension."

2 LODGE, DAVID. "The Modern, the Contemporary, and the Importance of being Amis," in his Language of Fiction: Essays in Criticism and Verbal Analysis of the English Novel. London: Routledge and Kegan Paul, pp. 245-49, 279.
     Reprint of 1963.B5.

3 PITT, VALERIE. "Readers and Writers," in her The Writer and the Modern World: A Study in Literature and Dogma. London: S.P.C.K., pp. 21-24.
     Discusses the religious implications of Braine's writings. Room at the Top is about sin. Although a naive novel, it is distinguished by a strong plot and a definite moral content. The Vodi is "bewildering to a literal minded reader."

4 STOKES, FRASER. "Current British Fiction." English Record, 16 (February), 7-12.
     Survey of British fiction after 1958. Finds in the writings of Braine, Amis, Fowles, and others a change "toward American tone, style and setting."

5 WILLY, MARGARET. "XIV: The Twentieth Century: 1. The Novel," in The Year's Work in English Studies. Vol. 45. Edited by T. S. Dorsch and C. G. Harlow. London: John Murray, p. 326.
     Braine departs from his usual themes of "ambition for power, wealth, and a room at the top" in The Jealous God.

1967 A BOOKS

1 LEE, J. W. John Braine. Twayne English Authors Series, edited by Sylvia E. Bowman. New York: Twayne Publishers, 127 pp.
     Focuses on plot, theme, characterization, setting, and style in this study of Braine's life, short stories, and first four novels. Since Room at the Top, Braine has matured considerably in his development of characters, style, themes, point of view, and focus. Plot construction is still weak, although there are signs of progress.

1967 B SHORTER WRITINGS

1   ANON. "John Braine," in <u>Contemporary Authors: A Biographical-
     Bibliographical Guide to Current Authors and Their Works</u>.
     Edited by James M. Ethridge and Barbara Kopala. Detroit:
     Gale Research, p. 111.
          Brief biographical data and listing of secondary
     sources.

2   ANON. "British novelists criticized." London <u>Times</u>
     (24 January), p. 1.
          Amis and Braine are criticized by Pravda for their sup-
     port of the United States in Vietnam. (<u>See</u> London <u>Times</u>,
     21 January.) Up until now, says the writer, these two
     novelists "'have striven in their works to evaluate con-
     temporary bourgeois society from a position of honesty and
     realism.'"

3   BURGESS, ANTHONY. "A Sort of Rebels," in his <u>The Novel Now:</u>
     <u>A Guide to Contemporary Fiction</u>. New York: W. W. Norton,
     pp. 147, 149, 152.
          <u>Room at the Top</u> (a study in "provincial hypergamy") and
     <u>Life at the Top</u> were received enthusiastically. <u>The Vodi</u>
     was less successful because it was "less rich in class
     overtones." Unlike the earlier heroes, the hero of <u>The
     Jealous God</u> is motivated by spiritual instead of material
     ambitions. Credits Braine, Amis, Wain, and Sillitoe with
     the return to popularity of the provincial setting in fic-
     tion. Includes a listing of primary sources through 1964.

4   LARRETT, WILLIAM. "A Brief Survey of the English Novel from
     Thomas Hardy to Graham Greene," in his <u>The English Novel
     from Thomas Hardy to Graham Greene</u>. Frankfurt/Main: Ver-
     lag Moritz Diesterweg, p. 9.
          Like George Gissing, Braine treats the working-class
     area of life.

5   SALE, ROGER. "Fiction Review." <u>Hudson Review</u>, 20 (Spring),
     141.
          Brief review of <u>The Jealous God</u>. Comments on the char-
     acterization and takes note of Braine's Catholicism in this
     novel.

1968

1968 A BOOKS - NONE

1968 B SHORTER WRITINGS

1   ANON. "PW Forecasts: Fiction." Publishers Weekly, 194
        (12 August), 46.
            Review of The Crying Game. This novel goes beyond
        Darling and Blow-Up because Braine's main characters are
        "arch-conservative, snobbishly reactionary Catholics, com-
        pletely amoral, but finding it very much the 'in' thing to
        do to prattle about their Papist background while knifing
        someone in the back or sleeping around." The reversal at
        the end is "slick and sardonic." This is Braine's best
        novel since Room at the Top.

2   ANON. "Fiction." Kirkus Reviews, 36 (15 August), 922.
            Review of The Crying Game. Frank Batcombe has none of
        the "calculating charm" of Lampton, but he is at times just
        as rotten. Readability has always been both an asset and a
        deficit of Braine's novels. This is a "momentarily involv-
        ing and essentially impermanent" novel.

3   ANON. "Rasping at Progs." Times Literary Supplement
        (29 August), p. 913.
            Review of The Crying Game. A readable novel sharing
        similarities to the thinking of Amis' Take A Girl Like You.
        Finds signs of a kind of "debased Puritanism" in Frank Bat-
        combe. He impresses one as "a humourless man glumly, bor-
        ingly, on the make." In all, this is a crude novel which
        might well be the "melancholy climax" to the Angry Young
        Men.

4   BURGESS, ANTHONY. "At Home in London." New York Times Book
        Review, 73 (27 October), 5, 70.
            Review of The Crying Game. Braine's first novel was a
        study of ambition, guilt, betrayal, hypergamy, and success.
        His latest theme, however, is bigger--getting on in the
        world. But because there is little story to it, the novel
        becomes boring. The hedonism and papistry are too self-
        conscious, and "the narrative style gives off the stale
        apple smell of old popular magazines."

5   DEPLEDGE, DAVID. "The Loving Game." Books and Bookmen, 13
        (April), 44.
            Interview with Braine on the occasion of the publication
        of The Crying Game. His new novel is the most complex and
        sophisticated he has written since The Jealous God. The

author predicts it will shock some readers. He comments on Catholicism in English writing, political and personal freedom.

6   EADE, D. C. "Contemporary Novelists: A Study of Some Themes in the Work of Stan Barstow, John Braine, David Storey and Keith Waterhouse." Master's thesis. University of Leeds.
    Focuses on the working-class themes in Braine's novels through to 1968.

7   GOSLING, RAY. "Just a Sensitive Lad." London Times (31 August), p. 19.
    Review of The Crying Game. Braine's first novel was enjoyable because Lampton was a real hero in a real world. The Vodi was "moving and uncomfortable." In The Jealous God, Braine was his most powerful. The Crying Game, however, lacks a "crisp and tense" plot and "cunning and incisive" writing. Recommends Braine travel more. Although the novel has all of the best-selling ingredients (sex, religion, materialism, ambition), the author is not a very perceptive prophet.

8   GREACEN, ROBERT. "Social Class in Post-War English Fiction." Southern Review, 4 (Winter), 148.
    Comments on class distinctions in Room at the Top and Life at the Top.

9   HAWORTH, DAVID. "More at the Top." New Statesman, 76 (30 August), 262.
    Review of The Crying Game. The development of Braine has been static. His trademarks are here, but his themes are confined. Comments on the (1) adroit handling of class behavior; (2) abundance of sex; (3) "narrative zest"; (4) rendering of Fleet Street; and (5) "obsessive" description of Kings Road. Although readable, clearly written, and very entertaining, the novel is "all Braine and no heart."

10 HEMMINGS, JOHN. "Sin is the Spur." Listener, 80 (29 August), 280.
    Review of The Crying Game. This is the Dick Whittington legend up-dated. Calls this a "plot très réussi, . . . with just the right blend of blandness and piquancy." The novel becomes "one glorious paper-chase."

1968

11   JACKSON, KATHERINE GAUSS. "Books in Brief." Harper's Maga-
       zine, 237 (November), 160-61.
           Review of The Crying Game. Despite its narrative pres-
       sure, the emotional content has been replaced by "facili-
       ty" and very unpleasant characters. The two central
       characters' lack of morality is more boring than shocking.
       The denouement is inevitable and irrelevant because of the
       crudity and sentimentality before. Comments on the repeti-
       tion of ideas and lack of editing.

12   KOHN, MARJORIE R. "Fiction." Library Journal, 93 (15 Sep-
       tember), 3154.
           Review of The Crying Game. An "engaging novel" with
       which Braine remains at the top. Written for sophisticated
       readers.

13   LeHAYE, JUDSON. "Fiction." Bestsellers, 28 (15 November),
       331-32.
           Review of The Crying Game. An "ambling" moral fable ex-
       ploring false gods and false values. The title comes from
       a song which states that "'before you know where you are,
       you are saying goodbye.'" Comments on the characterization
       ("a varying kaleidoscope"), settings (authentic), and
       themes (a look at the "machinations of the political world
       and some drearier aspects of journalism").

14   LEONARD, JOHN. "Books of the Times: Moral Calisthenics."
       New York Times (9 December), p. 45.
           Review of The Crying Game. Braine's Catholicism--
       apparent in his earlier fiction--is united with his new-
       found right-wing political position in a "cautionary tale"
       in which he kicks and talks to death morality. Its
       strengths are in the evocation of London and in convincing
       the reader that he, too, would like to indulge in material
       pleasures. Elsewhere, the novel fails. The Progflogging
       is "relentless and tedious"; women are reduced to "mindless
       and interchangeable pleasure mechanisms"; and Catholics
       make themselves known by word of mouth, not deed.

15   LODGE, DAVID. "The Rat Race." Tablet, 222 (14 September),
       914.
           Review of The Crying Game. An absurd novel, seemingly a
       parody of Braine but offered as a work of "serious preten-
       sions." Braine's treatment of Catholicism is absurd, be-
       cause his characters' professed beliefs are "grotesquely at
       odds with their actual moral behaviour."

1968

16 McGUINNESS, FRANK. Review of The Crying Game. London Maga-
    zine, NS 8 (October), 113-14.
        A vulgar novel filled with "cheap histrionics and
    'Braine' picture situations."

17 MARSH, PAMELA. "After Anger, What?" Christian Science Moni-
    tor (12 December), p. 9.
        Review of The Crying Game. Despite the uninhibited
    characters, this is "a moral book, a cautionary tale." It
    is the story of temptation. Frank escapes corruption, Adam
    does not. Braine's world is so realistic, it is nearly im-
    possible to leave it once one has entered.

18 PÉREZ GALLÉGO, CANDIDO. Literatura y rebeldia en la Ingla-
    terra actual: Los Angles "Angry Young Men," un movimento
    social de los años cincuenta. Madrid: Consejo Superior de
    Investigaciones Cientificas, 32 pp., passim.
        General study of the Angry Young Men, including bio-
    graphical material on Braine. (In Spanish.)

19 POTOKER, EDWARD M. "Fleet Street Frolics." Saturday Review,
    51 (2 November), 38, 43.
        Review of The Crying Game. Like O'Hara and his preoccu-
    pation with wealth, sex, class, and "boozy religiosity,"
    Braine is writing his first book over and over again. His
    writings are anti-climactic; his latest has too much "sham
    sex and sham politics." As a Catholic, Adam is the kind of
    character Greene could have made interesting. Although
    Braine is adult in his handling of the politics of reli-
    gion, unfortunately his tiresome parties obscure his social
    preoccupations.

20 PRICE, R. G. G. "New Fiction." Punch, 255 (4 September),
    346.
        Review of The Crying Game. Braine's knowledge of res-
    taurants and clothes is reminiscent of Arnold Bennett.
    This is a thin story, told well with great vitality.

21 RATCLIFFE, MICHAEL. The Novel Today. London: Longmans,
    48 pp., passim.
        Braine, Wilson, Amis, Drabble, and Johnson are concerned
    with "portray[ing] the individual less in the mesh of his-
    tory than in the more urgent context of contemporary
    society."

1968

22 SHAPIRO, STEPHEN A. "The Ambivalent Animal: Man in the Con-
    temporary British and American Novel." Centennial Review,
    12 (Winter), 15-16.
        Finds a "success-is-failure" theme in Room at the Top
    and Life at the Top with tragic overtones. This is a
    study of "the paradoxical man who wants to 'make it' but
    who realizes that success in the Establishment is a kind
    of failure."

23 TUBE, HENRY. "New Novels: Unreal City." Spectator, 221
    (30 August), 296.
        Review of The Crying Game. Comments on the "surface
    truth" to London city life and Braine's pleasant sense of
    humor. But the novel suffers from a too "real" sense of
    place, "so that the banality of the view produces a curious
    sense of unreality, similar to that conveyed by 'human'
    articles in newspapers."

1969 A BOOKS - NONE

1969 B SHORTER WRITINGS

1   ANDERSON, DAVID. "Phonies and Salauds," in his The Tragic
    Protest: A Christian Study of Some Modern Literature.
    London: SCM Press, pp. 49, 50.
        In The Crying Game, Jack Wales is the phony, "recognized
    by his social success, his insensitiveness, his censorious
    attitude, and the total lack of any reality of self behind
    the public personage."

2   ANON. "Briefly Noted: Fiction." New Yorker, 44 (18 Janu-
    ary), 97.
        Review of The Crying Game. The hero is reminiscent of
    "every provincial adolescent pressing his nose to the pane
    of the adult rich, and thrilling to the adventures of
    Profumo."

3   ANON. "Left do not fight fair--author." London Times
    (1 March), p. 3.
        Braine delivers a speech before students in Caxton Hall,
    Westminster. Says the Left does not "fight fair." Urges
    the students to counter with the truth every time the Left
    sets up a sacred cow. The nation is facing a concerted ef-
    fort to erode the will for survival. If Britain falls, so
    will the rest of the world.

1969

4   ANON. "BBC news attacked as 'leftist.'" London <u>Times</u>
      (24 June), p. 2.
           Braine says the truth is distorted daily on the BBC, for
      only the leftists are heard from the United States. Com-
      ments on John Fitzgerald Kennedy (the worst president),
      Robert Kennedy (would have been an even worse president),
      and Martin Luther King, Jr. ("a troublemaker and a very
      stupid man").

5   ANON. "Paperbacks: Fiction." <u>Publishers Weekly</u>, 196
      (1 September), 53.
           Brief mention of the paperback edition of <u>The Crying
      Game</u>. "A fairly entertaining and most sophisticated novel."

6   BONAVIA, DAVID. "Moscow looks back in anger." London <u>Times</u>
      (19 December), p. 1.
           Pravda attacks Braine and Osborne for letting themselves
      be "'ground down and corrupted by bourgeois propaganda
      machine.'"

7   KUEHL, LINDA. "Books: The Poor, the Power Structure, and the
      Polemicist." <u>Commonweal</u>, 90 (15 May), 269.
           In retrospect, it is clear that Braine, Wain, and Amis
      in the 1950s were not angry at social injustice as much as
      they were unhappy at being born lower class. Their anger
      is "sheer spleen." Comments on Braine's political change
      from left-wing idealism to right-wing pragmatism.

8   LEO, JOHN. "Books." <u>Commonweal</u>, 89 (24 January), 538.
           Review of <u>The Crying Game</u>. In this "interminable ser-
      mon," Braine advances the idea that permissiveness is ruin-
      ing both church and state. "The Catholic characters plod
      through a plotless underworld of betrayal, perversion and
      abortions."

9   MELLOWN, ELGIN W. "Steps Toward Vision: The Development of
      Technique in John Wain's First Seven Novels." <u>South At-
      lantic Quarterly</u>, 45 (Summer), 339.
           Sees Spade, in Wain's <u>The Young Visitors</u>, as almost a
      parody of Braine's Lampton, "the lower-middle-class male
      to whom nothing matters in his grab for money, position,
      and sex."

10   SCHLEUSSNER, BRUNO. <u>Der neopikareske Roman: Pikareske Ele-
      mente in der Struktur englischer Romane 1950-1960</u>. Bonn:
      H. Bouvier Verlag, pp. 6-8.
           Discusses the neopicaresque tradition in <u>Room at the
      Top</u>. (In German.)

1970

1970 A BOOKS - NONE

1970 B SHORTER WRITINGS

1   ANON. "How Normal Can You Get?" <u>Times Literary Supplement</u>
     (25 June), p. 679.
         Review of <u>Stay with Me Till Morning</u>. Had this followed
     <u>Room at the Top</u>, the novel might have been mistaken for a
     satire on provincial Conservative values. Especially fas-
     cinating are the details and asides. Although reminiscent
     of Amis' <u>Take A Girl Like You</u>, his posture seems false be-
     cause he has forced his attitudes upon his characters.
     "It is hard to believe that these ordinary conservative
     provincials would be so obsessed with their antagonism to
     equality, cooperation and deviations from their social
     norm."

2   ANON. "Fiction." <u>Kirkus Reviews</u>, 38 (1 November), 1208.
         Review of <u>The View from Tower Hill</u>. Braine seems to
     waver between censure and consent. Ever since <u>Room at the
     Top</u>, "calculation has yielded to compromise and incentive
     to complacency." Their "glossy illusion of substances"
     may account for his novels' readability.

3   ANON. "PW Forecasts: Fiction." <u>Publishers Weekly</u>, 198
     (28 December), 58.
         Review of <u>The View from Tower Hill</u>. In this ironic,
     rather tragic novel, Braine continues to write smoothly
     and sardonically about the affluent society in Britain to-
     day. The material he uses has been used hundreds of times
     before.

4   BAKER, ROGER. "Crisis." London <u>Times</u> (27 June), p. 22.
         Review of <u>Stay with Me Till Morning</u>. This is a debate
     on the nature of permanence in human relationships.
     Braine's attitudes are disturbing, but his narrative skill
     is ever-present and his prose is "pointed and entertaining."

5   BURGESS, ANTHONY. "A Sort of Rebels," in his <u>The Novel Now:
     A Guide to Contemporary Fiction</u>. Indianapolis: Bobbs-
     Merrill, pp. 147, 149, 152.
         Reprint of 1967.B4.

6   CAPITANCHIK, MAURICE. "New Novels: Late and Early." <u>Specta-
     tor</u>, 224 (27 June), 852.
         Review of <u>Stay with Me Till Morning</u>. Braine's listing
     of objects is tedious. Only the frankness about sex sepa-
     rates this kind of writing from that of women's magazines.

1970

7   DERRICK, CHRISTOPHER. "Books for the Week." <u>Tablet</u>, 224
    (1 August), 742.
        Review of <u>Stay with Me Till Morning</u>. Braine is a heavy-
    handed moralist. The moral is "platitudinous" and ambig-
    uous with an undercurrent of Manicheanism.

8   DUNKLEY, CHRIS. "<u>Man at the Top</u>: Thames Television." London
    <u>Times</u> (15 December), p. 7.
        Comments on the television version of Lampton. Finds
    that some of his complexity was lost in the movie version,
    and now for television "much of the serrated cutting edge
    . . . has been blunted." Lampton is older, more experi-
    enced now, but Braine has not altered his character radi-
    cally. Calls it "a British <u>Peyton Place</u> with strong <u>Power
    Game</u> overtones."

9   GARIOCH, ROBERT. "Mauriac's Twig." <u>Listener</u>, 83 (25 June),
    868.
        Review of <u>Stay with Me Till Morning</u>. Criticizes the
    lack of character development and the cataloguing of small
    details and manufactured goods. This is not a work of art.

10 HAMILTON, IAN. "Lumbering Adulteries." <u>London Magazine</u>,
    NS 10 (July-August), 190.
        Review of <u>Stay with Me Till Morning</u>. A "squalid tale of
    moneyed, middle-aged adulteries . . . . Braine's glossily
    titillating, wealth-fixated novel will have much appeal to
    the bored types he purports to scrutinize."

11 JORDAN, CLIVE. "Dogbitten." <u>New Statesman</u>, 79 (26 June),
    920-21.
        Review of <u>Stay with Me Till Morning</u>. Braine's early
    support for Labour has turned to Conservatism. His new
    novel belongs to "the dogbitten middle years--disillusioned,
    backward-looking, pragmatic in human relationships." His
    style is solid and blunt, "with no charm and precious little
    distinction." Finds most interesting Clive Lendrick's es-
    cape from materialism to art. "This messy attempt to define
    freedom hints at deep dissatisfactions behind Braine's can-
    tankerous public face."

12 LINDROTH, JAMES R. "Book Reviews: Facing Our Sexuality."
    <u>America</u>, 123 (26 December), 568.
        Brief mention of Braine who, along with Wain, Amis, and
    Osborne, ushered in the decade of England's Angry Young
    Men.

1970

13   McDOWELL, FREDERICK P. W.   "Recent British Fiction: Some Es-
      tablished Writers." Contemporary Literature, 11 (Winter),
      406.
           Review of The Crying Game. The moral line wavers be-
      cause the author fails to "hold his characters at suffi-
      cient distance for him to pronounce definitively upon them
      and their standards." Braine does "capture the very tone
      and texture of decadent London."

14   MOORE, REGINALD. "Accomplished Dredging." Books and Bookmen,
      15 (September), 48.
           Review of Stay with Me Till Morning. A disappointing
      novel because the characters are shallow and the plot is
      "drearily predictable." The disintegration of relation-
      ships and personalities is potentially tragic, if only the
      reader could care about the characters.

15   SHRAPNEL, NORMAN. "Trouble in t'Bedroom." Manchester Guardi-
      an Weekly, 102 (4 July), 19.
           Review of Stay with Me Till Morning. A novel which in-
      terests and involves the reader. Praises Braine's tech-
      nique: "it is adroit and enables Braine to engender
      sympathy for the hero in the reader's mind."

16   SOKOLOV, RAYMOND A. "Welsh Rarebit." Newsweek, 76
      (14 September), 110.
           Brief mention of Braine, Wain, and Amis for having re-
      vitalized the English novel in the 1950s.

17   SPANN, EKKEHARD. "'Problemkinder' in der englischen Erzähl-
      kunst der Gegenwart: Graham Greene, Angus Wilson, John
      Wain, Kingsley Amis, Iris Murdoch, William Golding, John
      Braine, Alan Sillitoe." Dissertation, University of
      Tübingen.
           Analyses of Braine's novels through 1969 with commentary
      on their themes and characters. (In German.)

1971 A BOOKS - NONE

1971 B SHORTER WRITINGS

1   ALAYRAC, CLAUDE. "Inside John Braine's Outsider." Caliban, 8
      (August), 113-38.
           A study of the composite hero found in Room at the Top
      and Life at the Top. Comments on The Vodi, The Jealous
      God, and The Crying Game, also. Sees Lampton as the heroic
      figure of our time; a whole generation has identified with
      him.

2   ANON. "Language and Literature: English and American."
      Choice, 8 (October), 1009.
           Review of The View from Tower Hill. In this dreary
      novel, Braine's "sociological detail is more impressive
      than the psychological analysis of character."

3   ANON. "Paperbacks: Fiction." Publishers Weekly, 200
      (13 December), 44.
           Review of The View from Tower Hill. Since Life at the
      Top, Braine's writing has gone downhill. His latest novel
      lacks any interest at all.

4   BARTLEY, EDWARD. "Fiction." Bestsellers, 30 (15 February),
      486.
           Review of The View from Tower Hill. Although Braine has
      included all the ingredients of a "now" novel, this reads
      like "adolescent graffiti." The style is repetitive; the
      cataloguing is boring and gets in the way of the dialogue
      and action. One has the feeling that the novel was written
      with the cinema in mind.

5   DAVIS, L. J. "A Conservative Novel." Chicago Tribune Book
      World (21 March), p. 4.
           Review of The View from Tower Hill. Many critics have
      recently paid equal attention to Braine's vocal Toryism and
      to the contents and qualities of his novels. This is a
      waste of time. In its mixture of disappointment and pessi-
      mism over the human condition, this is a conservative book.
      It is also "a very sad, intelligent, and deeply felt one."

6   GINDIN, JAMES. "Well beyond Laughter: Directions from
      Fifties' Comic Fiction." Studies in the Novel, 3 (Winter),
      357-58.
           The fiction of the 1950s is "comic, satirizing man's
      pretenses." Finds a comic iconoclasm that is both social
      and individual. However, the plain Englishman's point of
      view--never taken in by pretense or romantic aspiration--
      is explicitly visible in Braine's work.

7   LAMPORT, FELICIA. Review of The View from Tower Hill. Satur-
      day Review, 54 (27 February), 30, 32.
           In contrast to his earlier works, The View from Tower
      Hill is "a curiously tepid work" with a quieter mood and
      more leisurely pace. It is hard to believe in Robin and
      Clive as real characters because of interruptions by
      "superfluous characterizations, assessments, sociological
      analyses and . . . itemized catalogues." The shifting
      focus blurs the characters, and Braine's lack of involve-
      ment leaves the reader detached.

1971

8   McDOWELL, FREDERICK P. W. "Recent British Fiction: Some Es-
     tablished Writers." Contemporary Literature, 11 (Autumn),
     406-407.
          Review of The Crying Game. Finds this to be a more in-
     teresting novel than have most reviewers. In this morality
     novel, Braine contrasts the glamorous easy life in London
     with "its hollowness, its transient pleasures, and its ma-
     terialistic bias." The moral line wavers, however, because
     of insufficient distance between author and characters.

9   NELSON, BARBARA S. "Fiction." Library Journal, 96
     (15 March), 975.
          Review of The View from Tower Hill. Sees in Clive and
     Robin the counterparts of some of O'Hara's Gibbsville
     citizens. Although Braine's material is not new, his writ-
     ing is effortless. The characters are believable, and his
     eye for detail is true. Calls this a "skillful dissection
     of a modern marriage."

10   S., P. H. "The Times Diary: Intellectuals Go for EEC." Lon-
     don Times (17 May), p. 12.
          Braine says he is "bored stiff" by the subject of Brit-
     ain's relationship to Europe.

11   SAYRE, NORA. Review of The View from Tower Hill. New York
     Times Book Review (14 February), p. 6.
          This is a puzzling book; it seems Braine is repudiating
     Room at the Top in parts. Unclear whether it is intended
     to be a moral novel (indictment of the conservative life
     and the accumulation of material goods) or documentary
     (life can be violent and messy for both the cautious and
     the reckless).

12   WAGNER, GEOFFREY. "The Realistic and the Real." National
     Review, 23 (6 April), 378-79.
          Review of The View from Tower Hill. Like Allen Drury in
     The Throne of Saturn, Braine writes sociological or repor-
     torial fiction in "a rather more leaden prose. . . . Yet if
     the setting is clapboard, the characters drive far deeper
     into themselves than do Drury's, chiefly through sex."
     Robin is the most interesting character in the novel.

13   WEEKS, EDWARD. "The Peripatetic Review." Atlantic Monthly,
     227 (March), 111-12.
          Review of The View from Tower Hill. The abundance of
     sexuality and lack of much love help to explain the monot-
     ony in modern fiction. Sees similarities between this nov-
     el and John Updike's Couples. "The moral, if there is one,
     is that a marriage of convenience has little to rely on
     when sex intrudes."

14   WHITTEMORE, REED. "Preservers and Destroyers." <u>New Republic</u>,
       164 (13 February), 25.
         Review of <u>The View from Tower Hill</u>. Goes beyond explic-
       it sex to present a novel of manners with "grace and full-
       ness of perception." Finds striking the contrast between
       the assumptions about society in Braine's novel and almost
       any contemporary American novel.

15   ZAVARZADEH, MAS'UD. "Anti-Intellectual Intellectualism in the
       Postwar English Novel: Anatomy of A Metaphor." <u>Ball State</u>
       <u>University Forum</u>, 12 (Autumn), 68.
         Brief mention of Braine in a study of the Angry Young
       Men.

<u>1972 A BOOKS - NONE</u>

<u>1972 B SHORTER WRITINGS</u>

1   ANON. "Over the Counter." <u>Times Literary Supplement</u>
       (27 October), p. 1273.
         Review of <u>The Queen of a Distant Country</u>. Finally,
       Braine has written a novel "of real unforced style and
       feeling." However, Miranda's influence over the boy is
       unclear; this mystery is out of key with the novel's
       "tough naturalism." Also, the ending is overstated and
       Braine's prejudices show through too much. Praises
       Braine's recreation of time and place.

2   BRADBURY, MALCOLM. "The Novel," in Vol. 3, 1945-1965, of <u>The</u>
       <u>Twentieth-Century Mind: History, Ideas, and Literature in</u>
       <u>Britain</u>. Edited by C. B. Cox and A. E. Dyson. London and
       New York: Oxford University Press, pp. 331, 341.
         Finds social documentary and "a marked visionary or
       philosophical strain" in the postwar novels of Braine and
       his contemporaries. <u>Room at the Top</u> lacks "moral density."

3   BUCKMAN, PETER. "Doom and Decay." <u>New Statesman</u>, 84
       (27 October), 609.
         Review of <u>The Queen of a Distant Country</u>. Along with an
       airing of his public feelings, "there is this new and toxic
       element of self-justification on artistic grounds, which
       amounts to an apology for being, as he repeatedly claims,
       selfish, uncommitted to anything but writing, incapable of
       giving or feeling love." The novel is a "quasi-fictional
       essay in self-analysis."

1972

4   FRASER, G. S. "Cultural Nationalism in the Recent English
     Novel," in The Cry of Home: Cultural Nationalism and the
     Modern Writer. Edited by H. Ernest Lewald. Knoxville:
     University of Tennessee Press, pp. 28-29, 36.
          Braine, Wain, and others reflect the passing of the "rig-
     id hierarchy" of the traditional pattern of English life.
     Sees Room at the Top as a "frightening picture of the cor-
     rupting effect of a purely businessman's city" on a decent
     lad. Includes brief biographical background.

5   JONES, D. A. N. "Brown Studies." Listener, 88 (26 October),
     557.
          Brief mention of The Queen of a Distant Country. The
     story is weaker than earlier novels, but more plausible and
     likable.

6   McDOWELL, FREDERICK P. W. "Time of Plenty: Recent British
     Novels." Contemporary Literature, 13 (Summer), 368.
          Review of Stay with Me Till Morning. Braine is a master
     at analyzing conflicts within marriage, friendship, and
     professional life. "As moralist Braine's position is
     clear, but as an artist he perhaps gives the people and the
     milieu that he ostensibly condemns somewhat more than their
     due."

7   MECKIER, JEROME. "Looking Back at Anger: the Success of a
     Collapsing Stance." Dalhousie Review, 52 (Spring), 53-57.
          Sees Lampton as a working-class, male version of Emma
     Bovary. Both characters misunderstand the nature of happi-
     ness when they identify it with a place. This fact and the
     first-person narration complement Braine's satire. More-
     over, Lampton is shown to hold naive and conventional ideas
     lacking in taste, unaware of the unfavorable impression he
     is making on the reader. Although society doesn't punish
     Lampton in Room at the Top, it does in Life at the Top,
     where "living at the top proves harder than the ascent.
     . . . Nearly all the things Joe did to society in Room at
     the Top are done to him in this sequel."

8   PRYCE-JONES, DAVID. "Fiction." London Times (26 October),
     p. 10.
          Review of The Queen of a Distant Country. Braine "cun-
     ningly" reuses much of the material from Room at the Top
     for a different effect. "He could probably transmute it
     into something quite new again next year if he liked."

9   WAUGH, AUBERON. "Celebrating the Bourgeois." Spectator, 229
      (18 November), 797.
          Review of The Queen of a Distant Country. Finds that
      the literary queen's activities and attention paid to
      bourgeois society are peripheral. Braine's book about the
      life of a novelist is done so well, and catches so exactly
      "the strange mixture of callousness, selfishness, boastful-
      ness and untruthfulness which make someone wish to write
      novels, that one can forgive him his slightly-paranoid ob-
      servations about young people and about book reviewers."

1973 A BOOKS - NONE

1973 B SHORTER WRITINGS

1   ANON. "PW Forecasts: Fiction." Publishers Weekly, 203
      (12 February), 64.
          Review of The Queen of a Distant Country. Although a
      "pleasant, intelligent, eminently readable" novel, this is
      a reworking of the same scene once again. Finds most in-
      teresting the personal experiences of a novelist.

2   ANON. "Fiction." Kirkus Reviews, 41 (15 February), 203.
          Review of The Queen of a Distant Country. Interesting
      as "an audit of lapsed relationships." The hero becomes a
      writer while disqualifying himself as a human being. For
      the first time, Braine uses his sharp skills to relate an
      experience which seems "genuinely felt."

3   ANON. "Woolf letters fetch £4,600 at Cyril Connolly 'event'."
      London Times (5 April), p. 4.
          Braine sold the manuscript of Room at the Top for £650
      and of The Vodi for £200 at a book sale at Christie's.

4   ANON. "Briefly Noted: Fiction." New Yorker, 49 (5 May),
      149-50.
          Review of The Queen of a Distant Country. An "extremely
      pompous" book portraying "the artist as a middle-aged
      icicle." The ending is too convenient.

5   ANON. "Language and Literature: English and American."
      Choice, 10 (July), 772.
          Review of The Queen of a Distant Country. This appears
      to be a "thinly cloaked artistic autobiography." The nar-
      rator is not particularly likable; his conversion to life
      and love is not convincing. There is, however, much to re-
      flect on here.

1973

6   BROYARD, ANATOLE. "Room at the Bottom, Too." <u>New York Times</u>
      (23 May), p. 45.
          Review of <u>The Queen of a Distant Country</u>. Braine has
      become "a complacent old hen." This novel is filled with
      dogmatisms about writing as if the author believed them.
      Says Braine was better as an Angry Young Man. Perhaps he
      will become an angry middle-aged man when he reads the re-
      views of his new novel. "It may do him good."

7   DeFEO, RONALD. "Voice from a Distant Country." <u>National Re-
      view</u>, 25 (8 June), 643-44.
          Review of <u>The Queen of a Distant Country</u>. Like his
      earlier works, readability, recognizable characters, lucid
      prose, and unpretentious style are all virtues of this
      novel. However, in spite of its craftsmanlike, sincere,
      human work, it fails to impress the reader. Some of the
      plot elements are a reworking of <u>Room at the Top</u>, and the
      voice and concerns of the narrator seem rather dated, lack-
      ing in "urgency and originality." When he does try to deal
      with more sophisticated characters, as in <u>The View from
      Tower Hill</u>, his intensity focuses only on their sex lives,
      mechanical at best. Concludes that in his recent books,
      Braine hasn't had much to say. "Aside from its lack of
      complexity and resonance, and its annoying obligatory sex
      scenes, the new novel is not quite convincing." It lacks
      the tightness and intensity of his best book, <u>The Jealous
      God</u>. In <u>The Queen of a Distant Country</u> and many other
      works, Braine has "unfortunately retained a voice from a
      distant country."

8   DOYLE, PAUL A. "Fiction." <u>Bestsellers</u>, 33 (15 May), 86-87.
          Review of <u>The Queen of a Distant Country</u>. This book
      puts to rest the charge that Braine is a one-book writer.
      This is "a tough, frank, stinging, no-holds-barred novel--a
      book which is at times embarrassingly fascinating." Un-
      doubtedly, there is much that is autobiographical here.

9   FENBY, GEORGE. "The Organic Self (A Study of Selected English
      Working-Class Fiction)." Dissertation. University of
      Connecticut.
          Braine, Lawrence, Sillitoe, and Storey are all concerned
      with the stature of the self. In <u>Room at the Top</u>, the
      organic self is at its core, reflecting working-class
      values and attacking "people who allow their jobs, social
      position, material ambitions, class membership, purely
      physical tendencies, and social and cultural ideals to sub-
      vert their essential sensitive and loving selves." These
      writers promote "a faith in a highly sensual, primary rela-
      tionship," but unfortunately modern society is "too warped"
      to allow the organic desires fulfillment.

10   GORDON, JAN B. "Books." Commonweal, 99 (14 December), 301.
         Review of The Queen of a Distant Country. This Bildungs-
      roman seems inappropriate in an age when spiritual growth,
      too, is made to seem such a fiction. Although it shares
      similarities with the artist's arrival novel, this is
      really about a departure--and people leaving has always
      been the central metaphor of the Angry Young Men. Where
      the other writers seem dated now, Braine continues to speak
      with urgency, but now with a mellow voice. Murdoch's The
      Black Prince, together with the latest of Lessing, Spark,
      and Braine, suggests a revival in the British novel. All
      of these novels speak of a relationship between "personal
      and formal freedom." The threat of imprisonment is near;
      therefore, the writers deal with "spaces that lack commu-
      nity and hold out little hope for its restoration." The
      plot is clouded and the characters never change. Rather,
      they "develop new myths to explain their stasis."

11   GUNSTON, DAVID. "Growing Point: Man bites (or snarls at)
         man." London Times (25 July), p. 13.
         Lists the things Braine doesn't like about other men:
      bitten fingernails; long hair; dirty shirts; trendy gear of
      any kind; particularly medallions; identity bracelets;
      rings; an accent which is not native to the speaker; . . .
      left-wing convictions; men who mumble; men who come too
      near to you or touch you; non-smokers; teetotallers; men of
      my own age who're fitter than me. And above all, any trace
      of envy."

12   KUNA, F. M. "Current Literature 1972: II. New Writing:
         Fiction." English Studies, 54 (October), 480.
         Review of The Queen of a Distant Country. Although at
      home in a tough natural world, one senses a quality which
      adds "a poetic, almost spiritual dimension to the natural-
      istic setting." The novel's inner drama derives from the
      "process of self-discovery which is built like an indeter-
      minate, contrapuntal theme into the confident and deter-
      mined naturalistic structure of the book." Sees this as a
      new and promising departure from Braine's former, "often
      black and white technique."

13   LASATER, ALICE E. "The Breakdown in Communication in the
         Twentieth-Century Novel." Southern Quarterly, 11 (October),
         11.
         With its emphasis on materialism, Room at the Top is
      related to Eugene Ionesco's Le nouveau Locataire. Also, as
      in The Invisible Man, Lampton is unable to understand or be
      understood by society. He ends up dooming himself "to the
      world of appearances he had pursued."

1973

14   OWEN, JOAN. "Fiction." <u>Library Journal</u>, 98 (15 April),
      1305-1306.
            Review of <u>The Queen of a Distant Country</u>. "The con-
      scious manipulation and ultimate triumph over [its cliché
      theme] is both the novel's strength and its hero's quest."
      Tom and Miranda's love story is "northern, homespun, in-
      fused with Gothic suggestions of power, guilt, and politi-
      cal idealism." Comments on Braine's clear style.

15   S., P. H. "A Thousand Words a Day." <u>Newsweek</u>, 81 (30 April),
      82-83A.
            Review of <u>The Queen of a Distant Country</u>. This is a
      well-made novel with accurate observations about writers.
      The happy ending is a bit like a bedtime story. Lacks
      melodrama or sentimentality except for the last half-dozen
      pages.

16   THEROUX, PAUL. "Close Friends, Woman's Influence, Vegetarians,
      Femme Fatale." <u>New York Times Book Review</u> (27 May), p. 16.
            Review of <u>The Queen of a Distant Country</u>. Obviously
      about the writing of <u>A Room at the Top</u>, this novel lacks
      thought. "To write a widely-acclaimed novel is a good
      thing; to write about acclamation in this tedious way is
      bad manners."

17   VINCENT, LUCY. "Fiction." <u>Books and Bookmen</u>, 18 (January),
      83.
            Review of <u>The Queen of a Distant Country</u>. The later
      scenes of passion are disappointing to both Tom and the
      reader.

<u>1974 A BOOKS - NONE</u>

<u>1974 B SHORTER WRITINGS</u>

1   ALLEN, BRUCE. "Language Arts." <u>Library Journal</u>, 99
      (15 September), 2156.
            Review of <u>Writing a Novel</u>. Braine's advice for would-be
      novelists is pragmatic but "reductive" and "a bit program-
      matic."

2   ANON. "Commentary: Brainewaves." <u>Times Literary Supplement</u>
      (26 April), p. 444.
            Review of <u>Writing a Novel</u>. While somewhat enlightening
      on self-discipline, pacing, and the frustrations of writ-
      ing, Braine constantly avoids the question of ability. Re-
      calls an anecdote about Braine's visit with Lord Soper
      after the novelist's return from the United States.

1974

3   ANON. Review of <u>Writing a Novel</u>. <u>Times Educational Supple-
    ment</u> (3 May), p. 23.
        Braine draws on his experiences as a novelist for twenty
    years. Calls this "a sensible guide to the techniques of
    his trade."

4   ANON. "Room at the Bottom." <u>Economist</u>, 251 (25 May), 145.
        Review of <u>Writing a Novel</u>. An encouraging and practical
    book, valuable for Braine's analyses of passages from
    O'Hara, Powell, Fitzgerald, and himself.

5   ANON. "Non-Fiction." <u>Kirkus Reviews</u>, 42 (15 July), 771.
        Review of <u>Writing a Novel</u>. Braine seldom says anything
    worthwhile in this naive book.

6   ANON. "PW Forecasts: Nonfiction." <u>Publishers Weekly</u>, 206
    (29 July), 49.
        Review of <u>Writing a Novel</u>. "A sound, entertaining, use-
    ful middlebrow approach to writing a publishable novel."

7   IVASHEVA, VALENTINA. "Literary Encounters." <u>Anglo-Soviet
    Journal</u>, 35 (December), 26-31.
        Finds a division between writers before and after World
    War II and those writing in the 1960s. In Golding, Snow,
    Wain, Murdoch, Wilson, Wain, and Braine, finds a tired,
    pessimistic, conservative tone.

8   O'KEEFE, TIMOTHY. "Hubbub in the Piazza." <u>Guardian Weekly</u>,
    110 (4 May), 22.
        Review of <u>Writing a Novel</u>. One of Braine's most inter-
    esting chapters concerns improbability in the novel. His
    selections from Powell and Fitzgerald are deft, but he is
    overly fond of O'Hara. He is much better with his comments
    on dialogue. Questions the novelist's role as narrator and
    Braine's emphasis on the "mot juste."

9   S., P. H. "The Times Diary: Right on." London <u>Times</u>
    (4 June), p. 14.
        In a speech delivered before the Monday Club's Women's
    Group, Braine says the Conservatives are more in tune with
    the people than was the Left. Included in his speech are
    the following themes: (1) people's voting has little to do
    with their political beliefs; (2) the minority's gods were
    Freud and Marx; (3) never give in to terrorists; and (4) a
    cutback in the universities is essential.

10 THEROUX, PAUL. "Personal Products." <u>New Statesman</u>, 87
    (3 May), 631-32.
        Satirical response to <u>Writing a Novel</u>.

1974

11   WAUGH, AUBERON. "Cult of Boredom." <u>Books and Bookmen</u>, 19
         (June), 8-9.
             Review of <u>Writing a Novel</u>. Braine's rules are inept if
         not downright wrong. He is obviously unhappy with the re-
         views he has been getting and suffers from "an acute attack
         of writers' paranoia." His statements are often crass.

12   WEBB, W. L. "Spring Reading." <u>Manchester Guardian Weekly</u>,
         110 (19 January), 26.
             Brief mention of <u>Writing a Novel</u>.

1975 A BOOKS - NONE

1975 B SHORTER WRITINGS

1   ANON. "Fiction." <u>Kirkus Reviews</u>, 43 (15 December), 1390.
             Review of <u>The Pious Agent</u>. "A slew of poison-darted
         corpses . . . clutter up the obliquely transparent action."
         This novel is "superagent kid stuff in which [Braine] turns
         over an old new leaf."

2   FINGER, LOUIS. "Hit Parade." <u>Times Literary Supplement</u>
         (20 June), p. 689.
             Review of <u>The Pious Agent</u>. A routine plot lacking any
         real enthusiasm written in "nerveless prose" filled with
         clichés.

3   FORREST, ALAN. "Fiction." <u>Books and Bookmen</u>, 21 (November),
         53-54.
             Review of <u>The Pious Agent</u>. A highly readable tour de
         force, a "splendid right-wing fantasy in which nasty
         Lefties get their comeuppance with the author's evident
         relish." The beginning is reminiscent of John Gardner's
         first Boysie Oakes novel. The double-cross and exchanges
         are more sophisticated than one would expect in this kind
         of work. Enjoyable reading because the characters are
         skillfully drawn.

4   GLENDENNING, VICTORIA. "Seeing Red." <u>New Statesman</u>, 89
         (13 June), 782.
             Review of <u>The Pious Agent</u>. There are some surprises,
         but the novel has "a lot of completely unfictional matter
         in the way of sub-Bond sartorial detail," including an ob-
         session with floor-coverings. Concludes that it is good
         reading "of a routinely competent kind." His description
         of an England crawling with hostile elements is vivid.

5   KEATING, H. R. F. "Crime." London Times (12 June), p. 12.
        Review of The Pious Agent. The extramarital sex angle
    is not germane to the novel and adds nothing to the devel-
    opment of theme or character. The dialogue about contempo-
    rary artifacts is "trowelled on," the espionage details
    ring false, and his security precautions are "pure Sax
    Rohmer mumbo-jumbo."

6   LASKI, MARGHANITA. Review of The Pious Agent. Listener, 93
    (5 June), 748.
        The overall effect of the novel is nastiness as well as
    of a thriller "contrived rather than compelled."

7   S., P. H. "The Times Diary: Let it be." London Times
    (3 February), p. 12.
        Notice that Braine is working on The Stirrer, a play to
    be produced in the autumn in the West End. Although the
    play might be political, Braine denies this possibility.

8   _____. "The Times Diary: Novel thought." London Times
        (10 April), p. 16.
        Both Braine and Mary Wilson agree they like poetry that
    rhymes.

9   WILSON, COLIN. "The Varieties of Wish-Fulfillment," in his
        The Craft of the Novel. London: Victor Gollancz, p. 117.
        Sees Room at the Top as "a work of social criticism with
    tragic overtones." Both Amis' Lucky Jim and Braine's Room
    at the Top are "wish-fulfillment fantasies in the romantic
    tradition. Both have the air of freshness and excitement
    that always seems to accompany successful self-image
    projection."

1976 A BOOKS - NONE

1976 B SHORTER WRITINGS

1   ANON. "PW Forecasts: Fiction." Publishers Weekly, 209
    (5 January), 60.
        Review of The Pious Agent. Although a "neat idea," pos-
    sibly too British for American readers. Finds in the back-
    ground plenty of money and sado-masochistic torture.

2   ANON. "Brief Reviews." Critic, 35 (Fall), 94.
        Review of The Pious Agent. A "thriller with a twist"
    that seems a parody of Graham Greene.

1976

3   ARTHUR, BUDD. "Espionage and Intrigue." Booklist, 72
    (1 March), 960-61.
        Review of The Pious Agent. Written with style and suc-
    cess. The agent is "a hit-man whose second thoughts never
    interfere with his efficiency."

4   ASPLER, TONY. "Business Boy." Listener, 95 (3 June), 718.
        Review of Waiting for Sheila. The people in this
    "straight novel" are "selfish, deceitful, materialistic.
    . . . It would not be so bad if one didn't suspect that the
    Company has become beguiled by its own product, and that
    the novel applauds rather than queries Jim's resounding
    hardhat philosophy."

5   CALLENDAR, NEWGATE. "Criminals at Large." New York Times
    Book Review (2 May), pp. 62-63.
        Review of The Pious Agent. As a caricature of espionage
    fiction, there are no surprises; everything is predictable.
    Finds unbelievable the memo device and the Director's dia-
    logue. Although it is "derivative and eclectic," the novel
    is "exciting and stimulating" to read and is saved by its
    style. The killer agent and the Russians talk and act like
    real human beings.

6   GOSLING, RAY. "Fiction: Revisiting a Fifties' Phenomenon."
    London Times (4 December), p. 7.
        Like Room at the Top, Life at the Top is a superb,
    "moral, exciting, robust family story" and an inoffensive
    sexy book. In The Pious Agent, we see a different Braine--
    "violent, sexually explicit and kinky Catholic." But this
    is a superficial novel, lacking the depth of family life,
    man's inner battle between freedom and responsibility, and
    the efforts for self-advancement.

7   LeHAYE, JUDSON. "Fiction." Bestsellers, 36 (June), 67.
        Review of The Pious Agent. Braine continues to express
    his contempt for contemporary mores in what might be a
    spoof on the current mystery story craze. As in his other
    novels, the central character has "a predilection for aves
    and orisons, ingrained through early training, and now car-
    ried through varied episodes of mayhem, murder, and sex."
    Although the novel lacks credibility, Braine is to be com-
    mended for his style, description, format, and "imaginative
    use of omission."

8   MOUNT, FERDINAND. "The Durable Consumer." <u>Times Literary</u>
    <u>Supplement</u> (4 June), p. 665.
        Review of <u>Waiting for Sheila</u>. His first "straight" nov-
    el since his manual <u>Writing a Novel</u>, this is "a first-class
    working model of his own method." The plot, relationships,
    and celebration of sex are of "sound quality"; the narra-
    tive tone is "dour"; the observations are sharp and the
    pleasures sudden, and with the exception of Henry the char-
    acters are solid and consistent. However, Braine refuses
    to allow himself to be carried away. Some day, hopefully,
    he will write a book "700 pages long, rampantly self-
    indulgent, violently inconsequential--and irresistible."

9   S., P. H. "The Times Diary: Book Walk." London <u>Times</u>
    (24 June), p. 16.
        Braine participated in the book society's second annual
    sponsored walk around the London publishing houses. He
    complained of the heat.

10 VEIT, H. C. "Mystery...Detective...Suspense...." <u>Library</u>
    <u>Journal</u>, 101 (1 April), 927.
        Review of <u>The Pious Agent</u>. An unorthodox view of the
    British secret service. "The display of too many Bondian
    brand names is maddening and the multiplicity of murders
    cannot reflect accepted opinions of Catholic piety."

11 WADE, ROSALIND. "Literary Supplement: Quarterly Fiction Re-
    view." <u>Contemporary Review</u>, 229 (October), 214-15.
        Review of <u>Waiting for Sheila</u>. Braine "contrives to
    generate a kind of steamy excitement" with explicit sex
    scenes. The sequence of events is "brusquely unfolded,
    sometimes with crudity but always with humour and common-
    sense." Sees Jim Seathwaite as a man permanently hurt by
    his experiences as a child; hence, there's no final solu-
    tion at the end.

12 WINKS, ROBIN. "Robin Winks on Mysteries." <u>New Republic</u>, 174
    (26 June), 30.
        Review of <u>The Pious Agent</u>. Calls this "a distinctively
    bad book" which fails in its imitation of Len Deighton.
    The theological overtones and writing are obvious. Finds
    on page 212 a stunning moment which is "nicely tricky."

1977

1977 A BOOKS - NONE

1977 B SHORTER WRITINGS

1   ANON. "Break: Concretely spoken." <u>Times Educational Supple-</u>
     <u>ment</u> (24 June), p. 80.
          Statement by Braine that he is obsessed by a drive for
     perfection, but knows he will never reach it.

2   S., P. H. "The Times Diary: Still room at the top for nov-
     elists." London <u>Times</u> (28 September), p. 14.
          Announces that Braine is about to begin a 175,000-word
     epic to counter prophets who predict the death of the novel
     as a serious art form. Braine states: "'The English novel
     isn't dying. It's just that novelists have alienated them-
     selves from the public, and they don't try to find out what
     the reader wants.'" Says novels today are too "'introspec-
     tive, too narrow.'"

JOHN WAIN

Writings by John Wain
1951-1977

Mixed Feelings: Nineteen Poems (1951)

Contemporary Reviews of Romantic Poetry, ed. (1953)

Hurry on Down (1953; as Born in Captivity, 1954)

Interpretations: Essays on Twelve English Poems, ed. (1955)

Living in the Present (1955)

A Word Carved on a Sill (1956)

Preliminary Essays (1957)

The Contenders (1958)

International Literary Annual, No. 1, ed. (1958)

Gerard Manley Hopkins: An Idiom of Desperation (1959)

A Traveling Woman (1959)

Fanny Burney's Diary, ed. (1960)

Nuncle and Other Stories (1960)

Weep Before God: Poems (1961)

Sprightly Running: Part of an Autobiography (1962)

Strike the Father Dead (1962)

Anthology of Modern Poetry, ed. (1963)

Essays on Literature and Ideas (1963)

The Take-Over Bid (1963)

The Living World of Shakespeare: A Playgoer's Guide (1964)

Wildtrack: A Poem (1965)

The Young Visitors (1965)

Death of the Hind Legs and Other Stories (1966)

The Dynasts, ed. (1966)

Selected Shorter Poems of Thomas Hardy, ed. (1966)

Selected Stories of Thomas Hardy, ed. (1966)

Arnold Bennett (1967)

The Smaller Sky (1967)

Shakespeare: Macbeth: A Casebook, ed. (1968)

Letters to Five Artists (1969)

A Winter in the Hills (1970)

Shakespeare: Othello: A Casebook, ed. (1971)

The Life Guard and Other Stories (1971)

A House for the Truth: Critical Essays (1972)

The Shape of Feng (1972)

Johnson as Critic, ed. (1973)

Dr. Johnson out of Town (1974)

Samuel Johnson (1974)

Harry in the Night: An Optimistic Comedy (1975)

Johnson on Johnson: A Selection of the Personal and Autobiographical
    Writings of Samuel Johnson (1709-1784), ed. (1976)

Professing Poetry (1977)

Writings about John Wain
1953-1977

1953 A BOOKS - NONE

1953 B SHORTER WRITINGS

1   ALLEN, WALTER. "New Novels." <u>New Statesman and Nation</u>, 46
     (24 October), 496, 498.
          Review of <u>Hurry on Down</u>. "The picaresque, for Mr. Wain,
     is essentially the comic and the satiric; and Mr. Wain, in
     his grim and gritty and tough-minded way, can be very funny
     indeed." In Wain are the makings of a true satirist. Like
     Smollett, he has "the true churlish, curmudgeonly, deni-
     grating attitude towards human nature and institutions."
     Links Charles Lumley and Jim Dixon (in <u>Lucky Jim</u>) as expo-
     nents of "the new hero."

2   ANON. "Matters of Conscience." <u>Times Literary Supplement</u>
     (9 October), p. 641.
          Review of <u>Hurry on Down</u>. There are similarities between
     Wain and early Waugh and Linklater, but there is a differ-
     ence: Lumley is fleeing from parents, academic culture and
     gentility, a manner of speech and a way of living. Al-
     though rather clumsy in conception, the novel demonstrates
     Wain's "considerable powers of observation and a great fund
     of comic invention."

3   CHARQUES, R. D. "New Novels." <u>Spectator</u>, 191 (2 October),
     380.
          Review of <u>Hurry on Down</u>. "Terse and uncomplicated in
     his vein of absurdity, loose-muscled and witty in style,
     Mr. Wain scores most freely at his most anarchic moments
     of dissent from current social moralities. The fooling is
     sometimes a little weak, the wit of the dialogue is not al-
     ways in character, and here and there, rotating on the axis
     of school and university, Mr. Wain stretches the long arm
     of coincidence. But he has made a very good comic start."

1953

4   SHRAPNEL, NORMAN. "New Fiction." <u>Manchester Guardian</u>
     (2 October), p. 4.
          Review of <u>Hurry on Down</u>. "Chasing its sneering and suf-
     fering young hero from job to job is most stimulating, at
     any rate for part of the way; the book seemed to me to
     start well, go off in the middle, and recover brilliantly
     near the end." Although Wain's sharp eye and economical
     pen equip him well for modern comedy, his moods do not mix
     comfortably. "Perhaps they are not meant to."

1954 A BOOKS - NONE

1954 B SHORTER WRITINGS

1   ANON. "Fiction." <u>Kirkus Reviews</u>, 22 (1 February), 76.
          Review of <u>Born in Captivity</u>. Although Wain's first nov-
     el has wit and observation, it is not "consistently deft
     nor always palatable."

2   ANON. "Tradition and Originality." <u>Times Literary Supplement</u>
     (19 February), p. 122.
          Both Amis and Wain represent a reaction against the neo-
     romanticism of the 1940s. Because of his poetry in <u>Mixed</u>
     <u>Feelings</u>, Wain has been identified as a "member" of the
     "neo-metaphysical school." He writes within a framework of
     "tart colloquialism and tricky metrical form" under the in-
     fluence of Empson's <u>The Gathering Storm</u>.

3   ANON. "Fiction." <u>Booklist</u>, 50 (1 March), 280.
          Brief mention of <u>Born in Captivity</u>. Wain's characters
     are "Dickensian in their grotesqueness and vitality." As
     a modern picaresque novel, Wain's narrative is edged with
     "barbed commentary" on the frailties of the British middle
     class.

4   ANON. Briefly Noted." <u>New Yorker</u>, 30 (20 March), 114.
          Brief mention of <u>Born in Captivity</u>. "A bright, wry, in-
     telligent, and generally amusing book."

5   ANON. "New Books in Brief: Call of the Wild." <u>Nation</u>, 178
     (27 March), 264-65.
          Review of <u>Born in Captivity</u>. The novel has its amusing
     places, but "the total effect is dispiriting." None of the
     jobs performed by Lumley are productive; hence, his various
     trades are given "a slightly frivolous quality--as though
     they were wish-fulfillment." Somewhat reminiscent of
     Huxley's <u>Antic Hay</u>.

6   DOBRÉE, BONAMY. "English Poetry Today: The Younger Genera-
    tion." Sewanee Review, 62 (Autumn), 609-10.
        As a "University Wit," Wain is an extremely clever poet
    "whose realm seems to lie in emotions produced by the in-
    tellect rather than by the whole being." Quotes from
    "Eighth Type of Ambiguity" to illustrate Empson's influence
    on Wain.

7   FULLER, EDMUND. "The Unhappy Drifter." New York Times Book
    Review (21 March), pp. 5, 20.
        Review of Born in Captivity. Because Wain addresses
    himself to an unfunny subject, this is a book "occasionally
    hilarious, always interesting, but essentially unsatisfac-
    tory." Into a lightly satirical novel Wain injects "jar-
    ring elements irreconcilable with its general tone." For
    example, he allows Lumley to become contemptible instead of
    sympathetic; therefore, the readers are unable to identify
    with the hero. Wain apparently failed to decide clearly
    what kind of book he was writing.

8   HARTLEY, ANTHONY. "Poets of the Fifties." Spectator, 193
    (27 August), 260-61.
        Brief mention of Wain's essay about Empson's influence
    on the poets of the 1950s. Wain, Amis, Davie, and Gunn all
    share a similar tone ("'dissenting' and non-conformist,
    cool, scientific and analytical"), a distrust of rhetoric
    (influenced by Empson as well as Ogden and Richards' Mean-
    ing of Meaning, and the logical positivists), and a dislike
    of the "loose romanticism" of the war years.

9   HENDERSON, ROBERT W. "Fiction." Library Journal, 79
    (15 April), 775.
        Review of Born in Captivity. A brilliant satirization
    of "sophomoric-Bohemian university graduates who, in a
    naively sophisticated way, scorn the civilization in which
    they find themselves seeking a freedom from the 'captivity'
    of a bourgeois society, but actually leading to a futile
    nihilism."

10 SCOTT, GEORGE. "A bright first novel about a very bright
    young man." Truth, 154 (5 February), 185.
        Like the hero of Amis' Lucky Jim, Lumley in Hurry on
    Down is a comic conception in a recognizably contemporary
    world. Unlike Amis, Wain fails to reveal "a more intense
    'feel' of the contemporary scene." Perhaps the picaresque
    convention forced Wain to give "but a superficial impres-
    sion of the modern background to his comedy."

1954

11   SULLIVAN, RICHARD. Review of Born in Captivity. Chicago Sun-
       day Tribune (28 March), p. 8.
           Brief review including plot summary and character study.

12   W., J. "Among the New Books." San Francisco Chronicle: This
       World (22 August), p. 20.
           Brief review of Born in Captivity. Wain places Lumley
       in a "mildly allegorical world" abounding in coincidences
       with characters simultaneously individuals and types. "But
       the setting is fitting to a bourgeois Parsifal like Charles
       Lumley who seeks the grail in defiance of society." The
       outcome suggests that the world is reduced to a formula
       only for snobs.

13   WICKENDON, DAN. "Here, in a Manner of Speaking, Comes Tom
       Jones Again." New York Herald Tribune Book Review
       (21 March), p. 3.
           Review of Born in Captivity. Although basically a se-
       rious novel, this is also wildly funny and satirical. Wain
       manages to conjure up "the poetry, the anguish, the inci-
       dental absurdities of a man's first passionate love" to-
       gether with a throng of "sharply drawn" characters, "all of
       them wonderfully alive." In spite of its debt to Anthony
       Powell and the eighteenth-century models, this is a highly
       original novel with its "sinewy prose" and "devastating
       satire." Wain is as "hard-headed, as devoid of romantic
       and sentimental illusions, as any of his contemporaries,
       but he most refreshingly writes like a young man glad to
       be alive and rejoicing in his youth."

1955 A BOOKS - NONE

1955 B SHORTER WRITINGS

1   ALLEN, WALTER. "University Wits," in his The Novel To-Day.
       London: British Council, pp. 29-30.
           Wain, Amis and Murdoch express "a new attitude and
       values markedly different from those hitherto common in
       the contemporary novel." Their heroes are undoubtedly in-
       fluenced by George Orwell, Dr. Leavis, the logical posi-
       tivists, Robert Graves, and even P. N. Newby. As an ex-
       periment in the picaresque, Hurry on Down is reminiscent
       also of Smollett with its seriousness expressed through
       wild farce and its "pace and splenetic energy" of prose,
       all of which reveals an "exasperated fury at the world."

2   DERRICK, CHRISTOPHER. "Anti-Heroides." <u>Tablet</u>, 206
        (10 September), 256.
            Like Amis' <u>That Uncertain Feeling</u>, <u>Living in the Present</u>
        is a modern morality focused on an anti-hero. The wit of
        <u>Hurry on Down</u> is still present, but "the crossness seems to
        predominate and to be responsible for a wearisome amount of
        gross overstatement." This, together with "philosophic
        overtones conceived on somewhat callow lines," dulls an
        otherwise entertaining book.

3   KALB, BERNARD. "Three Comers." <u>Saturday Review</u>, 38 (7 May),
        22.
            Literary journalists often relate together Amis, Wain,
        and Murdoch because all three attended Oxford, write wit-
        tily, teach, and are of the same general age. Amis com-
        ments that although this attention is excellent publicity,
        it is inaccurate because all three writers are doing dif-
        ferent things. Brief biographical mention.

4   SCOTT, J. D. "The British Novel: Lively As a Cricket."
        <u>Saturday Review</u>, 38 (7 May), 23.
            Wain's <u>Hurry on Down</u> shows strong affinities with Wil-
        liam Cooper's <u>Scenes from Provincial Life</u>, Amis' <u>Lucky Jim</u>,
        and Murdoch's <u>Under the Net</u>, all of which are "Orwellian in
        the sense of being classless." Of the writers, Wain "is
        most specifically a disciple of Orwell, about whose work he
        has written some of the most penetrating things said on the
        subject."

1956 A BOOKS - NONE

1956 B SHORTER WRITINGS

1   ANON. "Poems Formal and Colloquial." <u>Times Literary Supple-</u>
        <u>ment</u> (8 June), p. 346.
            Review of <u>A Word Carved on a Sill</u>. Wain's poetic tone
        separates his writing from that of Thom Gunn and Elizabeth
        Jennings. This tone is "high and formal--what one thinks
        of as utterance rather than speech--and it is a public tone
        that can become stilted and self-conscious." Wain is at
        his best when "the sensual image is given rein among con-
        ceptual ones, enriching them, and, at the same time, being
        held in check by them." In these poems, the tone is re-
        served, the form is strict (<u>terza rima</u>), and the imagery
        "is never merely decorative but always an integral, sus-
        taining part of the whole."

1956

2   CARTER, THOMAS H. "Book Reviews." <u>Shenandoah</u>, 7 (Summer),
    57-58.
        Finds in the writings of Wain, Amis, and Murdoch, "high
    spirits, a cinematographic technique, and a flair for come-
    dy; each made a shrewd and knowing use of picaresque
    conventions."

3   CHAUCER, DAVID. "Book Reviews." <u>Shenandoah</u>, 7 (Summer),
    60-62.
        Review of <u>Living in the Present</u>. Finds some uncertainty
    of purpose. The initial situation is "splendid," but the
    move towards seriousness "numbs the comic sense" and even-
    tually smothers Wain's best instincts. It seems Wain is
    writing a novel which lies somewhere between the best of
    Arnold Bennett--suggested by the accurate social documenta-
    tion--and the early Waugh.

4   FRASER, G. S. "The Newer Poets." <u>New Statesman and Nation</u>,
    51 (2 June), 632.
        Review of <u>A Word Carved on a Sill</u>. Wain's earlier
    formula for poetry--neat, clear, authoritative, precise--
    sometimes seemed to write the poem. In his later poetry,
    however, there is a move "beyond a level of assured accom-
    plishment that was becoming mechanical."

5   HARTLEY, ANTHONY. "Poets of the Fifties." <u>Spectator</u>, 197
    (20 July), 100-101.
        General article covering the publication of <u>New Lines</u>
    and <u>The Chatto Book of Modern Poetry</u>. In the former, finds
    a "frustrated romanticism" lying at the bottom of Wain's
    intellectual poems. Wain's best poetry "takes its tone
    from the note of longing behind it, and the apparatus of
    modern culture gets in the way of this."

6   HYNES, SAM. "New School: The 'Poor Sod' As Hero." <u>Common-
    weal</u>, 64 (13 April), 51.
        Wain's epigraph to <u>Born in Captivity</u> defines both the
    nature of the new hero in English fiction and the role of
    the author in relation to him. Unlike Virginia Woolf, Wain
    is concerned with "the comic view of the sensitive soul."
    The new hero is a type--"the postwar Everyman"--who is
    trapped "by nature in a prison" caused partly by the Wel-
    fare State and partly by his own social and psychological
    situation. The hero emerges as a self-conscious, bumbling,
    "fragmented being" who either submits to the prison rules
    or escapes. He is, in essence, a moralist who must deal
    with an amoral or immoral world.

7   IGNATOW, DAVID. "Literary and Academic Themes." <u>Saturday</u>
    <u>Review</u>, 39 (15 December), 36-37.
        Brief mention of <u>A Word Carved on a Sill</u>. "Reflective
    and dramatic by turns, a self-defeating humanism emerges
    from the book." The only compensation appears in the
    whimsical, light poems.

8   MORSE, SAMUEL FRENCH. "Five Young Poets." <u>Poetry</u>, 89
    (December), 197-98.
        Review of <u>A Word Carved on a Sill</u>. Wain is the very
    anthithesis of poets Laurie Lee or R. E. Thomas. The title
    comes from a line by Robert Graves. In this celebration of
    "the pleasures and problems of a quotidian," an occasional
    shadow of "deliberate iconoclasm, or a show of assumed or-
    dinariness, recoils upon itself. One sees through the dis-
    guise a little too easily: the elaborateness is in the
    manner and not in the joke itself." Wain's real style is
    revealed in incidentals, such as the repetition of a line
    or the "off-handed manner" of Philip Larkin and Elizabeth
    Jennings. Unlike these poets, however, Wain takes greater
    risks by developing a "public" tone which, "when it does
    not come off, represents a more obvious failure. When it
    succeeds, the detachment it seems to depend upon gives the
    work its clear focus."

9   RIDLER, ANNE. "A Group of Poets." <u>Manchester Guardian</u>
    (13 July), p. 6.
        Review of <u>A Word Carved on a Sill</u>. Although Wain and
    D. J. Enright were grouped together with seven other poets
    in Robert Conquest's <u>New Lines</u>, this fact and the introduc-
    tion to the collection adds little to one's understanding
    of the poets. Wain's poems are "cleverly organised, some-
    times witty, but their total effect is rather dreary, as
    though a formula had taken the place of inspiration."

10 SCOTT, GEORGE. "Jolly Jack and Lucky Jim," in his <u>Time and</u>
    <u>Place</u>. London: Staples Press, pp. 215-17.
        Amis, Wain, and Murdoch share the following similari-
    ties: (1) they are disciples of Leavis; (2) they write
    comic novels expressing similar attitudes and objectives;
    (3) they use the stock figure of "the adolescent imagina-
    tion, the society nymphomaniac," suggesting "both a limit
    to their inventive powers and also a failure to create
    credible, normal women"; (4) they create heroes who are
    constantly running from some imaginary problem, "seeking
    escape in the <u>graffiti</u> of their private thoughts"; and
    (5) they resolve their novels by use of a <u>deus ex machina</u>.
    Of the three writers, Amis has the "most genuinely creative

1956

 talent." Both he and Wain find comedy is not satirical,
for "it has no firm basis, no coherent direction." Hence,
their farce becomes predictable and tedious in repetition.

11 TINDALL, WILLIAM YORK. "Disenchantment," in his <u>Forces in
Modern British Literature: 1885-1956</u>. New York: Vintage
Books, p. 119.
 As a "University Wit," Wain holds in esteem the "clever
verse of the dry, hard sort" of Empson and, later, T. E.
Hulme. Sharing this interest with Wain are Amis, Alvarez,
Gunn, and Davie.

12 WAUGH, EVELYN. "Dr. Wodehouse and Mr. Wain." <u>Spectator</u>, 196
(24 February), 243-44.
 Notices Wain's lack of manners in his review of Wodehouse's <u>French Leave</u>.

1957 A BOOKS - NONE

1957 B SHORTER WRITINGS

1 ANON. "Books: Lucky Jim and His Pals." <u>Time</u>, 69 (27 May),
106-107.
 General essay about the Angry Young Men and their con-
tributions to the revitalization of the 1950s British novel. Wain is "an Amis in whom the quinine water has changed
to straight quinine."

2 ANON. "Critical Approaches." <u>Times Literary Supplement</u>
(13 September), p. 546.
 Review of <u>Preliminary Essays</u>. Wain is a "no-nonsense
man." Like Lord David Cecil, he is out "to perceive ac-
curately in order to criticize justly." However, Wain's
essays are marred by "sudden outbursts of petulance or
plain silliness." Whereas Cecil concentrates on the clas-
sics, Wain is more worldly and excels in his writings on
contemporary writers.

3 CRISPIN, EDMUND. "Unlucky Us." <u>Observer</u> (8 March), p. 15.
 Seeks to correct misconceptions stemming from the British Press's attempt to lump together several writers under
the Angry Young Men heading.

4 GRANDSEN, K. W. "The Thirties and Us: Rebels and Time
Servers." <u>Twentieth Century</u>, 161 (March), 220-21.
 Responds to Morgan's essay (<u>see</u> 1957.B10) by examining
the relationship of <u>Lucky Jim</u> to <u>Hurry on Down</u> and other

contemporary novels. Concludes that the new writers are
"people who can't make up their minds whether to be rebels
or time servers."

5   HARTLEY, ANTHONY. "A Plain-Dealer." Manchester Guardian
    (20 August), p. 4.
        Review of Preliminary Essays. In these stimulating es-
    says, Wain's critical attitude is constant; it is, "by and
    large, part of the moral and intellectual tradition of Eng-
    lish Puritanism." With his serious concern for moral
    values, Wain combines "a sensitivity to literary techniques
    which is seen at its best in his analysis of individual
    poems." His study of Restoration comedy is the most suc-
    cessful example of his "half-dogmatic, half-empirical
    method."

6   HOGGART, RICHARD. "Plain Man of Letters." Nation, 185
    (26 October), 285-86.
        Review of Preliminary Essays. Wain's tone is typical of
    that of the 1950s generation of writers: "direct, relaxed,
    idiomatic, conversationally unbuttoned and strenuously un-
    genteel." Sometimes Wain's manner is "aggressively plain-
    man." His real strength may be in the range of his "in-
    telligent hospitality." Of any writer in his generation,
    he seems most likely to become "the general man of letters."
    Finds in him "a generous, high good sense which is not
    afraid of bold, comprehensive statement." His only short-
    coming is a tendency to engage in "bold generalizations."

7   HOLLOWAY, JOHN. "Tank in the Stalls: Notes on the 'School of
    Anger.'" Hudson Review, 10 (Autumn), 424-29.
        The Angry Young Men seem to have begun with Wain's Hurry
    on Down, although the name is actually taken from an ir-
    relevant context, Leslie Paul's Angry Young Man, published
    in 1951. Notes the lack of similarities between Amis,
    Wain, Osborne, and Braine, and concludes that there really
    is no new kind of hero at all.

8   HOUGH, GRAHAM. "Dons and Non-Dons." Encounter, 9 (December),
    76, 78, 80.
        Review of Preliminary Essays. Wain is an academic
    critic; that is, he "tends to look on criticism as an in-
    dependent rite rather than as a means to increasing the
    proper enjoyment of the arts." In his best essay--"Arnold
    Bennett"--Wain has something of which he wants to convince
    the reader when he says that Bennett has been undervalued.
    Also comments on Wain's essays on Restoration comedy
    (doesn't try to come to any conclusions); Ovid, Wordsworth,

1957

Tennyson, and Browning (covering old ground); Hopkins, Leavis, Bateson, Professor Knights (not very challenging opinions), and modern poetry (obsession with dates, something wrong with the tone).

9   MILLGATE, MICHAEL. "An Uncertain Feeling in England." New Republic, 137 (9 September), 16–17.
Wain's typical hero, like that of Amis and Murdoch, is the "irresponsible socially disruptive hero for whom everything turns out well at the end and whom one forgives, though often outraged," because he makes the reader laugh and because of his boyish innocence. What is unique about the hero is the area of society from which he comes. Moreover, as poets, both Wain and Amis display a deceptively casual approach, fondness for a conversational manner, humor (as a defense against an "over-organized and undersensitive world"), and rather rigid verse patterns.

10   MORGAN, W. JOHN. " Authentic Voices." Twentieth Century, 161 (February), 32–34.
Examines the origins of the Angry Young Men and the Movement. Responded to by Grandsen (see 1957.B4).

11   O'DONNELL, DONAT. "Island Intellectual." Spectator, 197 (16 August), 223.
Review of Preliminary Essays. Finds a "down-to-earth" style of writing and a lack of "intellectual stamina." Wain's essay on Bennett is possibly the best in the book.

12   PRITCHETT, V. S. "These Writers Couldn't Care Less." New York Times Book Review (28 April), pp. 1, 38–39.
Survey of the Angry Young Men. "These novelists regard the Welfare State with cynical detachment, revel in the bad manners, the meanness, the slackness, the caddish behavior and self-pity of their characters and have a chip on their shoulders. They like the limited region." Wain's novels are unromantic; his hero switches from "idealism" to a doctrine of "'self-interest.'"

13   RAYMOND, JOHN. "Talking Turkey." New Statesman and Nation, 54 (10 August), 179.
Review of Preliminary Essays. Wain is "earnest, provoking, didactic, highly intelligent and blessedly charmless." Finds a heavy influence of Leavis and Empson. Is concerned by Wain's superficiality (in "Restoration Comedy and its Modern Critics") and provincialism in some judgments. Above all, however, Wain cares intensely and intelligently about literature.

14 SPENDER, STEPHEN. "Notes from a Diary: The Young People's
    Crusade." Encounter, 8 (March), 70.
        Brief reference to Wain's speech at the Institute of
    Contemporary Arts. Wain said one great difference between
    the 1950s and 1930s was that during the earlier period
    there was more money around.

15 WATERMAN, ROLLENE. "A Gallery of Lucky Jims." Saturday Re-
    view, 56 (27 July), 9.
        Brief biographical details and a discussion of the
    theme in Hurry on Down. "Britain's new education and the
    way it leaves its products ill-equipped for the business
    of life seems to be [Wain's] chief concern."

1958 A BOOKS - NONE

1958 B SHORTER WRITINGS

 1 ALVAREZ, A. "Poetry of the 'Fifties: In England." Inter-
    national Literary Annual, No. 1. Edited by John Wain.
    London: John Calder, p. 97.
        In a survey of the Movement, refers to Wain's comment
    on poetry "of consolidation."

 2 ANON. "Taking It Easy." Times Literary Supplement
    (17 January), p. 30.
        Finds that both Wain and Amis have practiced "a learned
    and deliberate anti-stylishness." Unlike Waugh, whose nov-
    els are filled with cruelty, these writers are "more ten-
    derhearted." When Wain does resort to violence in Hurry on
    Down, it is not funny. Concludes that "the Wain-Amis moral
    climate is a highly salubrious one. A great deal of anx-
    ious knowingness is coupled with much groping after a rock-
    bottom decency." Predicts that Wain will turn serious
    eventually.

 3 ANON. "Fairly Serious." Times Literary Supplement
    (14 March), p. 137.
        Review of The Contenders. Unlike his first two comic
    novels, here Wain is more serious because he is concerned
    primarily with a character situation. However, the char-
    acters do "lack certain kinds of distinctness," and the
    narrator "rarely seems just what he is supposed to be."
    For example, Shaw is supposed to be a provincial journal-
    ist; yet he is familiar with "the metropolitan-literary
    smart talk."

1958

4   ANON. "Jovial Middle-Aging Man." Time, 71 (28 April), 102,
        104.
            Review of The Contenders. This is a "lively, funny
        story" in an essentially "American-style." Wain is good-
        natured, not angry, in this novel of character.

5   ANON. "Fiction." Booklist, 54 (1 June), 562.
            Brief mention of The Contenders. "A clever plot en-
        hanced by lifelike dialog and interesting, if not always
        admirable, characters."

6   BAILHACHE, JEAN. "Angry Young Men." Les Langues Modernes, 52
        (March-April), 31-46, also numbered 143-158.
            Brief biographical details and discussion of Hurry on
        Down and its relationship to the Angry Young Men. (In
        French.)

7   BALLIETT, WHITNEY. "Books: The Emergence of Clarence." New
        Yorker, 34 (31 May), 103-104.
            Review of The Contenders. In this "work of ridicule,"
        Wain's comedy is fresh, and his style abounds with similes
        and metaphors. The reader realizes at the end that Roper
        and Lamb are merely symbols of the war between Business and
        Art, and that all along Wain has been creating a convincing
        portrait of "a wholly good man" in Shaw.

8   BRINNIN, JOHN MALCOLM. "Young But Not Angry." Mademoiselle,
        46 (April), 150-151, 170.
            Background study of the origins and development of the
        Movement and Maverick poets. Wain and Amis are the best
        known of the new poets and novelists in England. Quotes
        Wain as saying that the new poet has a conservative tone,
        and that Larkin is recognized as the most highly esteemed
        poet of the group.

9   COSMAN, MAX. "John Wain Attacks Competitiveness in Our So-
        ciety." New York Herald Tribune Book Review (27 April),
        p. 7.
            Review of The Contenders. Like his earlier novels, this
        book is "a cross between burlesque and melodrama," but its
        greatest significance lies in Wain's contempt for what is
        about him. "Basically he is an inquisitor of belief and an
        irrepressible censor of behavior. But at the same time he
        is a writer fallible in his craft, still apt to contrive
        when he should perceive, and to verbalize when he should be
        subtle." Predicts that Wain will make a permanent mark in
        "the novel of attack."

10 COUGHLAN, ROBERT. "Why Britain's Angry Young Men Boil over: Most Talked about Writers of To-Day Reflect Frustration of Declining England." Life, 44 (26 May), 138-50.
    In a survey of the Angry Young Men, distinguishes between the Angries and the Beat generation. The English writers are not angry; rather, their attitude is one of "wry irritation and their weapon is more often satiric than polemics." Quotes Wain's comment that the 1930s were the last years when people felt a personal responsibility for society and its ills. Includes brief biographical details.

11 CRANE, MILTON. Review of The Contenders. Chicago Sunday Tribune (18 May), p. 2.
    Calls this a "swift, pointed, skillfully wrought satirical novel." Wain is best in his comic scenes, "imagined and executed in virtually dramatic terms."

12 CURLEY, THOMAS F. "Of Three Men." Commonweal, 68 (16 May), 189-90.
    Review of The Contenders. Wain subtly says what he does not mean in the opening line to the novel, for this is actually the story of three men--Lamb, Roper, and Shaw, the hero. His subtlety is also found in the names of Clarence (from Clarus, meaning clear or illustrious) and Pepina ("pep-in-her").

13 FELDMAN, GENE and MAX GARTENBERG. "Introduction," in their edition of Beat Generation and the Angry Young Men. New York: Citadel, p. 16.
    Wain's hero becomes pathetic when he thinks he can become an "Insider merely by donning the proper masks." Includes a brief reference to Walter Allen's review of Hurry on Down (see 1953.B1).

14 GINDIN, JAMES. "The Reassertion of the Personal." Texas Quarterly, 4 (Fall), 126-34.
    The fairy-tale endings to the novels of Wain, Amis, and Wilson signify a great difference from comic novels of a generation ago. Compared to Huxley or Waugh, Wain deals much more directly with the world as he finds it. He, like his contemporaries, uses comedy as a means of social criticism to attack fraud and pretense. In his first two novels, however, Wain exaggerates the comic gimmick. His parody of the picaresque dominates Hurry on Down, thereby preventing a meaningful treatment of Lumley and his world. Moreover, the hero's pursuit of the victim in Living in the Present detracts from the author's observations on the hero, society, and politics. Only in The Contenders does

1958

the movement of the narrator, who eventually becomes in-
volved in the action, give the novel "sharpness and sub-
stance." Concludes that a "twin insistence on limiting
values to the personal and yet affirming the existence of
value leads writers like Wain, Amis and Wilson to use the
comic as an essential instrument."

15 HARKNESS, BRUCE. "The Lucky Crowd--Contemporary British Fic-
    tion." English Journal, 47 (October), 387-92, 395-97.
        Finds in the early novels of Wain and Amis a composite
    hero. Similarities in characters, style, techniques,
    ideas, and subject matter are discussed in this survey of
    their novels.

16 HARVEY, W. T. "Have You Anything to Declare? or, Angry Young
    Men: Facts and Fiction." International Literary Annual,
    No. 1. Edited by John Wain. London: John Calder,
    pp. 47-54, 57-59.
        Maugham's review of Lucky Jim in The Sunday Times (Lon-
    don), Wain's article in The Twentieth Century (March,
    1957), and Declaration all contributed to the growth of the
    Angry Young Men myth. There is evidence of a "more overt
    moral interest" in Wain than in Amis. In Wain's first two
    novels, the author faces the problems of "reconciling comedy
    and seriousness or farce and realism" and of identifying
    for himself the center of his moral interest. The Con-
    tenders, Wain's best novel to date, is marked by "an over-
    explicitness in the way in which the protagonists recognize
    their own moral dilemma."

17 HURRELL, JOHN D. "Class and Conscience in John Braine and
    Kingsley Amis." Critique, 2 (Spring-Summer), 39-40.
        As one of several Angry Young Men, Wain writes against
    the background of the Welfare State. Class distinction is
    of primary concern to him. Like Braine, he seems satis-
    fied with "chronicling the times" he lives in. The hero
    rejects political solutions to his problems, although "a
    political assumption determines motivation throughout the
    novels."

18 LEHMANN, JOHN. "The Wain-Larkin Myth." Sewanee Review, 66
    (Autumn), 578-87.
        Seeks to explain why Wain's views on the development of
    English poetry (in "English Poetry: The Immediate Situa-
    tion") are wrong. Says that Wain's views of what happened
    between Auden's departure for the United States and Lar-
    kin's appearance are largely mythical. Contrary to Wain's
    position, a violent poetic revolution occurred.

19   MOORE, GEOFFREY. "Poets of the Fifties," in his <u>Poetry Today</u>.
      London: Longmans for British Council, pp. 45-51.
              Discussion of the Movement poets' manifesto and its ori-
      gins. Wain's and Amis' verse remind one of Osborne's
      drama. All three writers are "witty polemicists who, by
      poking fun at pomposity and conventional attitudes, give
      their audience intense and irreverent enjoyment, yet at the
      same time leave it with a rather troubling sense that this
      caricature has got to stop sometime." At times it is dif-
      ficult to distinguish Wain's work from that of Amis, except
      that Wain "tends to be brash where Amis is quizzical." The
      exception to this brashness is found in <u>A Word Carved on a
      Sill</u>, wherein the style is controlled. In "Usefulness of
      Light" and "This Above All is Precious and Remarkable,"
      Wain's aggressiveness is mellowed by the theme of love.
      It is then that Wain is at his best.

20   NICHOLSON, GEOFFREY. "Top People." <u>Spectator</u>, 198
      (28 March), 400.
              Review of <u>The Contenders</u>. Although it would be a
      pleasant surprise, Wain might become a J. B. Priestley of
      the 1960s if he isn't careful. Wain is a vigorous, very
      funny writer whose attitudes are sympathetic and intelli-
      gent. Through Shaw, he shows no reluctance about telling
      people what is wrong. Moreover, he manipulates his charac-
      ters and situations, "against all probability, to make his
      point more emphatically."

21   PESCHMANN, HERMANN. "Changes in Critical Climate." <u>English</u>,
      12 (Summer), 44-45.
              Review of <u>Preliminary Essays</u>. Eliot's <u>On Poetry and
      Poets</u> and Wain's latest collection signify a change in
      critical opinion. Both indicate a revival of interest in
      the Romantics and a move away from metaphysical complexity.
      Wain's writing is noted for its common sense and plain
      speaking, but sometimes these characteristics have their
      limitations, as in the case of his analysis of Dylan
      Thomas' complex poems. Concludes that Wain opts for "a
      care for plain, or at any rate straightforward, statement;
      a concern with the formal qualities of texture and shape;
      with structure, music, and over-all design."

22   PIPPETT, ROGER. "Rat Race To the Top." <u>New York Times Book
      Review</u> (27 April), p. 4.
              Review of <u>The Contenders</u>. This novel defies classifica-
      tion--as a novel of character, picaresque tale, social sat-
      ire, a modern morality, or simply "a cautionary tale."
      Wain's sense of humor is "wicked" and his hatred of preten-
      sion and pomposity is "relentless."

1958

23   SPENDER, STEPHEN. "Anglo-Saxon Attitudes." Partisan Review,
         25 (Winter), 112-13.
             Wain is influenced by Leavis (in his criticism) and
         Empson (in his poetry). Like Amis, he combines his criti-
         cal standards with "provincial toughness." He has a strong
         sense of the time and place in which he is writing. Wain's
         contribution to Declaration "is distinguished by scholar-
         ship, critical sense, and intellect from everything else
         in the volume."

24   _____. "When the Angry Young Men Grow Older." New York
         Times Book Review (20 July), p. 12.
             Wonders what the Angry Young Men will do, now that
         they have outgrown their anger. Both Wain's and Amis'
         training and critical values are academic. They exercise
         "independence of judgment." Moreover, both oppose "gen-
         tility" and "the cliquish standards" of universities and
         literary columns.

25   STANFORD, DEREK. "Beatniks and Angry Young Men." Meanjin,
         17 (Summer), 413, 417-19.
             Both Wain and Braine are "mesmerically possessed by the
         theme of careerism" and are critical, by implication, of
         the psychology of their characters. Moreover, one finds
         in their writings "a vein of fascination will all the de-
         tails of 'lifemanship.'"

26   TYNAN, KENNETH. "The Men of Anger." Holiday, 23 (April),
         117, 181-82.
             In a general article on the Angry Young Men and John
         Osborne, comments that Jimmy Porter (in Look Back in
         Anger) speaks in essentially the same idiom as Dixon (in
         Lucky Jim) and Lumley (in Hurry on Down). Wain's and
         Amis' "all-round academicism . . . makes their writing at
         once saner and tamer" than Osborne's.

27   WALZER, MICHAEL. "John Wain: The Hero in Limbo." Perspec-
         tive, 10 (Summer-Autumn), 137-45.
             Finds in Wain's novels a clear presentation of a new
         picaresque hero, one who is detached from political
         causes and from the progress of his own life. "Moving
         vaguely through a bourgeois world in decay, the hero of
         his picaresque seems a study in formlessness;" that is, he
         has no perceptible character at all as he is continually
         juxtaposed with a rigid social order. Of his three nov-
         els, Hurry on Down is the best. In Living in the Present,
         unlimited farce renders implausible the reconciliation,
         and in The Contenders, Shaw is not a believable person.

28 WEAVER, ROBERT. "England's Angry Young Men--Mystics, Provincials and Radicals." Queen's Quarterly, 65 (Summer), 185,
188-90.
Groups together Wain, Amis, and Braine as "provincial"
Angry Young Men--in contrast with "mystics" (Wilson, Hol-
royd, and Hopkins) and "radicals" (Osborne, Tynan, and
Anderson). The provincials are comic novelists who, like
their heroes, come from the provinces and are self-
conscious about it. They express some sentimentality about
working-class life, are not interested in Lawrence, and,
except for Braine, have been influenced by Orwell. Wain is
overrated as a novelist. Despite similarities, Hurry on
Down lacks the "verve, ambition and intellectual vitality"
of Bellow's The Adventures of Augie March. The Contenders
is "a respectable, drab and unimaginative novel." Concludes that all of the British authors in the 1950s are
little more than "a noisy and pretentious group of minor
writers."

29 WEEKS, EDWARD. "The Peripatetic Reviewer." Atlantic Monthly,
202 (July), 82-83.
Review of The Contenders. Shaw's efforts as peacemaker
for his two friends are a bit monotonous because the reader
participates in his own affairs only by inference. The
rivalry over Myra is carried beyond credibility; the ending
is "theatrical." Shaw's comments on life give the novel
"its salt and sanity." He knows how to handle anger, and
his irony has "a sharp and cutting edge."

30 WILLIAMS, D. Review of The Contenders. Manchester Guardian
(25 March), p. 6.
In this novel about rivalry, Myra is a "glossy, lifeless
figure who simply will not do as the bone of contention between two wideawake Staffordshire chaps." Hence, the book
fails as social comedy in spite of some clever touches
(Roper's addition to model railways, for example). "Fortunately, Mr. Wain modulates occasionally into farce (his
true bent as a novelist) and then writes racy, rackety, in-
vigorating stuff."

1959 A BOOKS - NONE

1959 B SHORTER WRITINGS

1 AITKEN, DOUGLAS. Review of A Traveling Woman. San Francisco
Chronicle (16 August), p. 28.
There is much food for thought in this "sensitive and
moral" book. A psychological novel "well worth reading."

1959

2   ANON. "Poet and Critic March in Ranks of Lively Novelists."
     London <u>Times</u> (5 March), p. 15.
         Review of <u>A Traveling Woman</u>. Calls this a "Restoration
     Comedy brought up to date." Technically, this short novel
     should be taken as a "<u>locus classicus</u>." Wain pairs the
     characters against each other "with a symmetry which soon
     becomes enchanting." He suspends all moral judgments;
     hence, the reader, too, "can feel as sympathetically wanton
     as he likes." Suggests that Wain might have made more of
     the goodness and wisdom of the good and wise man.

3   ANON. "The Man Inside." <u>Times Literary Supplement</u> (6 March),
     p. 125.
         Review of <u>A Traveling Woman</u>. Wain's most obvious char-
     acteristic is "vigour." The exposition is handled rather
     haphazardly, leading the reader to wonder why he wrote
     this. "He has hurled himself upon his narrative, and its
     otherwise unconvincing people are galvanized by the vio-
     lence in him, though what it impels them to do is nothing
     at all."

4   ANON. "Fiction." <u>Kirkus Reviews</u>, 27 (1 April), 274.
         Review of <u>A Traveling Woman</u>. Wain's manipulation of
     these surface characters is "slickly contrived." Moreover,
     his "humor is forced, and the situations dull and often in
     exceedingly bad taste."

5   ANON. "Mixed Fiction." <u>Time</u>, 73 (15 June), 98.
         Review of <u>A Traveling Woman</u>. Wain looks back in "lan-
     guor," not anger, in this novel with a "La Ronde-styled
     plot." His sharp eye for "the social fads and furbelows
     of suburban England" and his sharp ear for "the mannered
     vulgarities of middle-class speech" do not compensate
     for the book's lack of "either the pulse beat of anger or
     the tart shivers of satirical laughter."

6   ANON. "Combating Malevolence." <u>Times Literary Supplement</u>
     (20 November), p. 673.
         To some critics, the works of Wain and Amis seem marred
     by "an inability (or unwillingness?) to maintain a consis-
     tent narrative style: these writers tend to lapse, sud-
     denly and without warning--or any apparent justification--
     from sophisticated social comedy into music-hall slapstick,
     or from flat naturalism into the crudest melodrama."

7   BALAKIAN, NONA. "The Flight from Innocence: England's Newest
    Literary Generation." Books Abroad, 33 (Summer), 261,
    266-68.
        Wain is less the "spontaneous humorist" and more the
    consciously intellectual and philosophically oriented
    writer than Amis and other Angry Young Men. In his first
    four novels, his characters' dilemmas stem from "an erring
    concept of freedom." The conclusion to The Contenders is
    sardonic, whereas on the surface the novel is full of sur-
    prises and "satirical fun." Finds the novel to be "col-
    loquial, with aimless, idiomatic dialogue that speaks not
    only for the locale but for the professions it is depict-
    ing; it has an almost American flavor." In Wain's novels
    there exists a characteristic irreverence toward women as
    the weaker sex.

8   BODE, CARL. "The Redbrick Cinderellas." College English, 20
    (April), 332, 334-37.
        Although Wain is "a better storyteller" than Amis, Hurry
    on Down's characters are "scruffier" and the comedy is less
    distinguished than Lucky Jim's. Finds that as he writes,
    Wain "gains in adroitness" with promise as a novelist of
    ideas. His writings in Preliminary Essays show him to be a
    critic with "a fresh, unpretentious mind." His criticism
    is founded on common sense, though still rather shakily.
    He is a critic in the making who has yet to find his set of
    critical principles. His conservatism affects all of his
    writings.

9   BRADBURY, MALCOLM. "Botching Life Up." New York Times Book
    Review (24 May), p. 5.
        Review of A Traveling Woman. With each new novel,
    Wain's technical skills grow. He possesses "a real sense
    of the changing social scene of modern England." In this
    "docile and rather middle-aged" novel, Wain and his charac-
    ters need to work harder on their morality. "The con-
    science of these people is as slight as their misdemeanors,
    and means almost as little."

10 COLEMAN, JOHN. "Various Formalities." Spectator, 202
    (13 March), 380.
        Review of A Traveling Woman. In this novel, a "confu-
    sion of high comedy and dangling motivations" leaves the
    resolution unexpected and unsatisfying. Both the tone and
    the characters lose focus, and the plot becomes "increas-
    ingly formal." Asserts that "by playing for laughs at what
    seem almost wilfully inopportune moments and, as it were,
    spoofing George's feelings out of existence, . . . Mr. Wain

so effectively ensures the withdrawal of [the reader's]
sympathy that the crippling strokes at the end rain on
air."

11   FREMANTLE, ANNE. "The Wily Ways of the World." Saturday Re-
      view, 42 (27 June), 15-16.
            Review of A Traveling Woman. In this funny and serious
      novel, Wain displays his gift for conveying both "the mo-
      mentariness of love's pleasure, and the ridicule of love's
      positions, as well as a great capacity for showing how ex-
      pensive love is." He does all this without moralizing; the
      ethical laws operate competently and inevitably.

12   FULLER, ROY. "Between Generations." London Magazine, 6
      (November), 19-20.
            Sees in the new poets, including Wain, "an absolute vic-
      tory over the slipshod and barmy style of the immediate
      post-war years, [and] a resulting body of work which tran-
      scends the cut and thrust of cliques and tendencies."
      Notes Wain's acute hatred of what is phony in society in
      "Jardin des Plantes."

13   GERARD, MARTIN. "Goodbye to All That: A Child's Guide to Two
      Decades." X, A Quarterly Review, 1 (November), 114-20.
            Tries to make some sense of the Movement poets and of
      Wain's "old maidish analysing and influence-mongering and
      tendency-seeking" in Interpretations: Essays on Twelve
      English Poems. "The honest examination of 'literature' to
      see whether much of it had any value at all was abandoned
      in favour of a sort of low brow horseplay activity arising
      from the resentment those who were put through the learn-
      eries felt for literature in general."

14   GINDIN, JAMES J. "Comedy in Contemporary British Fiction."
      Papers of the Michigan Academy of Science, Arts, and Let-
      ters. Vol. 44. Edited by Sheridan Baker. Ann Arbor:
      The University of Michigan Press, pp. 389-91, 395-97.
            The Angry Young Men--Wain, Amis, Murdoch, and Wilson--
      all use comedy in the creation of their novels. They con-
      cern themselves with a wide area of English society in-
      spected from a single point of view. Finds a kind of
      "personal honesty and morality" with a touch of "insu-
      larity." Hence, they fit in with the major traditions of
      the eighteenth- and nineteenth-century English novel. The
      humanity of these writers "belies an easy application" of
      the Angry Young Men designation. Wain's hero in Born in
      Captivity is "honest, direct, naive, yet never restricted
      by preconceptions as he attempts to discover what various
      areas in this comic world are like."

15 GUTWILLIG, ROBERT. "An Oft-Told Tale." <u>Commonweal</u>, 70
    (12 June), 309-10.
         Review of <u>A Traveling Woman</u>. Careless writing and
    clumsy plot weaken this "familiarly disappointing and dis-
    appointingly familiar" novel. Wain's characters and situa-
    tions lack the "formidable and uproarious imaginative pres-
    sure" usually seen in his writings.

16˙ HOLLOWAY, JOHN. "The Two Languages." <u>London Magazine</u>, 6
    (November), 16.
         Brief mention of the influence of Empson, Graves, and
    Auden on the poetry of Wain, Amis, and others. Empson's
    verse "relied on throw-away timing and impeccable tone,"
    and Graves's poetry displayed a "dry, depreciatory yet
    often tolerant tone."

17 JEFFARES, NORMAN. "Sketch for an Extensive View." <u>London</u>
    <u>Magazine</u>, 6 (November), 35.
         Refers to Wain, Amis, Davie, Holloway, and Larkin as
    "satirists <u>manqué</u>" who take precautions "against false
    emotions."

18 KROLL, MORTON. "The Politics of Britain's Angry Young Men."
    <u>Western Political Quarterly</u>, 12 (June), 555-57.
         This survey of the Angry Young Men says that Wain's
    heroes, like Amis', "disengage themselves from the torn
    fabric of a society and end up in hopeful, detached,
    niches." Both writers argue for "the positive value of
    the struggle for self-realization, for the discovery, in
    essence, of the meaning of Being." Mentions that Wain's
    hero rejects "the radicalism and literary intellectualism"
    of the 1920s and 1930s.

19 LEMAY, HARDING. "The Wit Flashes, the Point Is Serious."
    New York <u>Herald Tribune Book Review</u> (21 June), p. 8.
         Review of <u>A Traveling Woman</u>. A "devastating comment"
    on marriage and promiscuity, achieved in "light, sure
    strokes." If Wain had started by stating his views more
    boldly, the results might be too appalling to contemplate.
    The novel is both comedic and serious. Wain's style and
    powers of invention locate the emptiness of his characters,
    but he never loses sight of their serious failures and "the
    dry sorrows of their self-inflicted defeats." His comedy
    is "tightly structured."

1959

20   MANN, JR., CHARLES W.   "Fiction."   <u>Library Journal</u>, 84
     (15 June), 2081-82.
          Review of <u>A Traveling Woman</u>. It is unclear whether Wain
     was trying to write farce or "mordant comedy." The novel
     seems to be "a school exercise in novel writing" told in a
     "theatrical manner." The dialogue is long, the scenes are
     staged, and the ending is inconclusive and depressing.

21   NAIPAUL, V. S.   "New Novels."   <u>New Statesman</u>, 57 (14 March),
     376.
          Review of <u>A Traveling Woman</u>. As Wain's most accomplished
     novel so far, this will sustain his reputation for "light
     romantic fiction." However, the novel lacks substance and
     could be shortened to an outline of its story.

22   PERROTT, ROY.   "An Author in Search of Real People."   <u>Man-
     chester Guardian</u> (6 March), p. 4.
          Review of <u>A Traveling Woman</u>. Wain's "inventiveness and
     his purposeful, lively attack" on adultery give this novel
     "a brisk, surface animation." However, Wain's attempt at
     tragicomedy fails because his characters are created from
     the outside; they lack a life of their own. Therefore, in
     the important scenes, like the hero's love for someone
     else's wife, "the emotions and actions tend to look wilful,
     fatally subject to the author's whim." Concludes that Wain
     is still in search of real people to represent his themes.

23   ROSS, T. J.   "A Good Girl is Hard to Find."   <u>New Republic</u>, 141
     (21 September), 17-19.
          Finds that the representation of the female in <u>The Con-
     tenders</u> and <u>A Traveling Woman</u> is banal. There is a "Fal-
     staffian humor, . . . a self-chiding" which stems from
     Wain's enjoyment of recreating humans as they are rather
     than as they should be. There is little to keep reader in-
     terest in these two novels. Both suffer from the same
     problem: at a vital moment, Wain introduces a "Nice Girl"
     as an alternative, but the reader never really cares, "for
     she remains a lifeless figurine rather than a vital figure."
     Finds that the strength of Wain in both novels "is his de-
     lineation of male friendships." Then, the story comes to
     life.

24   THWAITE, ANTHONY.   "Poetry Since 1950," in his <u>Contemporary
     English Poetry: An Introduction</u>. London: Heinemann,
     pp. 143-44.
          There are several definite differences between Wain's
     and Amis' poetry. Wain is more heavily influenced by
     Empson. When he stays within the strict limits of the
     Empsonian form, he is at his best; elsewhere, he is not
     successful. Moreover, Wain works best with what

1960

G. S. Fraser has called "'the bold drydenic line'"--iambic
pentameter, usually end-stopped, "so that each line becomes
a separate rhetorical unit." Finally, Wain's poems are
usually moral statements. The danger in this is that too
often his poems remain on a merely literary level, and
this, together with the strict cadence of the form, "makes
it possible for vague or arbitrary thinking to masquerade
as strict logic."

25 VAN DER VEEN, ADRIAAN. "Boze Jongelieden in een Zich Ver-
    nieuwend Engeland." Vlaamse Gids, 43 (April), 232-36.
        Wain, Braine, Amis, and Osborne express a disillusion-
    ment with the Welfare State but lack the desire to make a
    better world. Rather, they are concerned with how one gets
    on in the world. The essays in Declaration show their
    ideas more clearly than do their novels or plays.

26 WILSON, COLIN. "The Writer and Publicity." Encounter, 13
    (November), 9.
        Considers the case history of Hurry on Down as a way of
    showing that today, in literary England, the writer's per-
    sonality is involved in promotion. When Hurry on Down was
    published, it received "rave notices and sold extremely
    well." At the same time, Wain expressed himself a lot in
    reviews and books, and "his published opinions tended to be
    positive and pugnacious." When Living in the Present
    failed, Wain became more "irascible and pugnacious, and de-
    veloped a complex about critics." Wilson admits that Wain
    is a serious writer, but says that "the spotlight treatment
    followed by a chorus of boos and cheers is not the best
    stimulus to serious writing." This account of the success
    of Hurry on Down is refuted by Wain in Sprightly Running.

1960 A BOOKS - NONE

1960 B SHORTER WRITINGS

1 ANON. "New Fiction." London Times (10 November), p. 15.
        Review of Nuncle and Other Stories. As in his novels,
    Wain's humor in these stories is "both rollicking and
    shrewd." Compares and contrasts "Master Richard" to
    Christopher Morley's Thunder on the Left. Says that Mor-
    ley, with "a courtly and lyrical manner, points a decora-
    tive, elaborately chased pistol at imagination's head; Mr.
    Wain bludgeons it . . .--and the bludgeon has an ingenious
    delayed-action built into the business end."

1960

2   ANON. "Uncertainties." <u>Times Literary Supplement</u> (11 November), p. 721.
        Review of <u>Nuncle and Other Stories</u>. This collection shows that Wain is still searching for a style and a tone of his own. The title story's theme calls to mind Henry James's "The Figure in the Carpet" and "The Private Life." Like James, Wain aims for comedy but also has a literary parable in mind. However, the story fails because the farce is incongruous with any serious meaning. Brief mention of the other stories.

3   BLUESTONE, GEORGE. "John Wain and John Barth: The Angry and the Accurate." <u>Massachusetts Review</u>, 1 (May), 582-86, 589.
        Memoir of Wain's speech at the University of Washington in 1959. Calls him "a deeply conflicted" man whose "ripostes are curiously germane to all his fiction." In all four novels, there is a pattern: "an ingenious idea, massaged until the blood begins to course, a fumbling but engaging hero, a villain he can safely disapprove." The evils are "class lines, provincial hypocrisy, an insulated school system, Midland grubbiness, the conventional perils of success." The hope is "a rather righteous hero who tilts comically at Midland windmills." <u>A Traveling Woman</u> is disappointing because the denouement is pointless, and because Wain does nothing with the themes of the pain of adultery and the comedy of psychiatry. The problem in all of his novels, as Wain admits, is that he "has nothing fundamental to quarrel with." This may help to explain why his novels end inconclusively.

4   BRYDEN, RONALD. "Sweetness and Shame." <u>Spectator</u>, 205 (11 November), 741.
        Review of <u>Nuncle and Other Stories</u>. Although Wain displays intelligence and inventiveness, the stories lack "the ring of a distinctive voice." Perhaps this is because the stories are really adaptations of sophistication vs. innocence. Wain sets an "adult life of jokes, seductions, stratagems" against "a complementary imagery of childhood, domestic virtue and pastoral simplicity," each of which denounces and seeks to destroy the other.

5   DAWSON, S. W. "A Personal Report on the Literary Fifties." <u>Audit</u>, 1 (February), i, 14.
        Comments on the low level of British writing. The novels of Wain, Amis, and Murdoch "have disappointed all but the most moderate expectations."

1960

6 GLICKSBURG, CHARLES I. "The Literature of the Angry Young
    Men." Colorado Quarterly, 8 (Spring), 299, 301.
        Wain is a satirist whose bitterness over his social ori-
    gins is expressed as "moral indignation: those in power
    are willing to sacrifice everything that is decent and hu-
    mane for the sake of retaining their power and increasing
    their wealth." With his third novel, Wain's anger changes
    to disillusionment in the form of "mordant satire." Calls
    The Contenders "a high-spirited and delightful demonstra-
    tion . . . of the absurdity of the competitive mania that
    rules England." The struggle for success "turns all human
    relationships into calculated moves of expediency."

7 HOLLOWAY, JOHN. "'Tank in the Stalls': Notes on the 'School
    of Anger,'" in his The Charted Mirror: Literary and Criti-
    cal Essays. London: Routledge and Kegan Paul, pp. 142-44.
        Examines Wain's verse as a way of coming to terms with
    the so-called Angry Young Men phenomenon. The surface is
    "cool, self-depreciatory, ironical"--obviously influenced
    by Empson. Examines "Eighth Type of Ambiguity" and "Rea-
    sons for Not Writing Nature Poetry," and concludes that
    Wain's verse, and less clearly his novels, show a reversion
    back to English writing's "more indigenous traditions."

8 JENNINGS, ELIZABETH. "Poetry in the Fifties," in her Let's
    have some Poetry! London: Museum Press, pp. 96-97, 103.
        Finds a heavy influence of Empson on Wain's verse, no-
    tably a "rigorous intellectual honesty" in, for example,
    "Who Speaks My Language?" Quotes Wain as saying he se-
    lected such a "strictly formal, carefully intellectual and
    questioning way," partly in reaction to those who revolted
    against clarity and intelligent shaping. His earlier poems
    "'aim at poise, coherence, and a logical raison d'être for
    every word, image, and metaphor used.'" In the later
    poems, Wain, like Davie, widens his subject matter and ex-
    periments with various verse forms and rhythms without
    sacrificing honesty and truthfulness. Jennings concludes
    that the additional verse forms may be a "sign that the
    poet has new and perhaps more difficult things to say."
    In his poem on the Nagasaki bomb, for instance, Wain de-
    monstrates a "new authority over style" and a "deeper con-
    cern with human, moral and political problems."

9 LESLIE, ANDREW. "The Joker." Manchester Guardian (11 Novem-
    ber), p. 9.
        Review of Nuncle and Other Stories. Wain's variety of
    style and treatment signals a "creative uncertainty." Like
    his novels, the stories are notable for "the quite shrewd

1960

and astringent eye for analysing the pattern of an emotional situation." On the debit side--also like his novels--
his writing is "always a study of situations rather than of
people." His observations are "simply uninvolved, rather
than consciously detached." Wain enjoys the elaborate
joke, but unfortunately the jokes contain "neither people
nor point."

10   LEWIS, NAOMI. "Short Stories." New Statesman, 60 (26 November), 846-47.
Brief review of Nuncle and Other Stories. Comments on
the fantasy in "Master Richard," the theme in "Rafferty"
("an exact little study in behavior"), and two special
forms of "middle-class vulgarity" in "The Quickest Way out
of Manchester." The stories are written in the "English
tradition"; the subjects "experiment in a number of
directions."

11   O'CONNOR, WILLIAM VAN. "John Wain: The Will to Write." Wisconsin Studies in Contemporary Literature, 1 (Winter),
35-49.
Discusses Wain's career as it relates to his novels,
poetry, and criticism. In all three areas, Wain's search
for a subject has been toward "old-fashioned moral truths."
What is missing, however, is "a sense of moral ambiguities."
The novels are "curiously stilted," as though Wain willed
them into existence. Examines Hurry on Down (a pointless,
inert novel lacking any "significant inner life"), Living
in the Present (a combination of farce and melodrama in
which Wain's imagination is less than adequate), The Contenders (evidence that Wain has been searching for a "down-
to-earth morality" all along), and A Traveling Woman (a
step forward in technique, a step backward in theme, indicating that Wain wants to be a wit but needs to be a
moralist).
Wain's poetry, on the other hand, is clever after the
manner of Empson. This cleverness is apparent in "Gentle-
man Aged Five before the Mirror" and "When It Comes." Finally, his criticism is often "stiffly academic," although
he strives for "jauntiness and facility." In Preliminary
Essays, Wain quarrels with academic life but rationalizes
or oversimplifies his own situation. Overall, his criticism is oversimplified with a "too insistent tone."

12   PESCHMANN, HERMANN. "The Nonconformists. Angry Young Men,
'Lucky Jims,' and 'Outsiders.'" English (London), 13
(Winter), 14.
Unlike Osborne, Wain (in Hurry on Down) and Amis (in
Lucky Jim) are more objective. To lump the three writers

together is "a case of critical myopia, sheer laziness, or, quite frankly, of palpable insincerity." In his second novel, Wain actually attacks the despair and nihilism Porter gives voice to in Osborne's Look Back in Anger. With The Contenders, Wain is at his most objective. Shaw resembles Osborne's Cliff Lewis and Roper and Lamb remind one of Braine's Joe Lampton in A Room at the Top. In his poems and other writings, Wain shows "a discriminating traditionalism and a recognition of certain elements in the social and educational system which, without finding them wholly admirable, he accepts as answering a deep-rooted need."

13 WOOD, FREDERICK T. "Current Literature 1958." English Studies, 41 (February), 49-50.
     Review of The Contenders. Notes the irony of Wain's winning the Somerset Maugham Award for this novel. Wain's style is "lively" and at times "slick." The plot is "somewhat conventional" and the characters are not altogether authentic. Prefers Wain the critic to Wain the novelist.

1961 A BOOKS - NONE

1961 B SHORTER WRITINGS

1 ALVAREZ, A. "English Poetry Today." Commentary, 32 (Spring), 218-19.
     General discussion of and response to the Movement and its claims. The Movement was a reaction "against wild, loose emotion." Its academic-administrative verse is "polite, knowledgeable, efficient, polished and, in its quiet way, even intelligent," but its tone is flat.

2 ANON. "Fiction." Kirkus Reviews, 29 (15 April), 381.
     Review of Nuncle and Other Stories. The collection lacks a central focus. "Variety, rather than variations, here indicates that there is still a style to be achieved. However, the stories "add interest" to his other writings.

3 ANON. "A Way of Speaking." Times Literary Supplement (14 July), p. 434.
     Review of Weep Before God: Poems. Finds a blend of satire, tragedy, "righteous indignation and humility" in this collection. This blend is reflected in the title of the collection, taken from a Jewish proverb ("Weep before God, laugh before men."). "The two extremes of experiment are neatness and looseness, but these seem to be the result of the poet's overshooting, or falling short of, his mark."

1961

He is aiming at somewhere in between. His models seem to be Swift or Yeats--"poets whose language insists uncompromisingly on the reality beneath false appearance." Although the short lyrics are his most successful, the longer poems command serious attention. "A Song about Major Eatherly," for example, is a poem which gathers "complexity and breadth of meaning" as it advances. The middle of the poem is weak because Wain seeks drama at "the expense of a naturally expanding symbolism."

4   ANON. "Non-Fiction." Kirkus Reviews, 29 (1 August), 712-13.
       Review of Weep Before God: Poems. The thoughts, emotions, and ideas in these poems are sincere. The shorter lyrics are less successful, perhaps because the overly schematic form and structure are too confining, resulting in "rather trite truisms or parables." In his longer, more forceful and articulate poems, "it is Wain's strident criticism of modern man and his daily disillusionments and self-delusions that come off, whereas the attempts to convey compassion, understanding, and mature compromises are sapped by inadequate or unoriginal vocabulary and syntax." Concludes that Wain is still more effective as a prose writer.

5   BARO, GENE. "Four Modern Poets." New York Herald Tribune Books (5 November), p. 12.
       Review of Weep Before God: Poems. This is not typical of Wain's best. Lately, when he writes badly, Wain turns to "journalistic verse, versifying this and that." In the good poems, "the meaning radiates beyond the poem instead of being something tacked on to it."

6   _____. "Mr. Wain in New Form." New York Herald Tribune Books (10 September), p. 10.
       Review of Nuncle and Other Stories. A disappointing collection, for despite their intellectual clarity, the stories lack the insight of his poetry, the "down-to-earth vigor" of his essays, or the satire of his novels. The best stories are those in which he captures precisely the lower-middle-class British life--one of the contributing factors in the development of his reputation. Focuses on "Christmas at Rillingham's," "Rafferty," and "The Quickest Way out of Manchester." In all three stories, "there is the suggestion of a life that lies beyond the immediate situation pictured, a life and a system of values that exert pressures and produce tensions all too germane to the behavior of characters." The other stories, however, "tend rather to be abstract ideas, literary notions, worked out in fictional terms."

7   BERGONZI, BERNARD. "After 'The Movement'." <u>Listener</u>, 66
    (24 August), 284-85.
        <u>Mixed Feelings</u> was the first Movement book of poems.
    Wain's 1950 essay on Empson increased the attention paid to
    Empson by poets at Oxford and Cambridge. Some of Wain's
    poems--"Eighth Type of Ambiguity," for example--are very
    Empsonian in form and language, though less so in spirit.

8   BRADBURY, MALCOLM. "Living in the Present." <u>Manchester
    Guardian</u> (14 July), p. 5.
        Review of <u>Strike the Father Dead</u>. Comments on the con-
    trasting styles of father ("pedantic, dry, self-exposing
    prose") and son ("slangy, ironic, Holden Caulfieldish self-
    exposition"). Finds the son's style to be self-defeating
    because he lacks a system of values with which to encounter
    the father's. Moreover, Wain fails to hit the "mystic
    note," for the scenes where Jeremy comes to "'understand'
    strike false." Finds superb Wain's evocation of "the gen-
    eral jazz-playing ethos into which he penetrates, to give
    precise, clear social detail, and manage a hard commonsense
    note which destroys all pretenses, even the author's own.
    The whole, however, is given a warm, documentary reality
    which is its most pleasing quality."

9   BRYDEN, RONALD. "British Fiction, 1959-1960." <u>International
    Literary Annual</u>, No. 3. Edited by Arthur Boyars and Pamela
    Lyon. London: John Calder, p. 44.
        "The exasperated comedies of Kingsley Amis and John Wain
    have affinities with the work of an older generation, who
    found a middle way between hazards in the various London
    bohemias between the wars. They look back on the dead days
    when choice was possible to them with the elegiac, fatalist
    humour of middle-age; but they seem more relevant to the
    society which succeeded theirs than do most of their embat-
    tled contemporaries of the pre-war Left."

10 BURNETT, HALLIE. "It Takes All Kinds to Make a Tale." <u>Satur-
    day Review</u>, 44 (16 September), 31.
        Review of <u>Nuncle and Other Stories</u>. These stories are
    distinguished by "vigor and imagination" and a consistent,
    thoroughly contemporary point of view. Wain is at his best
    in the slower, more controlled tales "in which subtle irony
    and the hidden, destructive urges of his characters are
    savored by both author and reader." Includes a brief sum-
    mary of each story.

1961

11   CRANE, MILTON. Review of <u>Nuncle and Other Stories</u>. <u>Chicago</u>
       <u>Sunday Tribune</u> (16 July), p. 3.
          Brief mention of theme and plot.

12   DAVIE, DONALD. "Poems and Orations." <u>New Statesman and Na-</u>
       <u>tion</u>, 62 (21 July), 91.
          Brief mention of <u>Weep Before God: Poems</u>. Wain "exhorts
       to the act of imagination," whereas the French poet St.
       John Perse (in <u>Chronique</u>) "makes it." Both poets "work
       from the idea to the image."

13   DENNIS, NIGEL. "Still Waiting for the Magic Wand." <u>New York</u>
       <u>Times Book Review</u> (16 July), p. 4.
          Review of <u>Nuncle and Other Stories</u>. In "Nuncle," Wain
       stops where he should have begun. His study of the pain of
       literary work holds "deep secrets"--if he had sought them.
       Although "Master Richard" demonstrates that he can tap "the
       world of high imagination and fascinating mystery," the
       other stories in the collection "only show how dull and in-
       significant his present world is."

14   GREEN, MARTIN. "British Comedy and The British Sense of
       Humour: Shaw, Waugh, and Amis." <u>Texas Quarterly</u>, 7
       (Fall), 226.
          Wain is one of Amis' "collaborators" in the sense that
       Nancy Mitford is Waugh's.

15   HEPPENSTALL, RAYNER. "They Like It Here," in his <u>The Fourfold</u>
       <u>Tradition: Notes on the French and English Literatures</u>.
       London: Barrie and Rockliff, pp. 213-20, 244-46.
          A discussion of the "Wain-Amis phenomenon" during the
       1950s, with an analysis of each writer's first four novels.
       Although closely associated with Amis at the start of his
       career, Wain differs greatly from him in his attitudes
       toward criticism (Wain is serious, Amis is irreverent),
       his public and critical reputation (Wain's is more hap-
       hazard than Amis'), and his development of comedy (Wain's
       comedy is "less rapidly engaging" than Amis'). In looking
       back at past writers, Wain's comedy is more tender-hearted,
       whereas Waugh's comic effects often centered upon "some
       violent, ludicrous death or frightful accident." Moreover,
       both Wain and Amis practice "a learned and deliberate anti-
       stylishness." Concludes that Wain takes his critical writ-
       ings too seriously and his novel writing not seriously
       enough. His attitude toward his origins--Stoke-on-Trent--
       has been ambivalent. Includes some biographical details
       covering Wain's years at Oxford and his association with
       Amis while there.

16   K., H. T. "Books Reviewed." Canadian Forum, 41 (August),
     117.
          Review of Nuncle and Other Stories. Wain's picture in
     this collection of disturbing and disturbed children is
     much deeper and more complex than in his earlier stories
     and novels, and his insight into "the lot of his wasted or
     burnt-out adults" is more sympathetic. Calls Wain a master
     of "the paradoxical bon mot and of exaggerated invective."

17   MALOFF, SAUL. "The Contemporary British Comic Novel: Satiric
     Eyes on a 'Revolution-of-Sorts'." Saturday Review, 44
     (8 April), 25-26.
          Survey of the new novelists of the 1950s. Includes a
     discussion of Wain's use of the comic novel.

18   MOON, ERIC. "Fiction." Library Journal, 86 (August), 2686.
          Brief mention of Nuncle and Other Stories. Four of the
     stories display Wain's "skill, style and sincerity." Four
     others illustrate most of his weaknesses because they are
     "slick, routine magazine fiction with clever but empty,
     secondhand plots and a lot of polish."

19   RICHART, BETTE. "Literacy, Wit and the Courage of Tradition."
     Commonweal, 75 (27 October), 126.
          Review of Weep Before God: Poems. The verse is tech-
     nically traditional, contemporary in feeling, and literate.
     Wain has "fused his reading and his talents successfully."

20   ROBIE, BURTON A. "Poetry." Library Journal, 86 (1 December),
     4191.
          Review of Weep Before God: Poems. This is hardly angry
     poetry, for "the final result is not a bang but a whimper."
     In other words, the means do not serve the end. Says that
     the total effect of the poems is "too baldly didactic,
     technically monotonous, and tonelessly dry to persuade."

21   RODWAY, ALLAN. "A Note on Contemporary English Poetry."
     Texas Quarterly, 4 (Autumn), 66-72.
          Examination of the Movement—why it began, where it was
     headed—with a brief mention of Wain.

22   ROSENTHAL, M. L. "Everything Is Subject for Good Talk." New
     York Times Book Review, (12 November), p. 4.
          Review of Weep Before God: Poems. Wain's writing is a
     combination of "an uneasy self-consciousness," a "deft plat-
     form presence," and a "humane candor." He is "witty, wry,
     confiding," and very much part of the present English mo-
     ment. Finds in "Anecdote of 2 A.M." a "Yeatsian poignancy"
     and a suggestion of the emotional sources of Wain's ability
     to hold a reader.

1961

23   SPENDER, STEPHEN. "The Present Position of Poetic Writing in
      England." Cairo Studies in English, 3 (Spring), 9-15.
          Brief discussion of the Movement with reference to Wain.

24   THWAITE, ANTHONY. "Names and Images." Spectator, 207
      (28 July), 149.
          Review of Weep Before God: Poems. This marks an ad-
      vance since his earlier work. Wain has moved away from
      Empson's to Lawrence's influence. "A Song about Major
      Eatherly" is his most ambitious and most successful poem
      so far. In "Boisterous Poem about Poetry," Wain resorts
      to "too much of the tedious frenetic screeching one finds
      in some of his fiction."

25   WILLIAMS, RAYMOND. "Realism and the Contemporary Novel," in
      his The Long Revolution. London: Chatto and Windus,
      p. 284.
          Says Wain and others fail to deal with the real prob-
      lems of our society. Because they lack profound convic-
      tions, they tumble repeatedly into farce and sentimentality.

1962 A BOOKS - NONE

1962 B SHORTER WRITINGS

1   ALLEN, WALTER. "Rebels and Ancestors in a War That is Con-
      stantly Renewed." New York Times Book Review (23 Septem-
      ber), pp. 4-5.
          Review of Strike the Father Dead. Wain's best novel
      since his first. Although the interlude of Paris lacks
      conviction and although Aunt Eleanor is a stock character,
      this is "a very skillful piece of craftsmanship." Partic-
      ularly notable are its "honesty and sobriety" and a com-
      plete avoidance of sensationalism. In this "deeply
      pondered" novel, the irony is never forced, and the way
      in which Wain establishes Jeremy as his father's son, "at
      one with him in austerity and integrity, in a fastidious
      regard for excellence, is both pleasing and moving." The
      self-revelation of the father is noteworthy, also.

2   ANON. "New Fiction." London Times (22 March), p. 15.
          Review of Strike the Father Dead. Wain has outgrown
      his "youthful originality." In this novel he resorts to
      the familiar device of different narrators. His theme is
      the outworn stern father vs. rebellious son, and Notting
      Hill as a setting adds little to the life of the novel.
      Wain even makes jazz seem sad and dull. Concludes that it
      is hard to know what to make of Wain.

3   ANON. "After the Bombardment." <u>Times Literary Supplement</u>
    (23 March), p. 197.
        Review of <u>Strike the Father Dead</u>. This novel suffers
    from incoherence because the switch in point of view "de-
    tracts from a reader's sense of reality." The description
    of London during the war is "totally inadequate," Jeremy's
    love life is "cursory," his development as a jazz pianist
    is overdone, his colloquialism is unrealistic, and the
    symbol of Major Edwards is so direct it seems clumsy. "Not
    much is left now of the picaresque gaiety with which Mr.
    Wain began, and at present his constructive power as a
    novelist is hardly equal to expressing what he wants to
    say." The writing is "slack."

4   ANON. "Fiction." <u>Kirkus Reviews</u>, 30 (1 August), 710.
        Review of <u>Strike the Father Dead</u>. Although a "consis-
    tently lively" story, it is only the pianist himself who
    "rings true." Finds the aunt "a mere convenience," and the
    old man "utterly incomprehensible to blatantly hackneyed."
    Wain still has a long way to go.

5   ANON. "Hurrying On." London <u>Times</u> (13 September), p. 11.
        Review of <u>Sprightly Running</u>. This is a book of uneven
    interest and value. The descriptions of his childhood and
    his days at Oxford are the best. Much of the remainder is
    "dismayingly naive and lacking in self-criticism." Wishes
    there were more about Wain's intellectual development and
    about the writers who have influenced him. "The whole book
    produces a picture of an engaging, ebullient man, an ad-
    mirer of 'dramatic personalities' and a bit of a dramatic
    personality himself, who at the age of 35 . . . was still
    unsure of the nature and direction of his artistic talent."

6   ANON. "Interim Judgment." <u>Times Literary Supplement</u>
    (14 September), p. 683.
        Review of <u>Sprightly Running</u>. Finds Wain's arrogance
    irritating. The attack is expected, the style is slack and
    interrogatory, and the judgment and definition are lazy.
    Moreover, the book is "marred by cliché in attitude and
    phraseology." The only compensation is the chapter on life
    at Oxford. Concludes that the emerging portrait of Wain is
    "commonsense, conservative, Johnsonian, and emphatically
    English middle-class man-of-letters."

7   ANON. "Fiction." <u>Booklist</u>, 59 (15 September), 74.
        Review of <u>Strike the Father Dead</u>. The development of
    the theme and characters is a "little uncertain," but
    Percy's merit and the story's serious aim make this recom-
    mended reading for the student of serious fiction.

1962

8   ENRIGHT, D. J.   "Strong Feelings."   New Statesman, 64
     (14 September), 323.
          Review of Sprightly Running. A sincere, highly personal
     book that may concurrently bore, irritate, charm, and oc-
     casionally cheer the reader. Comments on Wain's "dispro-
     portionate violence" (of bullies, Communism, and the teach-
     ing profession), "compassionate understanding" (of E. H.
     Meyerstein and Wain's entire relationship with Oxford), and
     "self-awareness." Wain comes across as "an inveterate
     teacher: he must instruct, rectify, warn or denounce."

9   ENTWISTLE, WILLIAM J. and ERIC GILLETT. "Prose of Entertain-
     ment: Fiction," in their The Literature of England:
     A.D. 500-1960: A Survey of British Literature from the
     Beginnings to the Present Day. London: Longmans, Green
     and Company, pp. 231-32.
          Wain shows much promise as a novelist, poet, and critic,
     but so far his published work has fallen short of expecta-
     tions. His first four novels "are high-spirited and well-
     written but seem to lack a strong creative purpose."

10 GINDIN, JAMES. "The Moral Center of John Wain's Fiction," in
     his Postwar British Fiction: New Accents and Attitudes.
     Berkeley and Los Angeles: University of California Press,
     pp. 128-44.
          Examines Wain's first four novels and his collection of
     short stories, and finds that through them runs a constant
     commitment to the "moral worth of the individual." These
     works also indicate how difficult it is to understand and
     explain "what the human personality is like." Wain sets
     his moral statements in the contemporary English scene--a
     scene accepted in the first two novels but rejected in the
     second two "in favor of an older, moral, local tradition."
     For example, Hurry on Down is a mock picaresque novel sa-
     tirical of those "who commit themselves to class." Lumley
     seeks "the dignity of the personal and the humane."
          In Living in the Present, Edgar searches for, and finds,
     a reason for living--through such qualities as goodness,
     honesty, and love. In The Contenders, best of the four
     novels, personal value is projected into "a wider area of
     English society" as Wain attacks the competitive spirit
     motivating both the businessman and the artist. Further-
     more, the characters in A Traveling Woman learn that "man's
     nature . . . requires marital fidelity." The stories in
     Nuncle and Other Stories illustrate the power of personal
     love. Hence, Wain limits and defines the values he asserts
     through localism, difficulty of understanding the human
     personality, comedy, and diversity of the world. His weak-
     nesses are repetition and sentimentality. In the endings,

his "comic devices are often too brittle, too decorative,
and too occasional to prevent the weight of the emotion
from seeping through." Excerpted: 1974.B23.

11 HEALEY, ROBERT C. "New Fiction." New York Herald Tribune
Books (11 November), p. 11.
Review of Strike the Father Dead. Wain is not especial-
ly angry in this novel. Jeremy may be a rebel, but his
quarrel with society and his environment is "artistic rather
than social." Except for the jazz sequences, the novel is
curiously "bloodless and perfunctory." The background settings of Paris and London are "strictly utilitarian and
matter-of-fact."

12 HOLLOWAY, JOHN. "'Tank in the Stalls': Notes on the 'School
of Anger,'" in his The Charted Mirror: Literary and Critical Essays. New York: Horizon Press, pp. 137-45.
Reprint of 1957.B7 and 1960.B7.

13 HYNES, SAMUEL. "Books: Pitfalls in the Search for Identity."
Commonweal, 77 (5 October), 47-49.
Review of Strike the Father Dead. Wain has much in common with Amis, Braine, Sillitoe, and Storey, for all of
them are "interested in what happens to individuals in a
system which seems to deny individuality as a matter of social principle." Although not his best novel, Wain's latest
is typical of his weaknesses and strengths. In demonstrat-
ing the "Search for Identity" theme, for example, Wain has
written about unreal characters. Strength may be found in
the settings, the atmosphere, and the serious and important
ideas. "His book is a serious, intelligent, conscientious
piece of work, but that is not quite enough to make it a
good novel."

14 KARL, F. R. "The Angries: Is there a Protestant in the
House?" in his A Reader's Guide to the Contemporary English
Novel. New York: Farrar, Straus and Giroux, 304 pp.,
passim.
Wain's novels, together with those of many of his contemporaries, suggest a "narrow range, superficial analyses,
irresponsible and aimless protagonists, anti-heroic acts,
anti-intellectualism, and slapstick comedy." Although
Hurry on Down is more substantial than Amis' Lucky Jim, its
basic sentimentality compromises its point of view. The
key to understanding Lumley is in his reactions to class
stratification. Most of the angry protagonists "rebel and
then find some niche for themselves that fails to accommo-
date their former intention." Wain's later novels are rid-
dled with "conceptual clichés and examples of unimaginative

1962

planning that flawed his more artistically successful first
novel." Beneath the surface of his trivial characteriza-
tions are suggested important themes.

15 MANN, JR., CHARLES W. "Fiction." Library Journal, 87
(1 November), 4047.
Brief review of Strike the Father Dead. A sympathetic
work focusing on the conflict between the attitudes of a
professor ("a veritable Housman with his strict code of behavior and dedication to his scholastic discipline") and
his son ("softer in nature").

16 MITCHELL, JULIAN. "Landscape into Art." Spectator, 208
(23 March), 377.
Review of Strike the Father Dead. Finds in this, as in
all of Wain's novels, an inability to let the reader work
things out for himself. Although a thought-provoking, professional piece of writing, the novel never gets off the
ground because of Wain's "sledgehammer technique."

17 O'CONNOR, WILLIAM VAN. "Two Types of 'Heroes' in Postwar
British Fiction." Publications of the Modern Language
Association, 77 (March), 170.
The hero of Hurry on Down is similar to the hero in
Larkin's Jill. Both characters are ineffectual to begin
with, but their university training compounds their inabil-
ity to make a living.

18 PRESS, JOHN. "English Verse Since 1945," in Essays by Divers
Hands. Vol. 31. Edited by Peter Green. London and New
York: Oxford University Press, p. 145.
Quotes from Wain's 1954 review of Philip Toynbee's
Friends Apart to illustrate a note of "slight bitterness
and cynicism, a careful avoidance of high-sounding politi-
cal idealism, a determination to gaze cooly at facts."
Wain's attitude typifies that of the new generation of
poets.

19 PRICE, MARTIN. "The Complexity of Awareness and the Awareness
of Complexity: Some Recent Novels." Yale Review, NS 52
(Winter), 266-67.
Review of Strike the Father Dead. Although lacking
imaginative power, Wain's acute intelligence makes this one
of his best novels. Moreover, the experience of a jazz mu-
sician, and the world of Professor Coleman and the 1940s
London are all "vividly rendered." Wain's intelligence
proves "insufficient only to the fusing of these elements
into full characters who live out necessary lives."

20 QUINTANA, RICHARD. "Book Reviews." <u>Wisconsin Studies in Con-</u>
    <u>temporary Literature</u>, 3 (Winter), 84.
        Review of <u>Nuncle and Other Stories</u>. Wain is a clear
    writer in full control. He is himself as he conveys "the
    same sense of integrity that distinguishes his novels."
    Comments further on the gimmick ("Master Richard" and "A
    Message from the Pig-Man"). Best of all are the sketches
    with social humor and realism ("Christmas at Rillingham's
    and "The Quickest Way out of Manchester"). These are "dis-
    cerning, often humorous, and always free of anger." Wain
    is a "compassionate observer."

21 ROGERS, W. G. "From Beta to Bop." <u>Saturday Review</u>, 45
    (29 December), 39.
        Brief mention of <u>Strike the Father Dead</u>. Calls the al-
    ternating narrators a "clumsy technique," but the story is
    moving because of Jeremy's search "for the one right way
    for Jeremy."

22 ROSS, T. J. "'The Image of Another Creature': A Perspective
    on Contemporary English Poetry." <u>Connotation</u>, 1 (Winter),
    ii, 15-25.
        Survey of poetry of the 1950s, with mention of Wain.

23 SOUTHERN, TERRY. "Books and the Arts: Recent Fiction,
    Part I." <u>Nation</u>, 195 (17 November), 332.
        Brief review of <u>Strike the Father Dead</u>. "In putting
    aside his angry youth, Mr. Wain has also disposed of his
    power to surprise." This is "a calm and all too likely
    tale."

24 TAUBMAN, ROBERT. "Trad Man." <u>New Statesman and Nation</u>, 63
    (23 March), 419.
        Review of <u>Strike the Father Dead</u>. The title suggests
    Wain's "taste for violence," and indeed, Wain displays con-
    tempt for mid-twentieth-century living. The use of inte-
    rior monologue suggests more "psychological depth and sub-
    tlety than there actually is." Rather, Wain's interests
    are moralistic. Concludes that the novel is useful as an
    "inside account of the last twenty years of jazz."

25 TRACY, HONOR. "Lord of Imbecility." <u>New Republic</u>, 147
    (20 October), 45.
        Review of <u>Strike the Father Dead</u>. Despite its drawbacks
    (old themes, clichés, repetition), Wain's novel is written
    with "zest and humor and simply starry-eyed pleasure." Be-
    cause Wain identifies with Jeremy, both Professor Coleman
    and Aunt Eleanor "remain shadowy and unconvincing." How-
    ever, Wain writes so well that the reader may finish the
    book before perceiving the drawbacks.

1963

1963 A BOOKS - NONE

1963 B SHORTER WRITINGS

1   ANON. "Contemporary Poets Who Deserve a Reading." London
     Times (14 March), p. 17.
         Brief mention of Anthology of Modern Poetry. Calls it
     "a very enjoyable selection."

2   ANON. "Half a Life." Newsweek, 61 (13 May), 108.
         Brief review of Sprightly Running. This is an engaging,
     devoted, serious work, though rarely solemn. His devotion
     at times seems that of a very young man, but "he generally
     casts a cool eye on his subject and speaks with rousing
     candor."

3   ANON. "Biography." Booklist, 59 (15 May), 766.
         Brief review and summary of Sprightly Running.

4   ANON. "Antidisestablishmentarian." Time, 81 (24 May), 104.
         Review of Sprightly Running. "This unusual book sug-
     gests that most British intellectuals of his generation
     have settled into the admirable pattern of cultivated men
     of good will." His story of Oxford life is one of the best
     on education ever told, "because he was one of the few for
     whom education itself is a crucial experience."

5   ANON. "Books: Brief Reviews." Critic, 21 (June-July), 80.
         Brief mention of Sprightly Running. A "first-rate"
     autobiography whose "modest and sensible bit of self-
     reflection" contrasts with Wain's reputation as an Angry
     Young Man. "His quiet and honest style is as refreshing
     as a sundowner."

6   ANON. "Quick Guide to New Reading." London Times (3 October),
     p. 15.
         Brief mention of Essays on Literature and Ideas. Calls
     Wain one of the "soundest and least showing-off of the
     younger critics." Wain's comments on individuals are as
     satisfying as his encounters with a general theme.

7   ANON. "Discursive Critic." Times Literary Supplement
     (11 October), p. 799.
         Review of Essays on Literature and Ideas. Wain's essays
     reveal original insight, for he, like Orwell, "gathers much
     critical strength from a freshness and innocence in his ap-
     proach." Along with this, however, Wain is often "a slap-
     dash writer" whose perceptions are often juxtaposed to
     "great patches of critical impercipience." His generaliza-

tions are an easy way of avoiding a difficult argument.
Although he has an original mind, his fluency and readiness
to write on almost any subject "in the easy tone of a lec-
turer talking to a class of bright students, is by way of
being a curse."

8 BRAINE, JOHN. "The Penalty of Being at the Top." Time and
   Tide--John O'London's, 44 (3 January), 21, 23.
      Disagrees with John Davenport and Wain who say that an
   author's popularity and merits are connected. Says most
   young British novelists are worse than provincial; they
   are parochial.

9 COX, C. B. "Conclusion: The Modern Novel," in his The Free
   Spirit: A Study of Liberal Humanism in the Novels of
   George Eliot, Henry James, E. M. Forster, Virginia Woolf,
   and Angus Wilson. London: Oxford University Press,
   pp. 157-61.
      Finds that "destructive satire, ebullient farce, and
   sentimental romance are jumbled together in strange confusion" in the novels of Wain and Amis. At their worst, Wain
   and Amis "are either sentimental or hysterical; at their
   best, they honestly reject belief in heroic action and
   violently expose the hypocrisies of society." Hurry on
   Down suffers from a structural problem, that of the frus-
   trations of a liberal set on the hopeless goals of being
   independent of class. The novel lacks both a climax and a
   resolution. Finds more optimistic humanism in The Contenders.

10 ELLMANN, RICHARD. "Plain Mysteries." Encounter, 21
   (December), 88-89.
      Review of Essays on Literature and Ideas. Although Wain
   tries to make himself clear, there are inconsistencies of
   attitude, generalizations, and discriminations in this collection. Wain's attempt at literary history is provoca-
   tive, but often he leaves one with the impression of "sober
   recklessness." Moreover, his "method of isolating opposite
   strands of the same personality makes for a division which
   is hard to put right again."

11 GRAY, JAMES. "Never in Anger." Saturday Review, 46 (18 May),
   29.
      Review of Sprightly Running. This book reveals that
   Wain has always wanted to be a creative artist. As a
   writer, he is authentic, candid, without pretense, and
   "earnestly yet always humorously persuasive." The book
   leaves the reader feeling "the presence of a man whose
   spirit has been refined by suffering, by insight, by the

determination to be honest and, finally, by the benign influence of a mature, ironic outlook. Wain has gained in
stature by this modest examination of his far from angry
purposes."

12   HICKS, GRANVILLE. "Talks Along the Thames." Saturday Review,
      46 (14 December), 39.
         Review of Essays on Literature and Ideas. Wain attacks
      vigorously an astonishing variety of topics. Hicks offers
      comments on the essays covering Orwell and literary forms,
      and says the book is unified by a "sense of cultural
      change" and by a "strenuous effort to understand the nature
      of the present crisis" in society.

13   HOPE, FRANCIS. "Contender." New Statesman, 66 (1 November),
      616, 618.
         Review of Essays on Literature and Ideas. Wain is at
      his best when he stays close to the text. His "mixture of
      sympathy and tenacity" in the essays on Hopkins, Little
      Dorrit, and Eliot, for example, provides insight and in-
      struction. On the other hand, his writings on Byron, Pope,
      Shakespeare, education, India, and literary form are "gen-
      eral and less original."

14   HOWE, IRVING. "Mass Society and Postmodern Fiction," in his
      Decline of the New. New York: Harcourt, Brace and World,
      pp. 204-205.
         Wain, Amis, and Braine were blessed because they found a
      subject "urgently imposing itself upon their imaginations."
      This subject was contemporary life and the Welfare State.
      Through their comedy they were able to "structure" their
      complaints. Notes that many American critics scorned them
      because it was unclear whether the writers were looking for
      a better or bigger share of cultural and material goods in
      contemporary England.

15   KERMODE, FRANK. "The House of Fiction: Interviews with Seven
      English Novelists." Partisan Review, 30 (Spring), 77-79.
         Wain comments on reality and its relation to the author.
      The writer must have "a complete freedom of attitude [to
      select] the form that will take the piece of reality" that
      the writer has in mind. "The whole object of writing is to
      tell the truth." He "does not believe that myth has a free
      hand with reality; indeed reality is for him something you
      stand firmly outside of, that you select from."

16 LITTLEJOHN, DAVID. "Books and the Arts: The Misfit at Home."
     Nation, 197 (10 August), 75-76.
          Review of Sprightly Running. Labels this "autobiography-
     as-personal-therapy," but questions the usefulness. Wain
     is too anxious to find meaning in all of his torments from
     cradle to college. The most admirable chapters are Wain's
     account of Oxford and the literary chapter. His portrait
     of Meyerstein as a "mad and magnificent failure" is the
     finest thing in the book. Wain brings him to life and
     analyzes "both Meyerstein and his relationship to him with
     an artistry that is at once sympathetic, honest and keen."
     In the literary chapter, Wain is a man that matters: "the
     writer, the lover of man and life and letters who has never
     let his premature, self-indulged 'tragic vision' get in the
     way of his zest for living, his commitments to writing, his
     delight in the eccentric and wonderful in man." Finds "a
     good deal of angry editorializing" in Wain's other comments
     on literature. It seems that Wain writes with "consider-
     able less care when engaged in such rambling journalistic
     warfares."

17 McDOWELL, FREDERICK P. W. "'The Devious Involutions of Human
     Character and Emotions': Reflections on Some Recent Brit-
     ish Novels." Wisconsin Studies in Contemporary Literature,
     4 (Autumn), 342.
          Review of Strike the Father Dead. Jeremy's life in war-
     time London is the best section, whereas his retreat from
     Paris to London in the 1950s is the least successful be-
     cause "too much is compressed within too few pages" and
     because of an "inadequate delineation" of the protagonist.
     Although intermittently interesting and moving, this novel
     has "little of the gusto that imbued Hurry on Down and lit-
     tle of the psychological complexity" of The Contenders.

18 MOON, ERIC. "Bibliography--Personal Narrative." Library
     Journal, 88 (15 May), 1996.
          Review of Sprightly Running. Wain irritates in this su-
     perbly written collection only because he leaves the reader
     wanting so much more. "A Literary Chapter" puts Wain, as a
     writer, "into better focus than anything else on record."
     "Going Home" is a superb chapter and should be required
     reading for all creative writing courses.

19 NORDELL, RODERICK. "Wain vs. the Roughs." Christian Science
     Monitor (16 May), p. 11.
          Review of Sprightly Running. Discusses Wain's dispute
     over being called an Angry Young Man. Wain is trying to
     tell the truth, yet deliberately eliminates the more pain-
     ful or complicated experiences. The book is typical in its

vivid picture of a boy from Oxford at a loss for what to
do next, and atypical in his "articulate awareness of himself, of his melancholy in the contradictions of human life
even as he enjoys the moments that are gay." Notices a
similarity between Jeremy (in Strike the Father Dead) and
Wain: each chose his profession and finds himself "a con-
solidator, worthily assuming the large responsibility of
the artist."

20 O'CONNOR, WILLIAM VAN. "John Wain: The Will to Write," in
his The New University Wits and the End of Modernism.
Carbondale: Southern Illinois University Press, pp. 30-53.
In his poetry, Wain aspires to "passion, logic, and
formal beauty." In place of puzzles he gives the reader
cleverness--and in turn his critics are made uneasy. Wain
has turned to "old-fashioned moral truths" in his search
for a subject, but if he is to prove himself as a moralist,
he will have to find more complex moral problems. "He has
the Midlands City that Bennett had as a source for home-
grown characters and perennially engaging themes, and there
is London and the Continent for contrasts. What is missing
thus far is a sense of moral ambiguities." Excerpted:
1974.B23.

21 PRESS, JOHN. Rule and Energy: Trends in British Poetry Since
the Second World War. London: Oxford University Press,
245 pp. passim.
Discusses the characteristics of poets appearing in New
Lines. In his early verse, Wain is a disciple of Empson.
"Don't Let's Spoil It All, I Thought We Were Going to Be
Such Good Friends" is intended to be "a terse, poised commentary on a tragic situation." But no matter how serious
Wain's intentions, "the result is an uneasy mixture of
hard-boiled facetiousness, knowing cynicism, and facile
melodrama." Furthermore, "A Song about Major Eatherly" is
typical of its epoch, with its obsession about the destruction of Japanese cities. In it, "disgust and disillusion
mingle with a wry, stoical acceptance of the fact that we
live in barbarous and bloody times." Wain's review of
Toynbee's Friends Apart reveals a skepticism about the
course of public events since 1945.

22 PRYCE-JONES, ALLAN. "Early Days of the Melancholy Jacques
Wain." New York Herald Tribune Books (12 May), p. 4.
Review of Sprightly Running. A "bundled together" collection lacking sequence or a sense of proportion. Although the title is presumably taken from Dryden's Aureng-
Zebe, the reference is misleading. "Mr. Wain is at pains
to show himself a kind of melancholy Jacques. He describes

a natural propensity to look on the dark side, and early
resigns himself to be a tolerated outsider rather than a
natural member of the team." But Wain explains nothing of
his own talent. Concludes with comments about Wain's influence on other writers and his quickly growing reputation.

23 WILKIE, BRIAN. "Inner Visions." Commonweal, 78 (28 June),
    381-82.
        Review of Sprightly Running. "This book is a victim of
    its virtues. The first half has power, honesty, and
    beauty. Then, inexplicably, its Lehrjahre pattern sudden-
    ly disintegrates and the author begins to write editorials
    rather than real autobiography. At the end the reader al-
    most feels defrauded." Praises Wain for his "extraordinary
    ability to dramatize inner vision through setting" and for
    his portraits of Charles Williams, C. S. Lewis, and E. H. W.
    Meyerstein. These portraits are "lively, acute, and out-
    spoken." The literary discussions, however, are "too often
    superficial and stale," sometimes even naive.

1964 A BOOKS - NONE

1964 B SHORTER WRITINGS

1   ALLEN, WALTER. "War and Post War: British," in his Tradition
    and Dream: The English and American Novel from the Twen-
    ties to Our Time. London: Phoenix House, pp. 278-80, 282.
        In the early 1950s, Wain, Murdoch, and Amis were "strik-
    ing new notes in fiction." Hurry on Down was both an ex-
    ercise in the picaresque and a satire of this period of
    social change. But in spite of great promise, Wain has
    produced nothing to equal his first novel in either "attack
    or authority." Wain's "denigrating attitude" and his
    handling of comic situations reminds one of Smollett. Re-
    printed: 1965.B3.

2   ANON. "Briefly Noted: General." New Yorker, 39 (25 January),
    112.
        Brief mention of Essays on Literature and Ideas. These
    pieces are "learned, opinionated, sprightly" on a fairly
    wide range of literary subjects. The essay on India is
    "wonderful."

3   ANON. "Brief Reviews." Critic, 22 (February-March), 89.
        Brief review of Essays on Literature and Ideas. Wain's
    language is precise, and his meaning is unmistakable. "By
    contesting critical vagaries, he brings a new freshness to
    old subjects like Pope, Hopkins, Byron and Dr. Johnson."

1964

4   ANON. "To Please the Million." Economist, 212 (19 September),
     1138.
          Brief review of The Living World of Shakespeare: A
     Playgoer's Guide. Wain's book holds the reader's interest
     because of its "good sense and wide sympathies." The best
     chapters cover the great tragedies and late romances.

5   ANON. "Will For Everyman." Times Literary Supplement
     (15 October), p. 940.
          Review of The Living World of Shakespeare: A Playgoer's
     Guide. Although not offered as an academic study, the
     reader should get the "relevant facts" in Wain's sound and
     perceptive comments if he overlooks the "somewhat casual
     treatment of the historical material."

6   ANON. "Language and Literature: English and American."
     Choice, 1 (December), 314.
          Review of The Living World of Shakespeare: A Playgoer's
     Guide. Although Wain uses the current modes with "deftness
     and taste," he becomes absurd in his hunt for symbols and
     images. In addition, "he attempts to make Renaissance sto-
     ries and points-of-view available to the modern layman as
     expressions of the perennially human."

7   ANON. "Two More for the Bard." London Times (3 December),
     p. 23.
          Review of The Living World of Shakespeare: A Playgoer's
     Guide. The best chapter is "Blindness," in which Wain il-
     luminates the tragedies. This is a guide to the don and
     the undergraduate, and a source which will please and in-
     struct the common reader.

8   ARNOLD, W. E. "Critic in the Johnson Tradition." Commonweal,
     79 (31 January), 546-48.
          Review of Essays on Literature and Ideas with a summary
     of each essay. "Wain's hatred of journalism as a corrupter
     of art borders, at times, on obsession." However, for a
     former Angry Young Man, he does little shouting in this
     book. Comments further on Wain's balance and good sense.
     It is clear that he has learned much as a writer from
     Orwell. In his essay on Orwell, Wain gains "a better
     understanding of a man who was both committed to the mod-
     ern and the anti-modern at the same time." Concludes that
     Wain has a gift for sharing "the enjoyment of living and
     of reading."

1964

9   BALL, PATRICIA. "The Photographic Art." A Review of English
     Literature, 3 (June), 50-53, 56-57.
          Considers the standard of honesty in the work of Wain,
     Amis, and Larkin as a way of finding the true nature of the
     Movement. These poets take "realism to a new phase of
     crystallization, the time when it regards and knows it-
     self." The Movement's significant feature is its "aware-
     ness of honesty." Comments on "Reason for not Writing
     Orthodox Nature Poems" and the use of the villanelle verse
     form in "When It Comes" and "Gentleman Aged Five before the
     Mirror."

10   CAMPAIGNE, JR., J. G. "Books in Brief." National Review, 16
     (7 April), 291.
          Review of Essays on Literature and Ideas. Wain's criti-
     cal stand is "safe, polite and thin, a convention of ma-
     jority opinion culled from the literary handbooks and con-
     densed biographies." Because of this stand, Wain is com-
     mitted to an "imaginative timidity." His examinations are
     "unexcited, undernourished, and anonymous." Only in the
     essay on Hopkins does he leave behind the superficial
     approach.

11   DeMOTT, BENJAMIN. "Of Snobs and Taxes and Unimpressed Men."
     Harper's Magazine, 228 (April), 106.
          Brief mention of Wain, Amis, and Larkin's time together
     at Oxford in the 1940s. Wain dedicated a book to Larkin.
     Amis has since dedicated a book to Wain. Says their tastes
     are "likably low" and that they have been "baiting the
     gentry for years." Brief biographical mention that Wain's
     father was a dentist.

12   DUMAS, ROBERT. "Literature." Library Journal, 89
     (1 January), 111.
          Brief mention of Essays on Literature and Ideas. De-
     spite the rambling prose and loose thinking, the collection
     is "sprinkled with useful insights."

13   FRASER, G. S. The Modern Writer and His World. Baltimore:
     Penguin Books, 427 pp. passim.
          Wain differs greatly from Amis for the following reasons:
     (1) he is more of a moralist and romantic; (2) he is pres-
     ent as "a person, as a voice, in all his fiction"; and
     (3) his gifts of plotting and of producing "concentrated
     and eloquent expressions of strong emotions" are the gifts
     of a dramatist--perhaps his real medium. Like Amis, how-
     ever, Wain gives the reader "a sense of actual contemporary
     life." Living in the Present deserved more attention than
     it received. It is a very "gripping and uncomfortable

109

1964

study in the pathology of rage." As in his other novels,
this one does suffer from a "lack of critical distancing
between the author and hero." Finally, comments on the
characteristics of his poetry and his critical career, con-
cluding that Wain has become "a free-lance man of letters."

14   FULLER, JOHN W. "From the Bookshelf: John Wain: Judgment
       and Ideas." Christian Science Monitor (7 February), p. 9.
       Review of Essays on Literature and Ideas. For the most
    part, Wain is dynamic and charged with ideas, so that the
    reader is constantly fascinated. But this style can be
    disconcerting also, for it is marred by too many superla-
    tives and too many "semantic improbabilities." Because his
    critical method is always changing, it is difficult to cat-
    egorize him. "Wain's overstatements and his frankly sub-
    jective and familiar style, blended curiously with an ex
    cathedra overtone (somewhat reminiscent of Eliot's), seem
    to invite the reader's antagonism and dissent, but the pro-
    fusion of sprightly ideas, the surprising turns, the
    clarity of expression, the wit . . . invite the reader to
    keep on reading."

15   HAMILTON, IAN. "Four Conversations: Philip Larkin." London
       Magazine, 4 (November), 72, 76.
       Larkin says the Movement's beginning may be traced to
    Wain's succeeding John Lehmann on the BBC program. "John
    planned six programmes called First Readings including a
    varied set of contributors--they weren't all Movementeers
    by any means. It got attacked in a very convenient way,
    and consequently we became lumped together." Then an arti-
    cle in The Spectator and the appearance of New Lines in
    1956 lumped them together once again. But Larkin says it
    never occurred to him that he had anything in common with
    the other poets. Reprinted: 1975.B30.

16   HOLLOWAY, JOHN. "The Literary Scene," in The Modern Age.
       Vol. 7 in The Penguin Guide to English Literature. Edited
       by Boris Ford. Baltimore: Penguin Books, pp. 95-96.
       Finds a parallel between Wain's "Who Speaks My Language"
    and Auden's "Rimbaud." Concerning Empson's influence on
    the Movement, Holloway says: "At his most distinctive [he]
    has been least influential; and most influential at his
    most Audenesque."

17   KERMODE, FRANK. "Dialects of the Tribe." New Statesman, 68
       (18 September), 402.
       Review of The Living World of Shakespeare: A Playgoer's
    Guide. Finds a "conservative cast" in his celebration of
    order and his grasp of Shakespeare's pessimism. Wain is

less at home with the comedies. Is dubious about Wain's
commentary on earth and water imagery in Antony and Cleo-
patra, his defense of Eliot's essay on Hamlet, and his
essay on Timon.

18   McMANAWAY, JAMES G. "In Celebration of the Nature of Man."
     New York Times Book Review (1 November), p. 5.
         Review of The Living World of Shakespeare: A Playgoer's
     Guide. A stimulating guide into the development of Shake-
     speare's art and "the intense contemporaneity of some of
     his ideas." However, the book suffers from "tricks of
     faulty memory" and a defense of Eliot's discussion of Ham-
     let. Concludes that "few will read this book without a
     better understanding of Shakespeare's plays and a height-
     ened admiration for their author."

19   NEILL, S. DIANA. "The Nineteen Forties and After," in her
     A Short History of the English Novel. London: Collier-
     MacMillan, pp. 394-95, 399-400.
         In style, theme, technique, and subject matter, Hurry on
     Down, Lucky Jim, and Room at the Top display an attitude of
     "anti-authority and anti-tradition." The humor in Wain's
     novel recalls the frolic in Ivor Brown's Master Sanguine.
     The Contenders promised a more serious concern with satire,
     "a blending of sheer comedy with an awareness of the black
     depths in human personality." In place of the episodic
     plot in Hurry on Down, Wain used a plot "that gained mo-
     mentum from a conflict." Moreover, the novel is comparable
     to William Styron's This House on Fire in its concern with
     the "shoddy values so readily accepted in society."

20   PETTIGREW, JOHN. "Books Received." Canadian Forum, 44
     (April), 20-21.
         Review of Essays on Literature and Ideas. Most of these
     essays are "too light" to merit republication; hence, this
     collection will do little to advance Wain's reputation.
     Praises the essays on Pope, Byron, Hopkins, and India.
     Best of all are Wain's comments on Little Dorrit and George
     Orwell. At his worst, Wain makes "sweeping statements on
     sweeping topics." At his best, he focuses on particular
     authors or works. "Mr. Wain is still too much the review-
     ing journalist, still too much the perennial introducer of
     authors from all periods of literature, to have earned the
     title of critic. But in the essays on Dickens and Orwell,
     Mr. Wain shows that his apprenticeship could be over."

1964

21 PHELPS, GILBERT. "The Novel Today," in The Modern Age.
        Vol. 7 in The Penguin Guide to English Literature. Edited
        by Boris Ford. Baltimore: Penguin Books, pp. 488-90.
            As a novelist, Wain has written "in more or less con-
        scious revolt from all that is avant-garde and cosmopoli-
        tan." Says that the lack of commitment in Hurry on Down
        reflects the postwar political disillusionment. In spite
        of notable achievements, his first three novels do not
        succeed at a serious level. Only in Nuncle and Other Sto-
        ries are there "signs of a talent getting down to the hard
        work of creative detachment and control."

22 PICKREL, PAUL. "Unmixing Our Metaphors." Book Week
        (26 April), pp. 15, 19.
            Review of Essays on Literature and Ideas. Unlike Con-
        stantine, Fitzgibbon's writings in Random Thoughts of a
        Fascist Hyena, Wain's essays are nearly all literary; his
        mind is searching for "a unifying center." Therefore,
        Wain's attraction is to an age when writers like Swift and
        Pope could be both ironic and satiric because "they operat-
        ed from a consensus of thought or belief. They could at-
        tack because they had something to defend." But for Wain,
        it is difficult to find a consensus today. Sometimes his
        enthusiasm in searching for whatever unites leads him
        astray.

23 PRICE, MARTIN. "New Books in Review: Open and Shut: New
        Critical Essays." Yale Review, 53 (Summer), 597-98.
            Review of Essays on Literature and Ideas. Wain's prose
        is clear, direct, and sometimes simplistic. In his concern
        with the problems of the modern writer, Wain displays a
        great historical range. "Perhaps Mr. Wain is all too much
        a professional man of letters." His book has an institu-
        tional title, and the most pervasive note in the essays is
        the sense of the literary career. His essay on India is
        poetic.

24 RAINES, CHARLES A. "Literature." Library Journal, 89
        (15 December), 4915.
            Brief review of The Living World of Shakespeare: A
        Playgoer's Guide. Wain's attempt to elucidate Shakespeare's
        work to the masses is based on "reduction to the lowest com-
        mon thematic denominator." Most interesting of all is his
        Freudian approach to Hamlet.

25 THWAITE, ANTHONY. "Poetry of the 1950s," in his <u>Contemporary
English Poetry: An Introduction</u>. London: Heinemann Educational Books, pp. 149-51.
      Despite comparisons by critics, finds "definite and de-
finable differences" between the poetry of Wain and Amis.
Wain's early poems, in the form of villanelle and <u>terza
rima</u>, are more heavily influenced by Empson. At that time,
his poems were moral statements. More recently, Wain has
widened his scope and made freer his form. Now he is more
heavily influenced by Lawrence.

1965 A BOOKS - NONE

1965 B SHORTER WRITINGS

1 ADAMS, PHOEBE. "Potpourri." <u>Atlantic Monthly</u>, 216 (October),
174.
      Review of <u>The Young Visitors</u>. The results of the col-
lision between Soviet travelers and a fake English Commu-
nist are not quite as "amusing, surprising, or satirical as
they should be."

2 ALLEN, WALTER. "London Had Changed Since Dickens." <u>New York
Times Book Review</u> (24 October), p. 52.
      Review of <u>The Young Visitors</u>. Although an entertaining
novel written with intelligence and inventiveness, "it is
unlikely to compel the reader's complete belief." Because
of the narrative method, "a curious bias" creeps in, that
"nice young Russians shouldn't go to Britain because if
they do, they will be conned by crooks posing as Commies."
Two impulses--the satirization of professional literary
Communists in the West and the exploration of contemporary
Soviet youth--are in conflict and cancel each other.

3 _____. "War and Post War: Britain," in his <u>The Modern Novel
in Britain and the United States</u>. New York: E. P. Dutton,
pp. 278-80, 282.
      Reprint of 1964.B1.

4 ALVAREZ, A., <u>et al</u>. "An Appeal for Tolerance: Arrest of
Soviet Writers." London <u>Times</u> (24 November), p. 13.
      Letter signed by Alvarez, Cyril Connolly, Brian Glan-
ville, Goronwy Rees, Clancy Sigal, Philip Toynbee, John
Wain, C. V. Wedgwood, and Rebecca West, and addressed to
the editor of <u>The Times</u>, in which a protest is made over
the arrest of Andrei Sinyavsky and Yuli Daniel, Russian
writers, for publishing their manuscripts in the West under
the pen names of Tertz and Arzhak.

1965

5   ANON. "Fiction." <u>Kirkus Reviews</u>, 33 (15 July), 707.
         Review of <u>The Young Visitors</u>. Surprisingly, this is not
     an angry book; rather, it is an "innocuous, altogether
     bland comedy" about Cold War, cultural exchange, and naive
     politics. "Elena sounds like a character out of <u>Silk
     Stockings</u>, and Jack Spade lacks even comic dimension." The
     novel provides no surprises.

6   ANON. "Catching the Audience." <u>Times Literary Supplement</u>
     (29 July), p. 651.
         Review of <u>Wildtrack: A Poem</u>. Rather diffuse and lack-
     ing a "deliberate order or consistency in Mr. Wain's re-
     flections, except for the unity given by an underlying
     compassion." Calls this "a huge ragbag of a poem, with
     some moving moments, but also some unbelievable errors of
     tone."

7   ANON. "New Fiction." London <u>Times</u> (16 September), p. 14.
         Review of <u>The Young Visitors</u>. The stock caricatures are
     reminiscent of the worst kind of Hollywood film, and the
     clumsy protagonist destroys any humor in certain passages.
     But the greatest weakness is that the novel seems to begin
     as a satire on western attitudes toward the Russians, but
     then turns into a "stock cold war classic." One compensa-
     tion is that Wain does have "a good ear for adolescent
     language."

8   ANON. "Current and Various." <u>Time</u>, 86 (24 September), 114.
     Brief unfavorable mention of <u>The Young Visitors</u>.

9   ANON. "Spade Work." <u>Newsweek</u>, 66 (27 September), 108.
         Review of <u>The Young Visitors</u>. Wain wants to capture a
     note of innocence of a group of Soviet young people ob-
     serving Western society for the first time. "His visitors
     are among the truest modern Russians seen by a novelist,
     and his best achievement is to make it exquisitely clear
     how their loss of faith in an oppressive system is not nec-
     essarily political triumph, but human tragedy." The novel,
     therefore, is "a touching and perceptive quasi fable of the
     loss of one kind of innocence in our time."

10   ANON. "What Daisy Didn't Know." <u>Times Literary Supplement</u>
     (30 September), p. 850.
         Review of <u>The Young Visitors</u>. An ingenious story, but
     the plot collapses around "a political-sociological <u>conte</u>,
     whose types may perhaps crystallize some useful percep-
     tions." Spade, trivial and ridiculous, represents nothing
     at all. Elena is "just a grinning parody of a social
     realist heroine."

11   ANON. "Poems for the Good-Hearted." London <u>Times</u> (4 November), p. 15.
        Brief mention of <u>Wildtrack: A Poem</u>. Fails to hold much interest because it is too loosely written. This is a "rhetorical meditation on the world today."

12   ANON. "Non-Fiction." <u>Kirkus Reviews</u>, 33 (15 November), 1185.
        Review of <u>Wildtrack: A Poem</u>. Although Wain's seriousness of purpose and technical abilities are never in question, "the poem as a whole rarely achieves either passionate utterance or intellectual cohesion. . . . Energy is abounding throughout, and earnestness, too, but not the necessary dynamic, dialectical force."

13   BERNSTEIN, NORBERT. "Fiction." <u>Library Journal</u>, 90 (1 October), 4114.
        Review of <u>The Young Visitors</u>. "A few sexy sparks, with an overall satire of British stuffiness and communist ideological doubletalk, and enough to spare to make this a fairly amusing but unrequited love affair." Says Peter DeVries could have worked wonders with this situation.

14   BYROM, BILL. "Old Comrades." <u>Spectator</u>, 262 (17 September), 356.
        Review of <u>The Young Visitors</u>. The novel is neither critical nor amusing. The students' social and emotional attitudes are flimsily described and do not ring true; "these automatons are a travesty not merely of real Russians, but also of real human beings." Wain's comprehension of real attitudes is "false and shallow." The climax is unconvincing.

15   DAVENPORT, GUY. "The Puppet Masters." <u>National Review</u>, 17 (16 November), 1034.
        Brief mention of <u>The Young Visitors</u>. Calls this "a light and wispy bit of puppetry" which seems to be the first two acts of a comedy.

16   GRUBB, FREDERICK. "How Not to Fly: Robert Graves, Norman Cameron, William Empson," in his <u>A Vision of Reality: A Study of Liberalism in Twentieth-Century Verse</u>. New York: Barnes and Noble, pp. 128-29, 132.
        Wain's essay on Empson "signalled the counter-attack on the 'punch-drunk, romantic scribblers' of the 1940s." Includes a summary of Wain's major arguments.

1965

17   HAMILTON, ALEX. "On Killers and Socialists." Books and Book-
      men, 10 (June), 41.
           Review of the paperback edition of Nuncle and Other Sto-
      ries. In the title story are illustrated Wain's qualities
      as a writer: "the cerebral drive, the sense of being up to
      date, joined at times to a rather irritating knowingness,
      the strong physical awareness with which he lays out his
      backgrounds, his interest in the literary world as a ground
      for intrigue or range for manoeuvres." In each story
      there's a point made, and hence a satisfaction for the
      reader.

18   HOPE, FRANCIS. "Problem Poetry." New Statesman, 70 (August),
      222.
           Review of Wildtrack: A Poem. Wain's serious concern
      for contemporary issues "bulks too largely" in this poem.
      Best are the poems of Dr. Johnson and an eighteenth-century
      raree-show revolving around Dean Swift and a midget woman--
      "which suggest that Mr. Wain is at his best when senten-
      tiousness is balanced by formality and buttressed by eru-
      dition." His worst failures occur when he tries to be
      "simultaneously original and cosmic," as in "The Rib."

19   JACKSON, KATHERINE GAUSS. "Books in Brief." Harper's Maga-
      zine, 231 (December), 134.
           Brief mention of The Young Visitors. Wain goes to a lot
      of trouble for not very much in this "pleasant spoof." The
      outcome is amusing, not too predictable, and "somehow old
      hat."

20   JENNINGS, ELIZABETH. "Elusive Goddess." Spectator, 215
      (23 July), 109.
           Review of Wildtrack: A Poem. The most successful parts
      of this poem are the private sections--those which encom-
      pass significant portions of Wain's private life. The pre-
      dominant feeling is one of "compassion, . . . controlled by
      a fine irony and by a poetic skill which is flexible enough
      to express itself in many forms and cadences."

21   LEVINE, PAUL. "Reviews: Some Middle-Aged Fiction." Hudson
      Review, 18 (Winter), 592.
           Review of The Young Visitors. Calls this "a convention-
      al novel on the now unconventional theme of boy meets
      girl." Because the hero is "such a nasty egomaniac," the
      novel is "slight and the comedy is slightly grim."

116

22 MAYNE, RICHARD. "Travelling Man." New Statesman, 70
      (8 October), 528-29.
          Review of The Young Visitors. In his criticism, one al-
      ways knows what Wain's judgments are, and never has the
      feeling that he is "talking down." In this novel, Wain
      treats the theme of the Cold War, but the book doesn't live
      up to its promise. Spade's character goes wrong. Finds in
      the novel an "imaginative essay on East and West" from
      which Wain swings back to one of his primary themes--"a
      'picaresque' character who comes to grief because real hu-
      man beings can't sustain indefinitely the carefree pica-
      resque role." Concludes that Wain's attempt "to confront
      as forcefully as possible the quality of two ways of life"
      renders the book artificial.

23 MONTGOMERY, JOHN. "Young? Angry? Typical?" Books and Book-
      men, 11 (December), 86-87.
          A discussion of the social, political, and economic fac-
      tors contributing to the origins of the Angry Young Men.
      Brief biographical mention, and a reference to Sprightly
      Running in which Wain corrects the account of Hurry on Down
      given by Colin Wilson.

24 MURRAY, JAMES G. "Poor Moore, Worse Wain." Critic, 24
      (December-January), 70-71, 73.
          Unfavorable review of The Young Visitors. A "completely
      naive performance" lacking in sophistication and literacy.
      The narrative "not only aims low but sinks even more lowly."

25 POLLOCK, VENETIA. "New Novels." Punch, 249 (22 September),
      442.
          Review of The Young Visitors. Although one may not be-
      lieve in Elena or Spade as spokesmen for their countries,
      "as emotional beings they are honest enough to react vio-
      lently to each other first and think a long time after."
      Finds that the truth is "rather overstaged with excess of
      floodlighting; although jocular in expression and produc-
      tion, the book is sombre in the wings."

26 PRESS, JOHN. "Recent Poems." Punch, 249 (3 November), 665.
          Review of Wildtrack: A Poem. Wain explores many grand
      themes, but his sections on Swift and Johnson are the most
      moving and the closest to universality. Finds that Wain's
      poetry becomes "sharper and richer" when he moves from
      political and social developments to the lives of
      individuals.

1965

27   PRYCE-JONES, DAVID. "Soap-Box Derby." <u>Book Week</u> (17 October),
      p. 35.
         Review of <u>The Young Visitors</u>. This is a modernization
      of Daisy Ashford's period fable, <u>The Young Visiters</u> (<u>sic</u>).
      Complains about the repetition, inconsistent motives, and
      Wain's editorializing on Russia and Communism. Because
      Wain limits his characters to externals, he "makes them
      ciphers, not worth the recital."

28   SAMSTAG, NICHOLAS. "A Separation of Sex and State." <u>Saturday</u>
      <u>Review</u>, 48 (16 October), 52.
         Brief review of <u>The Young Visitors</u>. The novel comes
      dangerously close to a mere spoof on the reader. It is
      "shoddily done," and the ending is not a surprise.

29   SEYMOUR, WILLIAM KEAN. "Poets Young and Old." <u>Contemporary</u>
      <u>Review</u>, 207 (November), 275-76.
         Review of <u>Wildtrack: A Poem</u>. Wain's sincerity in this
      modern poem on "human interdependence" is both "powerful
      and appealing." Some readers may question "the self-
      conscious novelty of the method employed in its composi-
      tion." This is a blend of "journalism and creative
      writing."

30   WALSH, CHAD. "The Postwar Revolt in England Against 'Modern
      Poetry.'" <u>Bucknell Review</u>, 13 (May), 99.
         Tries to come to an understanding of what constitutes
      the new generation of poets. With the publication of <u>New</u>
      <u>Lines</u>, Wain, together with Jennings, Holloway, Larkin,
      Gunn, Amis, Enright, Davie, and Conquest, were "put on
      display." Cites Wain's "Anniversary" to illustrate how
      these poets are "newspaper columnists, commenting in tidy
      and urbane verse on the ordinary affairs of men." Since
      his beginnings, Wain has developed powerfully in the direc-
      tion of politics and social commentary. Empson's influence
      on Wain is obvious, judging by the example of "his own lean
      and stripped down, intellectually rigorous verse."

1966 A BOOKS - NONE

1966 B SHORTER WRITINGS

1   ANON. "Literature." <u>Booklist</u>, 62 (7 July), 1028.
         Brief mention of <u>Wildtrack: A Poem</u>. Wain contemplates
      man as "the enigma of nature" in a poem which is distin-
      guished by a "diversity of form and a tenuous unity of
      theme."

1966

2   ANON. "Language and Literature: English and American."
     Choice, 3 (October), 653.
          Brief mention of Wildtrack: A Poem. Wain's many voices
     and wide range of poetic techniques show him to be a "mas-
     ter craftsman."

3   ANON. "Hurry on Up." Times Literary Supplement (13 October),
     p. 933.
          Review of Death of the Hind Legs and Other Stories. To
     readers familiar with Wain's early novels, this will be a
     disappointing collection. "Most of the stories are con-
     ceived by sentimentality out of stock response." In "Man-
     hood," Wain demonstrates that he is still a writer of
     "vision and sensibility."

4   ANON. "Notes on Current Books: Fiction." Virginia Quarterly
     Review, 42 (Winter), x, xii.
          Review of The Young Visitors. The novel is a failure
     because "the characters are stereotypes without a breath of
     life; the language is an unironic rendering of Soho and So-
     viet clichés; and the underlying social criticism is banal
     and crude."

5   ANON. "Short Stories." London Times (8 December), p. 16.
          Review of Death of the Hind Legs and Other Stories.
     Comments on the "sticky sentimentality" of these stories,
     and says they "bear all the signs of having been set reluc-
     tantly in motion and whipped despairingly to a finish."

6   CROOK, ARTHUR. "John Wain," in his British Commonwealth Fic-
     tion Since 1950. London: The National Book League, p. 9.
          In Hurry on Down, Wain illustrates the humorous--and
     serious--effects of social conventions on Charles Lumley,
     a man to whom they are "foreign, incomprehensible and
     unpalatable."

7   DONOGHUE, DENIS. "The Long Poem." New York Review of Books,
     6 (14 April), 18-19.
          Review of Wildtrack: A Poem. The poem is held together
     by a few related themes and "a controlling concern." Finds
     the section on Johnson's childhood illness moving, but the
     Henry Ford segment is "flat and slack" because Wain has
     nothing new to say on this theme, and because "the lines
     are weary."

1966

8   EPSTEIN, JOSEPH.   "Sins of Omission."   <u>Book Week</u> (27 November),
     pp. 4, 19.
         Review of <u>Death of the Hind Legs and Other Stories</u>.
     Calls Wain both "a craftsman [and] a virtuoso" in this col-
     lection. He uses a wide range of subjects and techniques
     of construction. However, to claim the thread of these
     stories is alienation--as the publishers do--is to under-
     rate Wain, for they are about cruelty "of time and aging on
     people." It is an unconscious cruelty, "almost always inad-
     vertent, and sometimes even random." Together, the stories
     "constitute a delicate and remarkable probe of the modern
     heart of darkness."

9   FLEISCHER, LEONORE.   "PW Forecasts: Paperbacks: Literary
     Classics: January." <u>Publishers Weekly</u>, 190 (12 December),
     62.
         Brief mention of <u>Selected Shorter Poems of Thomas Hardy</u>
     and <u>Selected Stories of Thomas Hardy</u>. Says both collec-
     tions are compiled by one of Britain's best young novelists
     and critics.

10   GRAY, SIMON. "How Well Have They Worn? 5. <u>Lucky Jim</u>." Lon-
     don <u>Times</u> (3 February), p. 15.
         Brief mention of Wain. As an Angry Young Man, he has
     been identified and confused with Amis, Wilson, and Tynan.
     The hostile reactions in the press "are interesting now
     only as a demonstration of reflex rank-closing."

11   HECHT, ANTHONY. "Poetry Chronicle." <u>Hudson Review</u>, 19 (Sum-
     mer), 336-38.
         Review of <u>Wildtrack: A Poem</u>. Wain's poetic method is
     somewhat "discontinuous." Finds a weakness in the lan-
     guage, for at times Wain sounds "thinly" like Auden's
     poetry of the 1930s. Throughout, there is "a plain lack
     of energy not entirely obscured by flat and provocative
     pronouncements." As a whole, the poem is damaged by a
     "general limpness."

12   LITTLER, FRANK. "English Hybrid." <u>New York Times Book Review</u>
     (18 December), pp. 18-19.
         Review of <u>Death of the Hind Legs and Other Stories</u>.
     Wain's style, with its "comfortable garrulity, its alterna-
     tion of saloon patter with imported colloquialisms never
     less than 15 years old, is a familiar English hybrid." The
     stories are weak because they utilize "their promising set-
     tings merely to make a point." One leaves these stories
     with the feeling that Wain is living "on his abundant lit-
     erary capital."

13　MacMANUS, PATRICIA. "Probing with a Lyre." Saturday Review, 49 (3 December), 60.
　　Review of Death of the Hind Legs and Other Stories. Ever since his first novel, Wain's choice of subject matter has diminished his irony and pointed social comedy. In this collection, however, "he moves easily in diverse social directions, probing human pretensions and self-deceptions, though with less of the devastating comic put-down that so enlivens his novels." Finds a characteristic "variousness" in these stories.

14　MOON, ERIC. "Fiction." Library Journal, 91 (15 December), 6114.
　　Review of Death of the Hind Legs and Other Stories. Wain's reputation is waning, and this collection does nothing to rescue it. The plotting is routine, and the characters are stereotypic. Finds a kind of "heavy, sentimental nostalgia" in these stories. The only exception is "King Caliban," indicating that Wain "really has something."

15　MURDY, LOUISE BAUGHAN. "Introduction," in her Sound and Sense in Dylan Thomas's Poetry. Paris: Mouton, p. 11.
　　Brief mention of Wain's comment that "it is doubtful whether or not Thomas really cared much about any precise meaning as long as the sound of the poem satisfied him."

16　RABINOVITZ, RUBIN. "Reaction Against Experimentalism in the English Novel: 1950-60." Dissertation. Columbia University.
　　Mentions Wain's link, by chronology, with Amis, Wilson, Hinde, and Golding. Brief discussion of the characteristics they share as contemporary writers. Reprinted 1967.B17.

17　RAYMOND, JOHN. "Booking Office: Paperback Monsters." Punch, 251 (10 August), 233.
　　Brief mention of The Living World of Shakespeare: A Playgoer's Guide. Readers will find in this "thoughtful and perceptive study . . . the kind of consolation that poetry can offer life in the raw."

18　REGAN, ROBERT. "Poetry." Library Journal, 91 (1 May), 2345.
　　Review of Wildtrack: A Poem. Calls this a "compelling, compassionate poem." The theme is partly a meditation on the history of man and partly an examination of his uncertain current "estate." Although the language is frequently "an inadequate vehicle for its cosmic import," it is still surely "one of the most noteworthy accomplishments in recent English poetry."

1966

19   SEYMOUR-SMITH, MARTIN. "Good Intentions." Spectator, 217
     (21 October), 521-22.
         Review of Death of the Hind Legs and Other Stories. On
     the whole, these stories are "serious, responsible, sensi-
     tive and readable enough (some of them) to have appeared in
     Argosy and Ladies' Home Journal." But they fall far short
     of the classics by Maupassant, Chekhov, or Mansfield. In
     "Darkness," for example, Wain fails to communicate the
     man's panic urgently enough in his writing. Moreover, the
     title story is "sentimental and totally unconvincing." The
     overall failure of Wain is to achieve "authenticity." This
     failure is due to an "over-dependence upon the crude de-
     mands of a difficult market, and use of language which does
     not match his intentions and perceptions." Also, Wain
     lacks curiosity. He seems to use people "to create ef-
     fects." People don't interest him. Concludes by praising
     the humor and good-heartedness "that lies buried under the
     faults."

20   TAUBMAN, ROBERT. "Military Idiot." New Statesman, 72
     (21 October), 596.
         Brief mention of Death of the Hind Legs and Other Sto-
     ries. Says the stories are "occasionally sour about con-
     temporary habits, but the tone is set by what seem exer-
     cises in nostalgia."

21   WOLFE, GEOFFREY. "Objects and Emotions." Book Week (22 May),
     p. 8.
         Review of Wildtrack: A Poem. Wain has an appetite for
     variety. At his worst, he is "flat and bland;" at his
     best, he is "jocund and grave." Wain rarely says what is
     unnecessary to say. He "celebrates the subjective imagina-
     tion; his enemy is collective, 'homogenized' man. Yet he
     never ignores the imperative that language, and intuition,
     are printed to be shared."

1967 A BOOKS - NONE

1967 B SHORTER WRITINGS

1   ANON. "Fiction." Booklist, 63 (15 January), 522.
         Review of Death of the Hind Legs and Other Stories.
     These stories are concerned with "cruelty carelessly and
     unconsciously inflicted." They are "well-crafted, sensi-
     tive, and appealing."

2 ANON. "PW Forecasts: Paperbacks: Nonfiction." Publishers'
   Weekly, 191 (10 April), 83.
      Brief mention of The Living World of Shakespeare: A
   Playgoer's Guide. Throughout this study, Wain is alert to
   Shakespeare's artistry and his genius for "making his lan-
   guage work as drama and poetry simultaneously."

3 ANON. "Language and Literature: English and American."
   Choice, 4 (May), 293.
      Review of Death of the Hind Legs and Other Stories. As
   Wain grows older, his anger diminishes and his thoughtful-
   ness and stature increase. The most notable features of
   his writing are the range of subjects and the variety of
   points of view.

4 ANON. "Dropping Out." Times Literary Supplement (5 October),
   p. 933.
      Review of The Smaller Sky. Calls this a "shapely novel"
   developed from an ingenious idea: a study into the way
   people are labeled "mad" and the results of that labeling.
   Unlike The Young Visitors, this novel shows Wain seeming to
   understand the environment he is describing. The narrative
   is swift and readable, and the dialogue is sound and well-
   selected; however, readers may find a somewhat "shallow and
   pretentious" commentary on the modern world. His treatment
   of television journalists suggests the novel is intended as
   a moral fable with the journalist as the scapegoat, but
   Wain's treatment of him unbalances the story.

5 ANON. "Language and Literature: English and American."
   Choice, 4 (December), 1119.
      Brief mention of Arnold Bennett. A "readable apprecia-
   tion" that takes the conventional view of the English
   Realist.

6 BROICH, ULRICH. "Tradition und Rebellion: Zur Renaissance
   des pikaresken Romans in der englischen Literatur der
   Gegenwart." Poetica, 1 (April), 214-29.
      Discusses the revival of the picaresque novel in England
   with reference to Hurry on Down, Lucky Jim, and Under the
   Net. In both eighteenth-century and twentieth-century
   picaresque, realism, satire on class, and the grotesque are
   emphasized. (In German.)

7 BUFKIN, E. C. The Twentieth-Century Novel in English: A
   Checklist. Athens: University of Georgia Press,
   pp. 124-25.
      Lists Wain's novels through 1965.

1967

8   BURGESS, ANTHONY. "A Sort of Rebels," in his The Novel Now:
     A Guide to Contemporary Fiction. New York: W. W. Norton,
     pp. 144-46, 149, 153.
          Wain's early novels were hailed by the early critics who
     failed to notice the "atrocious construction and indiffer-
     ent" style. In Strike the Father Dead, jazz "carries the
     right nonconformist overtones," but as in The Contenders,
     "Wain evades the problem of narrative style by opting for a
     first-person colloquial which sounds weary rather than
     bright." His subjects are always excellent, but even in
     The Young Visitors there is no fresh departure. Wain is a
     fine poet and critic, but the novel form "hides his fine
     taste and his clarity of thought." Includes a listing of
     fiction and nonfiction through The Young Visitors.
     Reprinted: 1970.B7. Excerpted: 1974.B23.

9   CLIVE, GEORGE. "New Novels: Desert Victory." Spectator, 219
     (6 October), 398.
          Review of The Smaller Sky. Wain has dealt with the
     problems of the nonconformist in Hurry on Down, but his
     latest novel is much more pessimistic. Says Geary needs
     further development, for he is too much "the ordinary,
     persecuted man, the hero-victim of many other novels." By
     comparison, both his wife and the television personality
     are "far more real." Concludes that the climax has the
     right degree of "inevitability."

10   COX, C. B. "Paperback Fantasy." Spectator, 218 (10 February),
     173.
          Brief mention and summary of Wain's introduction to Se-
     lected Stories of Thomas Hardy.

11   DENNIS, NIGEL. "'Late Again, He Groaned.'" New York Review
     of Books, 8 (23 March), 13.
          Review of Death of the Hind Legs and Other Stories. "Mr.
     Wain has not stretched a single brain cell and has even, in
     the few stories that deal with more extraordinary people,
     managed to make them seem ordinary, too."

12   FREEMAN, GILLIAN. "Points of Departure." New Statesman and
     Nation, 74 (6 October), 440.
          Review of The Smaller Sky. Calls the novel "funny, per-
     tinent, and also very sad." Novels like this are not just
     original, "but bizarre launching pads for satire."

13 HEMMINGS, JOHN. "Certified." Listener, 78 (12 October),
    476-77.
        Review of The Smaller Sky. Apparently Wain does not be-
    lieve in his own argument, for Geary, though he quits his
    job and leaves his wife, cannot convince Wain of his sani-
    ty. At the end, "the novel, if not an outright failure, is
    a downright disappointment."

14 MARTZ, LOUIS L. "New Books in Review: Recent Poetry:
    Roethke, Warren, and Others." Yale Review, 56 (Winter),
    279-80.
        Review of Wildtrack: A Poem. Because Wain can write in
    any style and any form, this poem is exciting to read and
    technically "a remarkable achievement." However, it does
    not work because "it is too literary, too much of an exer-
    cise." Excerpted: 1974.B23.

15 O'HARA, T. "Books." Commonweal, 85 (10 February), 538-39.
        Review of Death of the Hind Legs and Other Stories.
    Says that "too often a flatulence and gross sentimentality
    perdures" in this collection, prompting one to ask how
    seriously Wain can be taken. "The recurrence of defeated
    men and women, the desolation motifs, the dislocated rela-
    tionships and the cultural and institutional collapses
    point out Wain's ambition. . . . Regrettably he failed to
    achieve it."

16 PRICE, R. G. G. "New Novels." Punch, 253 (11 October), 562.
        Review of The Smaller Sky. Enjoyable reading, but "the
    material really only justifies a short story and the para-
    ble element [is] unexpectedly trite."

17 RABINOVITZ, RUBIN. Reaction Against Experimentalism in the
    English Novel: 1950-60. New York: Columbia University
    Press, pp. 38-63, 174-76.
        Expanded reprint of 1966.B16.

18 RATCLIFFE, MICHAEL. "The Death of Privacy." London Times
    (5 October), p. 8.
        Review of The Smaller Sky. As readers, we are able to
    observe the hero "like guilty but compassionate eaves-
    dropper[s]." Moreover, as "a parable of escape and exploi-
    tation it is never tendentious because never forced, and it
    is written throughout with a deep sense of pain, tact, and
    immediacy."

1967

19   ROSENTHAL, M. L.   "Contemporary British Poetry," in his The
      New Poets: American and British Poetry Since World War II.
      New York: Oxford University Press, pp. 219-20.
          Brief discussion of Wildtrack: A Poem. Says it is weak
      because of an infrequent reliance on "his personal, ideo-
      syncratic voice of knowledge." Most of the poem becomes
      "an awkward machinery for the thematic contrasting of mass-
      man . . . and subjective man." Moreover, Wain's lyrical
      voice develops in a few powerful sections, notably "The
      Day-Self Contemplates the Defeat of Time" and "The Night-
      Self Sees All Women in One Woman." These, together with
      "The Twelve," are "as good as anything Wain has ever done."

20   TREVOR, WILLIAM. "Fiction: William Trevor Sees Paddington
      Afresh." Books and Bookmen, 13 (October), 46.
          Review of The Smaller Sky. Notes a recurrence in novels
      now of the "lone figure, saddened and maddened by the
      creeping threats of our bleak age." In Wain's new novel,
      Geary is the love figure. "With technical cunning that
      never affects his charity, [Wain] entices one into the
      slippery mind of Geary." Says Wain's ear is acute as ever,
      except when recording the "ramblings of an elderly Irish-
      man." Suggests the novel could be more economical.

21   URWIN, G. G., ed. "John Wain: A Traveling Woman," in A Taste
      for Living: Young People in the Modern Novel. London:
      Faber and Faber, pp. 134-44.
          Summarizes Wain's views on contemporary novelists and
      comments on Wain's use of the comic figure in Hurry on Down
      and A Traveling Woman. Finds in the latter, unlike the
      first novel, that "the picaresque structure has been re-
      placed by the close interweaving of different yet compara-
      ble themes: the events result from deeper, more plausible
      emotions. And the end is neither complacent nor humorous."
      Includes an excerpt from A Traveling Woman and a brief bio-
      graphical entry.

22   WORDSWORTH, CHRISTOPHER. "Man on His Own." Manchester Guard-
      ian Weekly, 97 (19 October), 11.
          Review of The Smaller Sky. Calls this "a compressed,
      intricate, and still eminently plausible" novel; its alle-
      gory isn't overbearing, the vignettes "are dove-tailed with
      great skill." Says Swarthmore is "a sharply defined con-
      temporary master" and Geary is the "crux" as he walks the
      "razor's edge of his condition where one clumsy touch could
      dislodge the whole book." Hopes it will be filmed as more
      than a pseudopsychological Hitchcock thriller.

1968 A BOOKS - NONE

1968 B SHORTER WRITINGS

1   ALBÉRÈS, R. M. "Renaissance du Roman Picaresque." Revue de
     Paris (2 February), 47-53.
          Finds themes of dissolution, indecision, guilt, uneasi-
     ness, and the need to kill the preceding generation in
     Strike the Father Dead. (In French.)

2   BEACHCROFT, T. O. "Moods After Two World Wars: III," in his
     The Modest Art: A Survey of the Short Story in English.
     London and New York: Oxford University Press, pp. 226-27.
          In Death of the Hind Legs and Other Stories, the title
     story is "a rare achievement: a story of Dickensian
     bravura, cast effectively in modern short-story form,
     brief, colourful, and controlled." Says that Wain's "in-
     vention of emotionally bizarre human situations" is Dick-
     ensian also. Often Wain's stories remind one of Stacy
     Aumonier and Pett Ridge.

3   LEE, JAMES W. "Introduction: VIII: John Wain," in his John
     Braine. Twayne English Authors Series, edited by Eliza-
     beth A. Bowman. Boston: Twayne Publishers, pp. 26-30.
          As a man of letters, Wain's influence on Braine and the
     1950s and 1960s is considerable. Traces the history of
     the publication and critical response given to his first
     three novels, and studies Wain's treatment of class struc-
     ture. Includes a plot summary of each novel.

4   MILLER, KARL, ed. "Introduction," in Writing in England To-
     day: The Last 15 Years. Baltimore: Penguin Books, p. 14.
          Brief mention of Wain as a member of the Movement. Re-
     fers to the poet's reversion "to ordinary speech and moral
     earnestness."

5   PEYRE, HENRI, ed. "Introduction," in Fiction in Several Lan-
     guages. Boston: Houghton Mifflin Company, p. xxiii.
          Surveys the development of the contemporary novel from
     Forster to Wain, Wilson, Spark, and Murdoch, and concludes
     that it may be "too subtly ironic, too self-conscious in
     its mastery of style, perhaps too thin in content, to ex-
     ercise a potent attraction on the man of other lands, en-
     deavoring with Arnoldian 'high seriousness' to understand
     life better and perhaps see it steadily through their
     literature."

1968

6   SCOTT-KILVERT, IAN. "English Fiction 1967." <u>British Book</u>
    <u>News</u>, 331 (March), 165-69.
        Brief mention of <u>The Smaller Sky</u> as a most original
    novel.

7   VALENCIA, WILLA F. "The Picaresque Tradition in the Contempo-
    rary English and American Novel." Dissertation. Universi-
    ty of Illinois.
        Analyzes Wain's early novels and finds them faithful to
    the historical picaresque tradition. In them, "roguish
    anti-heroes have been educated . . . above their lower
    middle-class families but are in a social no man's land
    because they retain a traditional hostility." This return
    to tradition signifies a reaction against the experimental
    novel. Gives several other reasons for this revival, in-
    cluding the following: (1) the fumbling anti-hero as an
    apparent spokesman for an age which has "rediscovered the
    fact of man's limitations"; (2) the current glorification
    of youth; (3) contemporary man's vulnerability to satire;
    and (4) the comic relief as good entertainment.

<u>1969 A BOOKS - NONE</u>

<u>1969 B SHORTER WRITINGS</u>

1   ANON. "Paperbacks." <u>Observer</u> (2 February), p. 34.
        Brief mention of the paperback edition of <u>The Young</u>
    <u>Visitors</u>. A "neatly told" though occasionally "pat" tale.

2   ANON. "As They Liked It." <u>Times Literary Supplement</u>
    (3 July), p. 725.
        Brief mention of <u>Shakespeare: Macbeth: A Casebook</u>.
    Wain's choice of essays is predictable.

3   ANON. "Bi-Focus." London <u>Times</u> (5 September), p. 11.
        Interview with Wain prior to the telecast of a four-part
    television adaptation of <u>The Contenders</u>. Wain says he was
    happy in the 1950s—the setting of much of the novel—for
    it was "'a kind of holiday between two disasters: the di-
    saster of having too little in the forties, and the disas-
    ter of having too much in the sixties.'" In retrospect,
    the 1950s are beginning to seem like the 1920s—both were
    postwar periods "'in which it was a delicious sensation to
    be able to live comfortable lives and not have to queue for
    every necessity; both were full of inventiveness and crack-
    le.'" Then, the years of hunger were still a memory; hence,
    "'[life] had not degenerated into the kind of lemming-rush
    towards money and goods that we have now, when the whole

nation openly worships Mammon.'" Sees the Angry Young Men
as a "'put-up job by non-writing journalists in an attempt
to make writers interesting enough for gossip columns.
The real time of "anger" was in the early thirties--in
George Orwell's first novels and Auden's poems--this was a
real anger against the stupid, immovable situation of the
moment.'"

4   BROWNJOHN, ALAN. "Rival Claims." New Statesman, 78
    (5 December), 830.
        Review of Letters to Five Artists. "The moments of
    clarity and control, patches of achieved imagery and coher-
    ent thinking, are swamped in banality and sententiousness."
    In his early verse, Wain barely held in his emotions. In
    Weep Before God, he broke loose a bit, but his "boisterous,
    extrovert, consciously wide-ranging persona" is present, as
    it is in Wildtrack: A Poem and Letters to Five Artists.

5   DAVIS, ROBERT M. "Market Depressed and Unstable: Surveys of
    the Recent English Novel." Papers on Language and Litera-
    ture, 6 (March), 211-23.
        Mentions Gindin's treatment of Wain in Postwar British
    Fiction. (See 1962.B10.)

6   KUEHL, LINDA. "Books: The Poor, the Power Structure, and the
    Polemicist." Commonweal, 90 (May), 269.
        Wain, like Braine and Amis, was not so much "voicing
    moral outrage against social injustice during the fifties
    as [he was] vocalizing personal pique at being born lower
    class." In retrospect, his anger seems to have been "sheer
    spleen." Today, Wain continues to prescribe "traditional
    English values for his characters."

7   MELLOWN, ELGIN W. "Steps Toward Vision: The Development of
    Technique in John Wain's First Seven Novels." South Atlan-
    tic Quarterly, 17 (Summer), 330-42.
        Focuses on the development of Wain's narrative technique
    as offering the most positive evidence of his potential
    worth. Hurry on Down is a picaresque adventure story, a
    pastiche, in which Wain develops one character completely
    and surrounds him with a host of lightly sketched charac-
    ters. Wain envisions life as "an impoverished existence
    devoid of memory or meaning." In Living in the Present, he
    is concerned with the problems of "Being and Not-Being."
    However, Banks and his troubles are unconvincing as Wain
    tries to complicate a simple story line with mystery. The
    Contenders is another wish-fulfillment with a sharper point
    of view. Shaw's monologue is a technical advance for Wain,
    as is its unity of theme and form. As in his other novels,

the central figure in A Traveling Woman is inadequate.
Wain turns to symbolism in this novel (the Cowley family
form a center round which the other figures revolve and
change), but it is a novel without moral values or meaning.
Strike the Father Dead succeeds because of an elaborate
organization, clear characterization, and the manipulation
of a large number of themes. These themes include "the
freedoms and dependencies of fathers and sons [and] the
values a man should live by." Wain's weakness here, and
in all of his novels, is "he believes that values depend
upon cultural standards and are subject to time's changes.
Hence, he himself does not judge his characters' values."
In The Young Visitors, a personal monologue, both Elena and
Spade are stock characters. The message is that "personal
relationships are the most important forces in society.
. . . Wain fuses understanding and technique as he develops
the conflict between personal and social values." Lastly,
Wain limits the action and characterization in The Smaller
Sky, and because of this limitation and the montage tech-
nique, "neither characters, events, nor settings intrigue
the reader." His symbolism is interesting, but as in
Strike the Father Dead, "the message is not stated in such
a way that it affects [the reader]," although it is obviously important.

Concludes there are two reasons for Wain's failure to
achieve artistic success. To begin with, although he can
draw interesting eccentrics, "he paints most skillfully the
humdrum, everyday, ordinary sort of person; and these per-
fectly delineated characters impress [the reader] no more
than do their real-life prototypes." Secondly, as a serious novelist, too often Wain tries to satirize, exhort, and
even retreat all at the same time, and "his confusion of
purpose results in artistic failure." The essential problem, therefore, is that "only in parts do [his novels] con-
vince one that they should be novels rather than stories,
or poems, or even essays." Includes biographical details.
Excerpted: 1974.B23.

8   PRESS, JOHN. "The Movement and Poets of the 1950's," in his
A Map of Modern English Verse. New York and London: Ox-
ford University Press, pp. 251-52, 254.
Discusses the Movement and says that Wain's essay on
Empson was important, for Empson was one of the "formative
influences" upon the Movement. The younger poets were
quite ready to accept Wain's praise of the greatness of
Empson.

9   TAYLOR, JOHN RUSSELL. "Enter the English Stage Company," in
     his The Angry Theatre: New British Drama. New York: Hill
     and Wang, p. 36.
         In Look Back in Anger, The Outsider, and the "extrovert,
     disenchanted novels of John Wain and Kingsley Amis, the
     under-forty readers found a rallying-point [which] was to
     prove short-lived."

1970 A BOOKS - NONE

1970 B SHORTER WRITINGS

1   ANON. "Accomplished Carpentry." Times Literary Supplement
     (12 February), p. 151.
         Review of Letters to Five Artists. A hardly humble book
     of "empty sophistication." Wain has come far away from the
     "closely argued Empsonian density" of his beginnings. This
     book has "the kind of flatness which [one] associate[s]
     with poetry designed . . . as a vehicle for major state-
     ments."

2   ANON. "Non-Fiction." Kirkus Reviews, 38 (15 February), 233.
         Review of Letters to Five Artists. Wain develops "the
     telling tensions of opposites within art" in a book marked
     by "a strong aggressive line, a clean imagery and vigorous
     conception."

3   ANON. "PW Forecasts: Poetry." Publishers' Weekly, 197
     (6 April), 60.
         Brief mention of Letters to Five Artists. These are
     "mature and often affecting poems, . . . clearly and
     quietly written."

4   ANON. "Notable." New Republic, 162 (25 April), 26.
         Review of Letters to Five Artists. Wain plays both his-
     torian and lyricist at the same time. His rhetorical
     tricks are reminiscent of "middle MacLeish," but he likes
     iambic pentameter, "thereby demonstrat[ing] how un-American
     a Britisher can be."

5   ANON. "Rebel with a Small Cause." Times Literary Supplement
     (30 April), p. 471.
         Review of A Winter in the Hills. Wain goes farther in
     defining and developing his basic concerns as a writer than
     he has before, and he does so "with a growing maturity and
     conviction." This development is apparent in Wain's "new
     depth of observation and compassion," seen in his Welsh

1970

village characters. His violence is less crude, his humor
less farcical. His strength continues to be in his acute
observations of social situations, "catching hints of character and motive in conversational habits, contriving elaborate and efficient plots." As before, his theme concerns
"the quality of individual living." Although Wain is an
excellent storyteller--his narrative is "blunt" and "vigorous"--he does falter at moments of high emotion. At those
moments, a "wooden unreality descends when characters begin
to explain exactly, sincerely, what it is they feel." None
of this is fresh, but Wain is able to work his ideas into
"a mature scheme of social criticism."

6   ANON. "Fiction." Kirkus Reviews, 38 (15 June), 657.
        Review of A Winter in the Hills. "Wain, no more innova-
     tional a stylist than the material he uses, still keeps his
     story signally well sustained while juxtaposing man's in-
     dividual . . . existence against the encroachments of the
     century (bullying bureaucracy, greed, materialism, etc.).
     The novel has both stamina and sympathetic concern."

7   ANON. "PW Forecasts: Fiction." Publishers' Weekly, 197
     (29 June), 98.
        Review of A Winter in the Hills. Calls this a "lovely,
     wintry, leisurely novel. . . . Wales, its dying past, its
     stubborn people, its expressive language breathe and en-
     dure, an unadorned backdrop to Roger's contemporary
     dilemmas."

8   BERGONZI, BERNARD. "VII: Beyond Fiction?" in his The Situa-
     tion of the Novel. Pittsburgh: University of Pittsburgh
     Press, pp. 199-200.
        Brief mention of Wain's "masterly analysis" of Flann
     O'Brien's At Swim-Two-Birds. Wain views the novel more
     seriously than does Bergonzi, and effectively shows "the
     way in which it is about the culture and destiny of Ire-
     land."

9   BIRKINSHAW, PHILIP. "Poetry," in his The Thinking Voice: A
     New View of Poetry. Johannesburg: Witwatersrand Universi-
     ty Press, pp. 177-78.
        Brief mention of Wain's essay about the poet's relation-
     ship to the public in Preliminary Essays.

10   BRADBURY, MALCOLM. "Welsh Wain." New Statesman, 79 (1 May),
     632.
        Review of A Winter in the Hills. Finds a "sharp moral
     vein . . . felt with a fierce sense of liberal integrity."
     However, the "plotty narrative of action" results in a

"loss of symbolic density" and a gain in a "social and emotional density." The sense of actuality in the book is enough to give meaning to the emotional life.

11 BRICKNER, RICHARD P. "A War Has Many Battles." New York Times Book Review (13 September), p. 58.
       Review of A Winter in the Hills. As it develops, this novel is "real, funny, scary, fully vivid and appropriately charming." But by the conclusion, the novel has given up in "a shower of good-guy victories." Notes that Furnivall's speech at the end summarizes all of the conflicts in the book. The strongest point about the novel is that the suspense develops from its central situation.

12 BURGESS, ANTHONY. "A Sort of Rebels," in his The Novel Now: A Guide to Contemporary Fiction. Indianapolis: Bobbs-Merrill, pp. 144-46, 149, 153.
       Reprint of 1967.B8.

13 CAPITANCHIK, MAURICE. "New Novels: Saddest Story." Spectator, 224 (16 May), 652.
       Review of A Winter in the Hills. Although Wain's intentions are honorable, his style is "hackneyed." Finds unsettling the overwhelming sentimentality about Christmas, minority cultures, and cripples. Wain splits the characters convincingly into the good and the bad, but "because of Roger's basic sexual coarseness, the love scenes are embarrassing and coy." Concludes that the novel, on the whole, is "glutinous, verbose and fey."

14 FULLER, JOHN. "Abandoners." Listener, 83 (26 March), 413-14.
       Review of Letters to Five Artists. Wain's attempt to turn the artist back into a hero seems a mistake here. Finds that "the public and the private, the cosmic and the therapeutic, lie uneasily together." Rather, the value of the book lies in "the adroit procedures of the poems, the sensible details, the intermittent flashes of description and observation which alleviate the heavy contrivance which his notion of the long poem leads to."

15 LINDERMAN, DEBORAH. "Three English Novels." Nation, 211 (5 October), 313.
       Brief mention of A Winter in the Hills. "Everything ends much too nicely; at best, Wain is atmospheric about Wales."

1970

16   LINDROTH, JAMES R. "Book Reviews: Facing Our Sexuality."
      America, 123 (26 December), 568.
           Review of A Winter in the Hills. In place of his ear-
      lier comic extravaganzas, Wain turns to "philosophic depth
      and a firm belief in the individual" to demonstrate that
      "youthful anger can lead to the balanced reflection of
      middle age."

17   LOPRETE, JR., NICHOLAS J. "Fiction." Best Sellers, 30
      (15 October), 276-77.
           Review of A Winter in the Hills. Wain alternates be-
      tween comedy and compassion. His characterization--
      Dickensian in focus--is strong, but he is guilty of "utter
      didacticism." Although Wain has written superbly of his
      people, he should have avoided the "peroration."

18   MOON, ERIC. "Fiction." Library Journal, 95 (August), 2723.
           Review of A Winter in the Hills. Wain's best novel
      since his first. This is a book to read for fun, with its
      "humor, warmth, very clever changes of pace and atmosphere,
      characters who breathe reality, and a honey of a story
      line."

19   MOORE, REGINALD. "Out of the Cold." Books and Bookmen, 15
      (June), 43.
           Review of A Winter in the Hills. With a setting in
      Wales, Wain is departing from his first seven novels, all
      of which are set in the English way of life. Wain reveals
      his deep feelings for the Welsh and "the 'hard, old and ob-
      stinate mountains' that have shaped them," but Moore calls
      this a very "wordy and densely written novel."

20   NYE, ROBERT. "Setting up the Targets." London Times Saturday
      Review (2 May), p. iv.
           Review of A Winter in the Hills. An "irresistibly read-
      able" novel with heavy moral overtones. This is Wain's
      most substantial achievement to date. As a realist, Wain
      is "motivated by care about 'small' people and the way they
      live, whose care dares to find direct and unfashionable ex-
      pression." This "Dickensian warmth" carries Wain through
      the weak spots in the novel without serious mishap. How-
      ever, the literary satire at the end belongs to another and
      lesser book.

21   REGAN, ROBERT. "Poetry." Library Journal, 95 (1 May), 1749.
           Review of Letters to Five Artists. Although this book
      is less unified than Wildtrack: A Poem, both represent "an
      effort to produce poetry of some magnitude and intellectual
      solidity." Comments on Wain's "stylistic variety," which
      is achieved without shifting his tone abruptly.

22 ROBSON, W. W. "Epilogue: Literature Since 1950," in his
    Modern English Literature. New York and London: Oxford
    University Press, pp. 154-55.
        Wain's touch is "less certain" in his fiction than it is
    in his verse and criticism. At his best, he "catches some-
    thing of the blend of severity and tenderness that is as-
    sociated with Chekhov." Moreover, Wain is both a humorist
    and a harsh and somber observer, preoccupied "with what is
    enduringly English in a world of transient shams and
    illusions."

23 ROSS, MAGGIE. "Painfully Recognisable." Listener, 83
    (30 April), 592.
        Review of A Winter in the Hills. This is a "visual"
    novel, and as such it would make a good movie. Admires
    Wain's power to combine a large cast of characters into a
    convincing story that builds to a cathartic climax. Is ir-
    ritated by Wain's "inevitable philosophising." In spite of
    his sentimentality and over-explanation, the setting--"an
    integral part of the lives of its inhabitants"--saves the
    novel somewhat. However, the more Wain's characters are
    delineated, the less believable they become. "Perhaps
    without the weighty description and the sermonising, and
    with the dialogue starkly cut, the sticky cosiness would
    disappear, leaving intact the atmosphere which one feels
    the writer really intended."

24 S., P. H. "The Times Diary." London Times (2 March), p. 10.
        Announcement that Wain is working on a screenplay of The
    Smaller Sky because of the persistence of Piers Haggard, a
    young director who has wanted to film the novel ever since
    he read it in Israel three years ago. "'The idea immedi-
    ately appealed to me,' says Haggard. 'It is a very strong,
    simple fable and very cinematic. I could see it picture
    for picture. I feed John Wain images and he goes away and
    writes.'"

25 SISSMAN, L. E. "The Aftermath of Anger." New Yorker, 46
    (November), 204, 206.
        It is inaccurate to call Wain an Angry Young Man, for
    Lumley showed his disapproval of society by dropping quiet-
    ly out of it. Wain's comedy is "softer" than Amis', and
    there is a reduction in the element of farce in his recent
    writings. A Winter in the Hills, for example, is "a
    straight, traditional, old-fashioned novel of character and
    event." Obviously, Wain loves Wales and its people, but
    the novel suffers from a couple of flaws: (1) most of the
    characters are "unintentional caricatures," and (2) the
    moral judgments are "black-and-white," and this leads to

1970

sentimentality. Although Wain is a talented man, the
promise of his original idea has been "submerged by his
sympathy for and identification with the people of North
Wales."

26 SOKOLOV, RAYMOND A. "Welsh Rarebit." Newsweek, 76 (14 September), 110.
    Review of A Winter in the Hills. Calls Wain a conserva-
tive of basic values. His new novel "is an unashamedly
romantic, heroic, plot-heavy, character-ridden, warm piece
of narration with a beginning, a middle, and an end."

27 STANFORD, DEREK. "Private Lives in Public." Books and Bookmen, 15 (February), 32.
    Review of Letters to Five Artists. Wain's verse is
marked by a "new maturity, with fullness of content and
richer feeling-tone." He has left behind the old provincialism and "paraded toughness" of the Movement to engage
the "literary integration of Europe, in imaginative terms."
Wain's theme--the relationship between art and life--shows
a fresh awareness of the influence of environment. It also
demonstrates that Wain "is responsible in an altogether new
way to what we once called Nature, which used to be one of
his blind spots."

28 WADE, ROSALIND. "Quarterly Fiction Review." Contemporary
Review, 217 (July), 43-44.
    Review of A Winter in the Hills. Calls this a "long,
capacious novel" in which Wain puts to use all of his pow-
ers of observation and narrative experience. Apparently
his early farcical characters have matured, "deepening in
the process to embrace subtle comedy and, on occasion,
pathos." Because of the length, Wain is able to develop
the characters and build up scenes and situations. Wain
contrasts passing seasons and the boundless seascape to a
setting which could easily have become drab and monotonous.

29 WALL, STEPHEN. "Love from Gwynnedd." Observer Review
(3 May), p. 34.
    Review of A Winter in the Hills. Although a novel "with
its heart in the right place," the poor writing doesn't
allow Wain to make the best of inspiration. It seems "too
dilatory." The sympathetic point of view toward Welsh life
lacks the intensity needed to make it "register sharply."

1970

30 WEBSTER, HARVEY CURTIS. Review of <u>A Winter in the Hills</u>.
    <u>Saturday Review</u>, 53 (19 December), 33.
        A much better novel than Wain's first, but no more than
    "mildly edifying entertainment." Roger is a "sympathetic
    if not deeply realized character." Parts of the book—such
    as Roger's loneliness and imperialism's cruelty—are valu-
    able, but the novel is marred by flat narrative action
    (like a combination western and sexual adventure), clichés
    and "showy phrases," and a lot that is "clumsily jointed."
    Wain's ideas are important, but he should have presented
    the themes "more engagingly."

31 WEST, PAUL. "Eisteddfodder." <u>Chicago Tribune Book World</u>
    (13 September), p. 15.
        Review of <u>A Winter in the Hills</u>. Finds that the central
    image is the setting of Caerfenai and the Welsh hills; this
    fact is similar to the central structural image of <u>The
    Smaller Sky</u>—London's Paddington station. Wain stresses
    the anthropological aspect of Roger's involvement with a
    small community; that is, this novel "does almost insidi-
    ously what Eliot summed up as dreams crossing and moments
    in and out of time: Roger Furnivall discovers the race he
    belongs to, as well as its breadth, its beginnings, its
    variety, and its frightful, arbitrary power for good and
    evil alike." Rhiannon dominates the novel more in repose
    than the other girl does in action.

32 _____. "Milch Poems, Mousse Poetry." <u>Chicago Tribune Book
    World</u> (12 July), p. 5.
        Review of <u>Letters to Five Artists</u>. Finds in Wain's cur-
    rent poetry some evocation of C. Day Lewis' middle period:
    "unstrident, of even consistency, and journalistic." The
    writing is slack, "diffuse and glibly undetaining." Com-
    ments on how odd it is to find Wain "confirming fustian
    with holy emphases instead of exploiting a word's new but
    ineffaceable significances."

33 WORDSWORTH, CHRISTOPHER. "Reflections from the Gutter."
    <u>Manchester Guardian Weekly</u>, 102 (16 May), 18.
        Review of <u>A Winter in the Hills</u>. Wain is clever and
    entertaining, but his Welsh characters are "stock" and his
    Englishmen "are the sum of their ravelled impulses not
    their characters. . . . That old dark magic certainly ex-
    ists, and the friendliness, given a decade or so to take
    soundings, but Mr. Wain seems in a romantic hurry."

1970

34   YVARD, P.   "John Wain: révolte et neutralité." Études
     Anglaises, 23 (October-December), 380-94.
          Although Wain has been identified with Amis, Osborne,
     and Larkin in the 1950s, they have little in common. Sees
     Wain as a severe judge of the world in which his heroes
     seek an escape to neutrality. Brief mention of Hurry on
     Down. (In French.)

1971 A BOOKS - NONE

1971 B SHORTER WRITINGS

1   ANON. "Fiction." Booklist, 67 (1 January), 355.
         Brief mention of A Winter in the Hills as a "pleasant
    story."

2   ANON. "The Case of the Casebook." Times Literary Supplement
    (30 April), p. 500.
         Review of Shakespeare: Othello: A Casebook. Wain's
    selection is "judicious." However, it is unclear that
    Empson's essay is only an excerpt, the notes to the intro-
    duction are inconsistent and unspecific, and the page ref-
    erences within the essays are not properly modified. Also,
    questions the use the book will be put to and Wain's motive
    for compiling it.

3   ANON. "University News: Oxford." London Times (25 June),
    p. 17.
         Announcement that Wain is to become the first holder of
    a fellowship in the creative arts at Brasenose College,
    1971-1972. "The conditions of the fellowship provide that
    the fellow shall continue his creative work and should give
    at least one undergraduate lecture or demonstration in each
    full term and should generally contribute to the life of
    the college."

4   ANON. "Language and Literature: English and American."
    Choice, 8 (September), 836.
         Review of A Winter in the Hills. Since his first novel,
    Wain's theme has not changed substantially. He still dem-
    onstrates an interest in the survival of marginal cultures
    and in details of the most peripheral people. More notice-
    able in his latest novel, however, is "the superb realistic
    treatment of the affairs of relatively unimportant people
    in order to add credibility and a sense of purpose to their
    lives." Calls this the "most important achievement" of
    Wain's eight novels.

5   ANON. "A Sense of Uneventfulness." <u>Times Literary Supplement</u>
     (19 November), p. 1439.
         Review of <u>The Life Guard</u>. The moments are not particu-
     larly memorable, nor are the characters believable in this
     heavily didactic novel. Rather, finds the characters are
     "figures of convenience, and the end seldom justifies the
     means." Except for "The Innocent," feels that "art wafts
     out through the window, with craftsmanship not far behind."

6   BRADBURY, MALCOLM. "Modernity in England," in his <u>The Social
     Context of Modern English Literature</u>. New York: Schocken
     Books, p. 29n.
         Refers to Wain as editor of the <u>International Literary
     Annual</u>.

7   GINDIN, JAMES. "Well Beyond Laughter: Directions from Fif-
     ties' Comic Fiction." <u>Studies in the Novel</u>, 3 (Winter),
     357-58, 362-64.
         Examines the "comic iconoclasm" in the works of Wain
     and his contemporaries. Wain exaggerates the uncomfortable,
     but beneath this comedy there "is a sense of the difficulty
     of survival, of the effort and consciousness necessary to
     preserve oneself in an intrusive and demanding world." In
     Wain's recent fiction, one finds that the characters are
     far more responsible for their own discomfort, and the
     theme of human dignity is applied to wider areas of expe-
     rience. Moreover, the characters become less passive, and
     the comedy becomes less provincial. As Wain's fiction be-
     comes "less sheltered, less wrapped in the defensiveness of
     a comic and iconoclastic stance, the fiction has increas-
     ingly acknowledged the existence of violence both individ-
     ually and socially."

8   HAMILTON, IAN. "The Making of the Movement." <u>New Statesman</u>,
     81 (23 April), 570-71.
         The Movement was a "concerted reaction against the
     tangled and pretentious neoromanticism of the postwar
     years." Wain's "Reason for not Writing Nature Poetry,"
     "Who Speaks My Language," and "Eighth Type of Ambiguity"
     are "mini-polemics against the standard romantic postures
     of the Forties." Reprinted: 1973.B13.

9   JONES, D. A. N. "Give and Take." <u>Listener</u>, 86 (18 November),
     697.
         Review of <u>The Life Guard</u>. The story about the artist's
     model is not very funny, but "it tries hard." The story of
     the old actor is "miserable." And, in the story about mal-
     ice among schoolchildren, Wain "seems over-determined to

1971

avoid sentimentality about children." The other three stories "succeed very well in conveying a sensation of physical fear while motoring, swimming or driving a tractor."

10   JORDAN, CLIVE. "Mini-Briefs." New Statesman, 82 (5 Novem-
       ber), 625.
          Review of The Life Guard. Finds the prose "simple and
       colloquial" with a sense of life "seen from the outside, of
       subjects chosen, not choosing themselves." The one excep-
       tion is "The Innocent." Here at last is "an obsessive,
       personal feeling."

11   KUNA, F. M. "Current Literature 1970: II. New Writing:
       Fiction." English Studies, 52 (March), 476-77.
          Review of A Winter in the Hills. Wain combines the tra-
       ditional techniques of the realistic novel with a "mix of
       lyricism, melodrama and firm plot-outline with the typical
       behaviourisms and speech-inflections of contemporary peo-
       ple." The novel is pervaded by "a warm humanism" and a
       "web of symbolism." The reader will readily identify with
       the book, for it is "thoroughly contemporary."

12   LEVERENZ, VERGENE F. "John Barrington Wain," in Encyclopedia
       of World Literature in the Twentieth Century. Vol. 3. Ed-
       ited by Wolfgang Bernard Fleischmann. New York: Frederick
       Ungar, p. 484.
          Brief biographical notes, including Wain's connection
       with the Angry Young Men, his predominant themes, and a
       listing of primary works up to 1967.

13   McLEVIE, ELAINE M. "The Hero in the Post World War II Novel:
       Some Differences of Concept in the Works of English and
       American Novelists." Dissertation. Michigan State Uni-
       versity.
          Mentions Wain as following a pattern found in the works
       of Greene, Sillitoe, and Durrell. That is, sees in the
       hero his ability to "draw others to him in love or admira-
       tion, his awareness of his place in society, and his aim to
       discover himself in terms of that society or a manifesta-
       tion of that society which he will work to bring about."

14   MAHOOD, M. M. "A Shakespeare for All Seasons." Encounter, 37
       (December), 61.
          Brief review of Shakespeare: Othello: A Casebook.
       "John Wain surveys the findings and adds some aperçus of
       his own in a crisp and lively introduction."

15   MAY, DERWENT. "Never Knowingly Understated." <u>Observer</u>
       (7 November), p. 34.
          Brief review of <u>The Life Guard</u>. A "workaday collection"
       which, at best, is "a rough guide to a few contemporary
       goings-on." Wain's satire is "neither genial enough nor
       sharp enough."

16   P., J. K. "John (Barrington) Wain," in <u>The Penguin Companion
       to English Literature</u>. Edited by David Daiches. New York:
       McGraw Hill, p. 537.
          Brief biographical mention with a listing of Wain's
       poetry to 1965, novels and short stories to 1966, and
       critical essays to 1964. Comments on the picaresque
       qualities in <u>Hurry on Down</u>.

17   RIES, LAWRENCE R. "The Response to Violence in Contemporary
       British Poetry." Dissertation. Southern Illinois Uni-
       versity.
          As a neohumanist, Wain, like Peter Porter, Peter Red-
       grave, and George MacBeth, has not made as deep a commit-
       ment to the study of violence as have Sylvia Plath, David
       Gunn, and Ted Hughes. Wain and the others insist on "the
       dehumanizing quality of violence and see it as their duty
       to warn the public of the dangers of violence." This is a
       weak response, because "their prejudging of the issue pre-
       vents the neohumanists from examining the violence of their
       world with honesty and openness. Indeed, their timidity of
       response is perhaps one of the most damaging effects of the
       violence of the age." Reprinted with additions: 1977.B7.

18   SHRAPNEL, NORMAN. "At Short Range." <u>Manchester Guardian
       Weekly</u>, 105 (13 November), 19.
          Brief mention of <u>The Life Guard</u>. Wain's "concentrated
       realism of style makes him good on themes of physical and
       mechanical crisis, but he is most telling when the confi-
       dence dulls or cracks into a note of loss."

19   WILLIAMS, DAVID. "A Most Enjoyable Volume." London <u>Times</u>
       (4 November), p. 14.
          Review of <u>The Life Guard</u>. "These show him as a writer
       of wide-ranging sympathy, technically most adroit, whose
       work even at its least successful never fails for lack of
       lucidity or intelligence." Doubts the melodramatic title
       story, for Agnes seems to belong to a different story.
       Wain is not persuasive about her. His sense of comedy is
       strong, especially in "You Could" and the last story, a
       novella.

1971

20   ZAVARZADEH, MAS'UD. "Anti-Intellectual Intellectualism in the
      Postwar English Novel." <u>Ball State University Forum</u>, 12
      (Autumn), 68.
           Both Wain and Amis rejected literary modernism to pro-
      mote "the cause of simple, straightforward, and essentially
      premodern writing." <u>Hurry on Down</u> was one of several nov-
      els to strike "a new note in the anti-modernist movement"
      in English literature. Both Wain's novel and Amis' <u>Lucky
      Jim</u> are noteworthy for being among the first to manifest
      the new postwar sensibility--a "cultivated Philistinism,"
      and a "deliberately anti-intellectual approach to life and
      literature." To develop his alienated hero, Wain took "the
      working-class attitudes and values, stylized them, and used
      them as a sort of persona, a defensive shield," out of
      which emerged a new life-style and a new morality.

<u>1972 A BOOKS - NONE</u>

<u>1972 B SHORTER WRITINGS</u>

1   ADELMAN, IRVING and RITA DWORKIN. "John Wain," in their <u>The
      Contemporary Novel: A Checklist of Critical Literature on
      the British and American Novel Since 1945</u>. Metuchen, New
      Jersey: The Scarecrow Press, pp. 528-30.
           Listing of primary and secondary sources from <u>Hurry on
      Down</u> through <u>A Traveling Woman</u>.

2   ANON. "Fiction." <u>Kirkus Reviews</u>, 40 (15 January), 97.
           Review of <u>The Life Guard</u>. The point made by these situ-
      ation stories is self-evident and made "effortlessly rather
      than incisively." Wain suggests a mood in each (a little
      terror, sadness, humor, or cynicism), but does not extend
      himself in any way.

3   ANON. "PW Forecasts: Fiction." <u>Publishers' Weekly</u>, 201
      (24 January), 57.
           Review of <u>The Life Guard</u>. All seven stories lead to
      "turning points, a place where something has been accom-
      plished, [and] will not need to happen again." In "A Man
      in a Million," the reader laughs and mourns at the same
      time; he also rejoices at Wain's "sharp and wicked eye for
      the absurdity of all poseurs, of ourselves as role players."

4   ANON. "Briefly Noted: Fiction." <u>New Yorker</u>, 48 (13 May),
      146.
           Review of <u>The Life Guard</u>. Calls this a "well-made but
      rather sour little book." In "A Man in a Million," the
      hero is ridiculed to the point that the reader expects the
      story to deflate itself, but it never does.

1972

5   ANON. "The Pagan Roots." <u>Times Literary Supplement</u>
        (22 September), p. 1112.
            Review of <u>Interpretations</u>. Announcement of the second
        edition with a new introduction. Says the essays are still
        "obdurately polemical and egocentric: exhilarating, but
        useful for parenthetical insights only."

6   BAYLEY, JOHN. "Common Sense and the Common Reader." <u>New</u>
        <u>Statesman</u>, 84 (24 November), 777-78.
            Review of <u>A House for the Truth</u>. Wain has the advantage
        of being a novelist and poet; therefore, he can discuss
        literature as a fellow-craftsman, "without the intervention
        of a critical persona." These essays are excellent because
        Wain gives his perception of truth directly and simply.
        Wain shows enthusiasm for the way the author's work was
        written. He wants to share this pleasure.

7   BRADBURY, MALCOLM. "The Novel," in <u>The Twentieth Century</u>
        <u>Mind: History, Ideas, and Literature in Britain</u>. Vol. 3.
        Edited by C. B. Cox and A. E. Dyson. New York and London:
        Oxford University Press, pp. 331, 341.
            One main stream of the postwar English novel is "social
        documentary," often from the perspective of a lower-middle-
        class or working-class individual. This perspective is
        seen in the novels of Wain and others. Next to Amis, Wain
        is "a more irritably ironic novelist." In many ways he has
        a much more "traditionally liberal sense of the private in-
        tegrity that must be preserved against the explored social
        world." Wain is adept at evoking the moral confusion of a
        changing society, but is often thin and melodramatic in
        his sense of moral evil.

8   BRICKNER, RICHARD P. "Two in the Modern Tradition." <u>New</u>
        <u>Leader</u>, 55 (15 May), 23.
            Review of <u>The Life Guard</u>. Wain is very good at render-
        ing panic in the title story. Calls it a complete story
        with excitement and subtleties, "resolved in resounding
        dilemma." The ending to "While the Sun Shines" involves "a
        tainted moral victory with repercussions that extend the
        story outside itself in time." Moreover, Wain is casual
        in a fine sense: "His natural narrative voice has tricks
        down its throat that are as surprising as men and women
        are." Wain satisfies the reader's need for tension, for
        unforeseen predictability, and for "reverberant resolu-
        tion." In the other stories, however, Wain is too casual,
        too slight (as he is in <u>A Winter in the Hills</u>) to keep the
        reader interested.

1972

9 BROWN, F. J. "Fiction." <u>Books and Bookmen</u>, 17 (January), 58.
      Review of <u>The Life Guard</u> with plot summaries. "Altogether, John Wain has maintained his usual high standards in this new collection."

10 CASEY, JOHN. "House upon Sand." <u>Spectator</u>, 229 (4 November), 716.
      Review of <u>A House for the Truth</u>. Although Wain demonstrates a broad range of interests, the collection is a disappointment. He mixes social comment with literary criticism in a cliché-ridden ramble through his latest reading.

11 COX, C. B. and A. E. DYSON, eds. "Literary Criticism," in <u>The Twentieth Century Mind: History, Ideas, and Literature in Britain</u>. Vol. 3. New York and London: Oxford University Press, p. 462.
      Brief mention of Wain as critic. "Among critics in the humanist tradition, John Wain . . . has written lucidly and persuasively in support of the supreme value of literature."

12 DIXON, TERRELL F. "The Use of Literary History in <u>Hurry on Down</u>." <u>Notes on Contemporary Literature</u>, 2 (March), 6-7.
      Sees Edwin Froulish as the hero who attempts to find himself through literary history. Starts by trying to write modern, experimental works, rejects the Victorian style, and eventually feels at home with the Romantics and eighteenth-century picaresque hero. Along with this he develops an awareness and acceptance of himself.

13 FRASER, G. S. "Cultural Nationalism in the Recent English Novel," in <u>The Cry of Home: Cultural Nationalism and the Modern Writer</u>. Edited by H. Ernest Lewald. Knoxville: University of Tennessee Press, pp. 25-28, 37.
      Both <u>Hurry on Down</u> and <u>Lucky Jim</u> raised serious questions about class structure in England. Finds less control over emotion and impulse and more concern with conscience and doubt, as these novels question the traditional pattern of English life. Some biographical details.

14 GINDIN, JAMES. "John Wain," in <u>Contemporary Novelists</u>. Edited by James Vinson. New York: St. Martin's Press, pp. 1289-93.
      Discussion of Wain's developing themes, comedy, characterization, and structure. Includes a listing of primary sources. Reprinted with additions: 1976.B7.

15 HAMILTON, IAN. "The Making of the Movement," in British
      Poetry Since 1960: A Critical Survey. Edited by Michael
      Schmidt and Grevel Lindop. Oxford: Carcanet Press,
      pp. 70-73.
          Reprint of 1971.B8. Reprinted: 1973.B13.

16 KUNA, F. M. "Current Literature 1971: II. New Writing:
      Fiction." English Studies, 53 (April), 479-80.
          Review of The Life Guard. Wain is able to find meaning
      in a variety of plots. He is a sort of "moral pointillist."
      Even in his novels, there is a sense that they are composed
      of a series of "converging stories." Some of Wain's favor-
      ite preoccupations are highlighted in this collection:
      (1) people pushing themselves to the limits of their moral
      and physical strength; (2) "problems of adjustment after a
      crisis"; (3) "social and intellectual rat-race in a terri-
      tory where literature, journalism, sex and money combine to
      an odd confrontation in the thicket of the human jungle."

17 LEVIN, MARTIN. "New and Novel." New York Times Book Review
      (19 March), p. 41.
          Review of The Life Guard. In spite of the role changes
      in these stories, human frailties remain constant. Wain is
      no longer angry. Now, through a spokesman, he is "cluck-
      clucking and tut-tutting, like an élitist, at the new
      existential establishment of proles and young folks." How-
      ever, the "old Wain" comes through in "Wait Till the Sun."

18 MANO, D. KEITH. "Fiction." National Review, 24 (9 June),
      646.
          Review of The Life Guard. The first three stories are
      Wain's best, for events happen with "terrific consequence"
      as a man is challenged by death in each. For example, "The
      Life Guard" is as dynamic and unresolved "as a bad dream,"
      leaving "residual morning tics of fear." "While the Sun
      Shines" is both "harrowing (in two senses) and triumphant,"
      and "The Innocent" is both "wistful and profound."

19 MECKIER, JEROME. "Looking Back at Anger: The Success of a
      Collapsing Stance." Dalhousie Review, 52 (Spring), 50-51,
      57.
          Seeks to explain the causes for the decline of the Angry
      Young Men by showing that both Wain and Amis portray anger
      as an incomplete approach to life. In Strike the Father
      Dead, Wain (like Amis in Lucky Jim) tries for a viewpoint
      larger than anger, seeking anger only as a phase in the
      hero's growth. The novel serves as "locus classicus for
      anger as both a generating force and a collapsing stance."
      Includes brief biographical details.

1972

20 OPPENHEIM, JANE. "Fiction." <u>Best Sellers</u>, 32 (15 June),
149.
Review of <u>The Life Guard</u>. Each story has "poignancy and
delicacy." Wain concerns himself with the realities and
frailties of life and with humanity's changing roles. Both
his characters and situations are real; "his people are
ordinary folk who learn ordinary truths."

21 OSTERMAN, ROBERT. "A Pair of Pros: Revelations and Surprises
Abound in Fine British Story Collections." <u>National Ob-
server</u> (24 June), p. 23.
Review of <u>The Life Guard</u>. Wain works indirectly, and
like a performer slips in and out of different roles. Like
Elizabeth Taylor in <u>The Devastating Boys</u>, Wain does not
strive for "electrifying effect." His stories are "artful,
not arty" in his concern with contemporary anxieties and
follies.

22 PENNER, ALLEN RICHARD. "Introduction," in his <u>Alan Sillitoe</u>.
Twayne English Authors Series, edited by Sylvia E. Bowman.
New York: Twayne Publishers, pp. 20-21.
Although Wain's Charles Lumley is angry, his anger does
not approach the quality or intensity of Sillitoe's heroes.
"Lumley most resents the boorish nature of 'the respect-
able,' those who 'wear a uniform' of purposefulness." His
is a rebellion against middle-class values.

23 SWINDEN, PATRICK. "English Poetry," in <u>The Twentieth Century
Mind: History, Ideas and Literature in Britain</u>. Vol. 3.
Edited by C. B. Cox and A. E. Dyson. New York and London:
Oxford University Press, pp. 398-99.
Typical of Movement poetry, "The Last Time" is distinguished by a clever play on the title, an easy movement
within a traditional meter, a serious feeling, and "utilitarian" imagery. Finds in many of his poems a Johnsonian
"general air of good sense, empirical temper, and a certain
unruffled pessimism." In his later volumes, he becomes
repetitious or unnecessarily experimental. Fortunately,
Wain has sought to break away from the standards imposed
by the Movement.

1973 A BOOKS - NONE

1973 B SHORTER WRITINGS

1 ANON. "Non-Fiction." <u>Kirkus Reviews</u>, 41 (January), 52.
Review of <u>A House for the Truth</u>. Wain's truths are
firmly founded in "tradition, continuity, totality." His

criticism is respectable because his values are respectable. Moreover, he is "pertinent, precise and instructive in the largest sense, reinvesting literature with both an urgency and a magnitude often overlooked in the '70's."

2   ANON. "John Wain joins Oxford poetry chair contest." London
    Times (11 April), p. 4.
        Announcement that Wain has come forward for election to
    the Professor of Poetry at Oxford, to join Hugh Sykes
    Davies, Stephen Spender, Dan McNabb, John Jones, George
    McAllister, Nigel Frith, and Francis Warner. Wain is spon-
    sored by Peter Levi and Philip Larkin, of whom he says:
    "'They are the poets I most admire and they have had a lot
    to do with my decision to stand.'"

3   ANON. "Commentary." Times Literary Supplement (18 May),
    p. 557.
        Commentary on the current Oxford Professorship of Poetry
    election and the addition of John Jones' name into the
    running.

4   ANON. "Commentary." Times Literary Supplement (1 June),
    p. 617.
        Wain is elected to the 27th Oxford Professorship of
    Poetry. This commentator objects to Wain's reaction to his
    election. "Photographed carousing in his garden with
    youthful admirers and looking cannily out from under his
    gaffer-style peaked-cap, Mr. Wain reputedly intends to con-
    tinue his 'informal seminars' in the Oxford pubs and, what
    is more, to waste one lecture a year discussing work sub-
    mitted to him by undergraduate poets." Had Wain been
    elected by the University instead, "we might perhaps be
    spared this strenuous informality--and with it this idea of
    poetry as just another of the things soulful and exuberant
    people get up to."

5   ANON. "Explicitness and Art." National Observer, 12
    (30 June), 23.
        Review of A House for the Truth. Like Johnson and so
    many other writers, Wain writes literary essays for the
    common reader, uncorrupted by literary prejudices. He pro-
    vides the intelligent nonspecialist reader with equally
    nonacademic criticism of books and their authors. Quotes
    from Wain's essay on the current epidemic of the obscene
    and pornographic in art.

1973

6   BRADBURY, MALCOLM. "The Postwar English Novel," in his <u>Possi-
     bilities: Essays in the State of the Novel</u>. London and
     New York: Oxford University Press, p. 177.
         Like a number of other novelists, Wain has a realistic
     manner "heavily concerned with making over into fiction the
     new social alterations and viewpoints of postwar Britain,
     often from a lower-middle-class or working-class perspec-
     tive."

7   BRENDON, PIERS. "Literature and Criticism." <u>Books and Book-
     men</u>, 18 (January), 100-101.
         Review of <u>A House for the Truth</u>. Like his namesake,
     John Wayne, this writer transforms his enemies into "malig-
     nant caricatures in order to shoot them down." Wain comes
     dangerously close, in his "puritanical and inhibitory" way,
     to the reactionary position held by Storm Jameson in <u>Par-
     thian Words</u>--that of "condemning the whole modern movement
     in literary experimentalism . . . especially when it
     touches on areas of sex and violence, on moral grounds."
     Questions the value of collecting these essays under one
     cover. However, in Wain's articles on Johnson's poetry,
     <u>Dr. Zhivago</u>, and Orwell, he is "a sensible and fastidious
     critic."

8   CAREY, JOHN. "The Gentle Art of the Dentist." <u>Listener</u>, 89
     (15 February), 218.
         Review of <u>A House for the Truth</u>. According to Wain, the
     status of imaginative literature is under attack. "The
     feeling that Mr. Wain enjoys a snarl shouldn't deceive any-
     one into thinking that his worries can be laughed off."
     Includes a summary of Wain's critical positions.

9   CARTER, ALAN. "The Breakthrough," in his <u>John Osborne</u>. New
     York: Barnes and Noble, p. 28.
         Brief mention of the meaninglessness of attaching the
     Angry Young Man tag onto Wain, Amis, Nigel Dennis, Os-
     borne, or Wilson.

10   DUECK, JACK. "Uses of the Picaresque: A Study of Five Modern
     British Novels." Dissertation. University of Notre Dame.
         <u>Hurry on Down</u>, <u>Lucky Jim</u>, <u>Under the Net</u>, <u>Herself Sur-
     prised</u>, and <u>Murphy</u> all employ the picaresque in the most
     traditional manner. The authors use the picaresque "to
     picture truths about mid-twentieth-century society and
     then to dramatize specific options to the chaos and mean-
     inglessness of the times."

11   GREFRATH, RICHARD W. "Literature." <u>Library Journal</u>, 98
         (1 March), 744.
            Review of <u>A House for the Truth</u>. A "curiously engross-
         ing collection" offering an intellectual change of pace.
         Wain studies literature from a "poetic and moral stand-
         point." The essays on Johnson's poetry and <u>Dr. Zhivago</u>
         are especially noteworthy.

12   HALSEY, A. H. "Professor of Poetry and the Social Order."
         <u>Times Higher Educational Supplement</u> (14 September), p. 2.
            Disagrees with Wain's diagnosis of the educational ills
         in English society as stated in "Swing High, Swing Low:
         Reflections on a Saturday Night Out" (<u>Encounter</u>, July,
         1973, pp. 3-12). Wain prescribes proposals for attaining
         a society more just, equal, and humane. Although Halsey
         agrees with Wain's ends in view and the means toward them,
         he disagrees with Wain's diagnosis. Wain suggests that the
         fate of the individual both materially and spiritually is
         determined by genetic forces and schooling. This is more
         than the evidence warrants, however. In Halsey's view,
         "the determining fates are more capricious and more envi-
         ronmental and consequently more complex and more amenable
         to social reform than Wain's diagnosis would suggest."

13   HAMILTON, IAN. "The Making of the Movement," in his <u>A Poetry
         Chronicle: Essays and Reviews</u>. New York: Barnes and
         Noble, pp. 128-33.
            Reprint of 1971.B8 and 1972.B15.

14   JOHNSTON, ALBERT H. "PW Forecasts: Nonfiction." <u>Publishers'
         Weekly</u>, 203 (12 February), 63.
            Review of <u>A House for the Truth</u>. Wain searches for
         "permanent values--human truth chief among them." Finds
         notable that Wain is concerned with "poetry's essence re-
         gardless of technique or formal vehicle."

15   KUNA, F. M. "Current Writing 1972: II. New Writing:
         Poetry." <u>English Studies</u>, 54 (October), 489.
            Brief mention of Wain's aspiration for clarity and
         "formal perfection" in his poetry. Says the Movement poets
         believed that "the time did not require new world-schemes,
         personal philosophies, or an indulgence in the symbolical
         or allegorical." Although the Movement's program sounded
         admirable enough, soon it consolidated into "a set of re-
         actionary beliefs."

1973

16   LEIBOWITZ, HERBERT. "Literary Odds and Ends, Fine and
       Failed." New York Times Book Review (29 July), p. 7.
          Review of A House for the Truth. A "modest, comfortable
       and generally well-proportioned, if old-fashioned," collec-
       tion. In these essays one finds "the thoughtful melancholy
       of a donnish humanist."

17   MUGGERIDGE, MALCOLM. "Books." Esquire, 79 (April), 10.
          Brief mention of A House for the Truth. These essays
       are well up to Wain's standards. The essay about his trip
       to Russia is "extremely funny and perceptive." Likes very
       much the article on Orwell.

18   SEYMOUR-SMITH, MARTIN. "British Literature," in Funk and
       Wagnall's Guide to Modern World Literature. New York:
       Funk and Wagnall, p. 131.
          Anthony Burgess was about the only critic to notice that
       Hurry on Down is "an inept performance, ill-written and al-
       most insultingly badly constructed." The subject matter is
       "fashionable" and "well-meant." His later novels are even
       less distinguished. As for his poetry, Wain has degenerat-
       ed because of lack of direction. In the short stories,
       however, Wain demonstrates some of the control so badly
       needed in his other works.

19   THWAITE, ANTHONY. "7," in his Poetry Today: 1960-1973. Har-
       low: Longmans for the British Council, pp. 38-39, 99.
          Wain has progressed from "metronomic Empsonian measures
       to free-ranging and sometimes garrulous inconclusiveness."
       Finds in Wildtrack: A Poem and Letters to Five Artists "an
       irritably impatient self-importance which lunges towards
       'major statements' without earning the right to make them."
       Wain's most impressive poems are still to be found in Weep
       Before God. Brief bibliographical listing through 1969.

20   YVARD, P. "Literature and Society in the Fifties in Great
       Britain." Journal of European Studies, 3 (March), 36-37,
       39-40.
          Wain, Amis, Braine, and Osborne show that literature can
       have a social, moral, and even metaphysical impact on a
       "disturbed postwar audience," at a time when most tradi-
       tional values were already being challenged. In Hurry on
       Down, Wain illustrates the difficulty of "a sound and ef-
       fective relationship between the individual and society."
       In Living in the Present, the reader sees the "classless
       hero in an uncomfortable social position suffer[ing] from
       a passive dejection." In Strike the Father Dead, hierarchy
       is rejected and the individual turns away from "the ruling
       structures of his everyday life and escapes, far from his

past and tradition." But the hero still falls under the
tyranny of a majority of people, and this "crisis of au-
thority is another illustration of the conflict between
the individual and society."

1974 A BOOKS - NONE

1974 B SHORTER WRITINGS

1   ANON. "Humanities." Choice, 10 (January), 1706.
         Review of A House for the Truth. Wain is not totally
     coherent with his theme--that all imaginative writing which
     resists artificial divisions into poetry and fiction is
     unified. Wain has outgrown the "'backslapping mateyness'"
     style seen in his earlier essays.

2   ANON. "The Doctor's Favourites." Times Literary Supplement
     (8 March), p. 244.
         Review of Johnson As Critic. As an introduction to
     Johnson's work, this survey is generally sympathetic and
     fair. Finds, however, too many mistakes and simplifica-
     tions; its editing is "slapdash in presentation." For ex-
     ample, Wain misquotes Johnson from his preface to the
     Shakespeare editions. Instead of "what I have here not
     dogmatically but deliberately written," it should read
     "what I have here not dogmatically but deliberatively writ-
     ten." Wonders how the reader can trust Wain to give reli-
     able text if he cannot get right such a famous phrase.
     (See 1974.B28 for Wain's reply.)

3   ANON. "Paperback Short List." London Sunday Times (2 June),
     p. 39.
         Brief mention of the paperback edition of A Winter in
     the Hills. Calls it "top-class Wain--funny, poetric,
     shrewd and irreverent."

4   NO ENTRY

5   ANON. "Non-Fiction." Kirkus Reviews, 42 (15 December), 1341.
         Review of Samuel Johnson. As an advantage over Boswell,
     Wain has the distance of time from which he can define the
     motivating psychology behind Johnson--"the imposing moral-
     ist, the rationalist, the lawgiver." This biography af-
     fords Wain the opportunity to lament the decline of values

and to defend the virtues of the literary life. "Wain is
an eloquent and astute critic whose enthusiasm is affecting
and whose work is every bit the measure of the man."

6 ANON. "Reason's Champion." Economist, 253 (21 December),
99-100.
Review of Samuel Johnson. In his presentation of Johnson as a great literary figure and a great Christian hu-
manist, Wain has written a "wonderfully satisfying and
uplifting book." He defends Johnson as a good man of
reason and makes a statement of his own views on the state
of society, a society which needs Johnson's qualities "ex-
hibited before it as an example . . . if it is to save it-
self from unreason." This is "a new and racily styled
account of Johnson."

7 BAKER, SHERIDAN. "Alive and Well: The Contemporary British
Novel." American Libraries, 5 (October), 488.
Brief mention of Wain as a "clumsy, even boring" novelist in Hurry on Down. "His first-person anti-hero reports
his tours down or up the social strata in an idiom never
fully natural or brilliant."

8 BUCKLEY, JEROME HAMILTON. "Later Novels of Youth," in his
Season of Youth: The Bildungsroman from Dickens to Golding. Cambridge: Harvard University Press, pp. 267-68,
327.
Stylistically, Strike the Father Dead seems at times "a
bit flat in its breezy colloquialism and overfacile in its
brash humor." Yet, Wain manages to sustain its theme and
bring it to a full resolution. However, the novel falls
short of being a full-scale Bildungsroman. More needs to
be told of Jeremy's early conditioning if his adolescent
rebellion is to be fully understood.

9 CAREY, JOHN. "The VAT of Human Wishes." Listener, 92
(21 November), 678-79.
Review of Samuel Johnson. Wain's lament about the hor-
rors of the twentieth century gives a clear sense of the
difference between him and Johnson. Carey disagrees with
Wain's judgments on Johnson as a literary critic (Wain ex-
cuses Johnson's blunders), as political thinker (Wain sees
him as far-sighted and consistent), and as a strong character (Wain de-emphasizes Johnson's sentimentality and "ti-
tanic aloneness"). Moreover, Wain avoids "the scorn with
which Johnson greeted human aspirations." Most appealing
is Wain's characterization of the various misfits Johnson
befriended. Obviously, Wain is attracted to Johnson as a
man and desires to share his friendships. Does find some

awkwardness in his handling of Johnson's masochism. "If
the general thrust of Mr. Wain's study is to rescue Johnson
from the status of lovable mascot, and reinstate him as a
human being, he must be granted a full complement of sexual
appetites, however 'degrading' they may seem."

10   CHALKER, JOHN. "A New View of Old Johnson." Times Education-
     al Supplement (20 December), p. 18.
          Review of Samuel Johnson. Johnson is presented to the
     modern reader sympathetically yet with toughness. Wain's
     hypothesis about Johnson is fashionable but of little use
     in his psychological speculations. Because the book lacks
     documentation, the reader will have trouble testing Wain's
     views. Hence, the good effects of the book will not be as
     far-reaching as they might have been.

11   FIRCHOW, PETER, ed. "John Wain," in The Writer's Place:
     Interviews on the Literary Situation in Contemporary Brit-
     ain. Minneapolis: University of Minneapolis Press,
     pp. 313-30.
          Wain comments on writers in England, poets in residence,
     the publishing business, the social problems dealt with in
     Hurry on Down, The Young Visitors, and The Smaller Sky, and
     his experiences in the Soviet Union. Also examines the
     relationship between the modern writer and his audience in
     England and the U.S. Includes a brief biographical sketch.

12   GALE, GEORGE. "A Great Hack." Spectator, 233 (30 November),
     704-706.
          Review of Samuel Johnson. There is much to be said for
     the picture Wain gives of life and times in eighteenth-
     century England. Although the book begins by irritating,
     it develops and builds to establish the magnitude of John-
     son, thereby "justifying its own weighty seriousness." By
     the end, the biography "is seen to be a very substantial
     work of synthesis, intuitive understanding and intellectual
     grasp." Beyond a doubt, the book establishes a "heroism"
     about Johnson.

13   GREEN, ROGER LANCELYN and WALTER HOOPER. "VI: Inklings and
     Others," in their C. S. Lewis: A Biography. New York and
     London: Harcourt Brace Jovanovich, pp. 145, 154, 156, 158.
          Says Wain creates the wrong impression of Lewis' coterie
     at Oxford in Sprightly Running.

1974

14   GREENE, DONALD. "Johnson without Boswell." <u>Times Literary</u>
      <u>Supplement</u> (22 November), pp. 1315-16.
            Wain recognizes and tries to convey "the deeply humani-
      tarian Johnson" in a biography which is "unpretentious,
      excellently written and highly readable." Wain succeeds
      in putting Boswell in the proper perspective and in using
      new scholarship. This is a much needed biography. In-
      cludes a lengthy discussion of the pros and cons of Bos-
      well's <u>Life</u> and a comparison and contrast of Wain's study
      to that of Joseph Wood Krutch. Excerpted: 1975.B31.

15   HODGART, MATTHEW. "A Thunderous Reverberation." <u>New States-</u>
      <u>man</u>, 88 (15 November), 702.
            Review of <u>Samuel Johnson</u>. Finds this unsatisfying and
      "massively padded with picturesque detail and leisurely
      comment." Wain is found lacking as a biographer. He might
      have omitted attempts to make Johnson relevant to modern
      life. Concludes that there is no need to write about John-
      son: it's all there in Boswell. Excerpted: 1975.B31.

16   KENNEDY, ALAN. "Conclusion: A Quick Look Around," in his <u>The</u>
      <u>Protean Self: Dramatic Action in Contemporary Fiction</u>.
      New York: Columbia University Press, pp. 272-73.
            Compares <u>Hurry on Down</u> to <u>Lucky Jim</u>, and discovers that
      Wain's sense of comedy and the potentiality of dramatic
      action is not as subtle as Amis'. Moreover, Wain's novel
      ends in despair, unable to transcend a rigid society. "The
      novel cannot progress any further because its metaphorical
      terminology is limited by the conception of 'role-playing'
      as something that can go on only inside society."

17   LONSDALE, ROGER. "An Incomplete Johnson." <u>Manchester Guard-</u>
      <u>ian Weekly</u> (7 December), p. 20.
            Review of <u>Samuel Johnson</u>. Wain's vagueness about minor
      facts limits this biography. Although his primary source
      is Boswell, his portrayal of Johnson is in many ways the
      orthodox one for our age. However, at times his sense of
      personal involvement with Johnson seems too explicit, and
      his use of Johnson to comment on the ills of the twentieth
      century is over insistent. The narrative is readable, but
      there are some "rather lumpy patches of background mate-
      rial" and the critical chapters are occasionally "unexpect-
      ed or limited in emphasis but lively and often shrewd."

18   MADDOX, DONALD L. "Perspectives on World Literature." <u>Books</u>
      <u>Abroad</u>, 48 (Spring), 426.
            Review of <u>A House for the Truth</u>. Wain's analyses are
      "superb," but his constant cries against the evils of the

twentieth century are redundant and bordering on hysteria. Summarizes parts I and II, and comments on Wain's "remarkable flexible" critical faculties.

19   MILES, ROSALIND. "Sexual Themes," in her The Fiction of Sex: Themes and Functions of Sex Difference in the Modern Novel. Barnes and Noble Critical Studies. New York: Barnes and Noble, p. 115.

Finds in the early novels of Wain, Sillitoe, and Braine a revival of the "free, clever, sensitive, resourceful young man fending off a dim, grim, suppressive female. . . . Any female, no matter how good or bad, is primarily a landmark on the hero's road to self-definition, and must never be allowed to get ideas above this station."

20   MORRIS, JOHN N. "John Wain's Samuel Johnson." Hudson Review, 28 (Summer), 279-84.

Review of Samuel Johnson. As suggested in the epigraph and confirmed in the text, Johnson "is at once more and no more than we are, he is our master, instructor and exemplar, and he is these things by right not only of his strength . . . but of his weakness." Wain thereby modifies the picture Boswell gives of Johnson.

21   MORTIMER, RAYMOND. "In Praise of Dr. Johnson." London Sunday Times (24 November), p. 38.

Review of Samuel Johnson. Accepting Wain's position as advocate and not judge--he has great sympathy for Johnson--the book suffers from too few dates and no bibliography. Summarizes the life of Johnson.

22   RATCLIFFE, MICHAEL. "Nourished in Dark Soil." London Times (21 November), p. 12.

Review of Samuel Johnson. Wain shows that the key to Johnson is his "vigorous Christianity," for he was a man who detested cruelty and injustice of any kind. This is far from a gloomy book. In Johnson, Wain sees epitomized the battle for reason.

23   RILEY, CAROLYN and BARBARA HARTE, eds. "John Wain," in Contemporary Literary Criticism. Vol. 2. Detroit: Gale Research Company, pp. 457-59.

Excerpted: 1962.B10; 1963.B20; 1967.B8; 1967.B14; 1969.B7.

1974

24   SALWAK, DALE FRANCIS. "Kingsley Amis: Writer As Moralist."
     Dissertation. University of Southern California.
         Brief plot summary of Hurry on Down and a discussion of
     Wain's relationship to the Angry Young Men and the Move-
     ment. Mention of Wain's friendship with Amis during their
     years at Oxford.

25   SOULE, GEORGE. "Reviews." Carleton Miscellany, 15 (Fall-
     Winter), 140-44.
         Review of Samuel Johnson. Unlike Boswell's Life, this
     is a sustained narrative. Wain's storytelling is excel-
     lent; his prose is plain and strong. Moreover, Wain tells
     the whole story and puts Boswell's account into perspec-
     tive, bringing to life many formerly shadowy figures in the
     process. However, a side of Johnson's life seems to be
     missing because Wain omits reflections on much of Boswell's
     material. Also, because Wain seeks to counter the clichés
     about Johnson as a reactionary, at times the picture of
     Johnson seems tailored for the 1970s. For example, he pays
     little attention to Johnson's admiration for London's com-
     mercial life. Concludes that "Wain is as strongly present
     as Boswell, yet his presence is as wise, lucid, judicial,
     reasonable, and sympathetic as the portrait of Johnson that
     he draws." Includes a memoir of a trip taken with Wain and
     family in Britain, and later during a press party celebrat-
     ing the publication of Samuel Johnson.

26   TADMAN, BETTY. "Witty and Wise." Manchester Guardian Weekly
     (22 March), p. 27.
         Brief mention of Johnson As Critic. Wain's study re-
     veals Johnson's "intellectual energy and the variety of his
     interest and knowledge." A sustained study of his literary
     criticism rewards by contact with a mind so "keen, wise and
     humane."

27   VANSITTART, PETER. "Radio: Be Alive." London Times
     (7 September), p. 8.
         Review of Wain's radio drama, Dr. Johnson out of Town.
     Wain chiefly treats Johnson's trip to Scotland, emphasizing
     "his grand sympathies, his concern for suffering."

28   WAIN, JOHN. "'Johnson as Critic.'" Times Literary Supplement
     (15 March), p. 265.
         Reply to 1974.B2. Is worried that the reviewer's com-
     ment may discourage prospective readers from buying his
     book. "I would be far from claiming that there are no er-
     rors in my book, but if they are all as insignificant as
     this one, perhaps intending readers need not worry." Ex-

plains the error by saying he took the quotation from the
second of two texts.

29   WEBB, W. L. "Spring Reading." Manchester Guardian Weekly,
     110 (19 January), 26.
         Brief mention of Samuel Johnson.

30   WILSON, ANGUS. "The Great Cham." Observer (24 November),
     p. 33.
         Review of Samuel Johnson. Wain's "loving biography" is
     written with good sense from a personal viewpoint. Wain
     credits Johnson's extraordinary achievements and corrects
     distortions. Using a few thematic threads from start to
     finish, Wain maintains a structure. Moreover, he shows the
     interconnection between Johnson's outer and inner lives,
     and shows convincingly how his conservatism "was shot
     through by a constant and intense compassion for the lost
     and the destitute." A weakness is found in Wain's attempt
     to use Johnson to comment on the contemporary world, for
     his lamentations get in the way of his account of Johnson's
     life. Also, Wain's lack of sympathy for Johnson's Christi-
     anity (because of the agonies it caused Johnson) leads him
     to a misplaced Freudian analysis to explain a trauma that
     is basically religious.

1975 A BOOKS - NONE

1975 B SHORTER WRITINGS

1   ANON. "PW Forecasts: Nonfiction." Publishers' Weekly, 207
     (6 January), 55.
         Review of Samuel Johnson. A fresh, insightful, sympa-
     thetic study in which Wain treats Johnson's anguish of
     spirit with both candor and tact. This biography of the
     man and his mind "bristles with shrewd assessments" of his
     writings.

2   ANON. "Classified Books: Literature." Booklist, 71
     (15 February), 592.
         Brief mention of Samuel Johnson. "Wain's exhaustive
     portraiture assimilates previously unearthed knowledge into
     an exact but invigorating life history."

3   ANON. "James Tait Black Book Prizes." London Times
     (22 March), p. 16.
         Announces Wain's winning of the James Tait Black Memori-
     al Book Prize for Samuel Johnson, awarded by Professor
     Fowler.

1975

4   ANON. "Language and Literature: English and American."
     Choice, 12 (July), 686.
          Review of Samuel Johnson. "Wain has achieved that great
     rarity, a colorful and trustworthy literary biography, com-
     prehensive in its sources, judicious in critical and humane
     judgment, and, above all, a work that captures the profes-
     sional dimension of its subject's life."

5   ANON. "Non-Fiction." Kirkus Reviews, 43 (1 July), 770.
          Review of Feng. Wain is far removed from the "contempo-
     rary British idiom" here. Even the subject of this anti-
     heroic epic is "archaic."

6   ANON. "Notes on Current Books." Virginia Quarterly Review,
     51 (Autumn), cxxxvi.
          Brief mention of Samuel Johnson. "A serviceable account
     of the life of Johnson which is notable less for new schol-
     arship than for its readable, unpretentious style."

7   ANON. "1975: A Selection of Noteworthy Titles." New York
     Times Book Review (7 December), p. 70.
          Brief mention of Samuel Johnson.

8   ANON. "Prize Collection." London Sunday Times (7 December),
     p. 41.
          Announces that Wain shares the Heinemann Bequest (Whit-
     bread Award) for Samuel Johnson with Robin Furneaux for
     William Wilberforce.

9   BACHE, WILLIAM B. "Recent Books on Modern Fiction: General."
     Modern Fiction Studies, 21 (Summer), 332.
          Review of A House for the Truth. In these essays, Wain
     is direct, lucid, and generous with his praise. The writ-
     ings on Orwell, O'Brien, Johnson, and Pasternak are "compe-
     tent journalism" only. His complaint in the epilogue
     against the intellectual and moral climate in Europe and
     America has been heard before. Unfortunately, although
     this essay has merit, it does not follow a "stronger,
     tougher book."

10   BASNEY, LIONEL. "Books." Western Humanities Review, 29
     (Autumn), 375-77.
          Review of Samuel Johnson. Calls this the finest popu-
     lar biography since Joseph Wood Krutch's in the 1940s. It
     offers "fresh insight" and "a personal perspective." Wain
     relies heavily on his talents as a novelist. His sympathy
     for Johnson is powerful, as is his "sense of milieu."

11   BOULTON, MARJORIE. The Anatomy of the Novel. London and
        Boston: Routledge and Kegan Paul, 189 pp., passim.
            Like Malamud's A New Life, Wain's A Winter in the Hills
        is a story of redemption. The structure suggests "the
        family hearth and warmth of heart," and the novel recounts
        Furnivall's developing responsiblity and affection. In
        Strike the Father Dead, all three characters have merit in
        their values. Pathos arises because although they are aim-
        ing for the good, they cannot communicate. Each character
        tells his story in a style suited to his "age, mode of life
        and attitudes."

12   BROWNJOHN, ALAN. "Hymenoptera." New Statesman, 89 (30 May),
        732.
            Review of Feng. Calls this a "bloated absurdity, a
        heavy-handed shot at an epic" loaded with banalities and
        errors of tone. The modern parallels are neither striking
        nor apparent.

13   BROYARD, ANATOLE. "Thawing the Monument." New York Times
        (13 February), p. 32.
            Review of Samuel Johnson. Wain's biography humanizes
        Johnson and pays tribute to his monumental accomplishments.
        Also, Wain boldly redeems Johnson's poems "from the charge
        of dullness." He creates a brilliant picture of eighteenth-
        century England. "Best of all . . . is its rendering of the
        melodrama, or tragicomedy, of the literary life in any age."
        Summarizes the contents.

14   CHAPMAN, ROBERT L. "What, No Effusions of Reverence?"
        Nation, 220 (19 April), 469-70.
            Review of Samuel Johnson. Recommends this book to new-
        comers and to those already familiar with the man. Wain
        calls upon his talents as a novelist and dramatist to give
        a detailed account of Johnson's life. Thus, the character
        seems to take over, as in a novel. Johnson begins as "a
        great man palatable to liberals," but by the middle he is
        "the last towering bulwark of European humanism."

15   CLARK, JR., LINDLEY H. "Looking Over the Year's Books." Wall
        Street Journal, 186 (5 December), 16.
            Excerpt: 1975.B27.

16   CLEMONS, WALTER. "Dr. Sam." Newsweek, 85 (17 February), 90.
            Review of Samuel Johnson. The prime merit is Wain's
        emphasis on Johnson as a writer. Finds annoying Wain's
        "rather fat prose, which might be described as Johnsonian
        vulgarized." Johnson is a moralist, but Wain is a moral-
        izer, and "his orotund pronouncements keep toppling over
        into abject banality."

1975

17   COOK, BRUCE. "In Praise of Dr. Johnson, the King of Grub
        Street." National Observer (29 March), p. 21.
            Review of Samuel Johnson. In spite of Wain's claim of
        kinship with Johnson, on almost every count Wain had the
        advantage over him. "Few writers have overcome as much in
        the way of adversity as [Johnson] did, and fewer still have
        achieved more." It is his personality, above and beyond
        his works, that ultimately attracts biographers and readers.

18   COSGRAVE, MARY SILVA. "Outlook Tower." Horn Book Magazine,
        51 (August), 404-405.
            Brief mention of Samuel Johnson with summary. Calls
        this an "engrossing, well-documented" biography written
        with precise, clear language.

19   CRONIN, JR., GROVER. "Celebrating the Arts: Critic, Novel-
        ist, Poet, Painter." America, 132 (10 May), 362, 364.
            Review of Samuel Johnson. Focuses on the virtues of
        this study by saying that Wain: (1) appreciates the
        strengths of Boswell; (2) acknowledges Boswell's relation-
        ship to Johnson and how that shaped Boswell's biography;
        (3) perceives and celebrates "the heroic dimensions of
        Johnson's struggles with himself"; (4) has found new facts
        and new material, thereby modifying the reader's picture of
        Johnson; (5) exposes many misconceptions; and (6) recog-
        nizes Johnson's remarkable poetic sensibility. All of
        these merits go to provide today's general reader with "the
        most reliable introduction to Johnson that has ever been
        attempted." Wain gets to the heart of the man.

20   DAMROSCH, JR., LEOPOLD. "Word Lover." New Republic, 172
        (15 March), 29.
            Review of Samuel Johnson. Wain understands that Johnson
        was above all a professional writer. He writes of the man
        with respect and love. He is excellent on Johnson's early
        journalism, his qualities as a traveler, and his Rasselas
        and Dictionary. Wain skillfully tells the story of John-
        son's life, but unfortunately ignores some important schol-
        arship. Less impressive is his treatment of Johnson's
        mind. The most serious defect is that he presents Johnson
        "sentimentally as a hero from the golden age through whom
        to strike at modern barbarism."

21   DODSWORTH, MARTIN. "The Old, Old Story." Manchester Guardian
        Weekly, 112 (26 April), 22.
            Review of Feng. A conventional treatment of the theme
        of power and the emptiness of power. Although his rhetoric
        is fluent, Wain never goes beyond the obvious. His writing

is cliché-ridden. Had this been set in the age of Hitler,
Stalin, or Nixon, the truths about power and sanity might
have emerged. But because the poem is set in the remote
past, they do not.

22 EHRENPREIS, IRVIN. "A Misunderstood Genius." New York Review
    of Books, 22 (20 February), 4, 6.
        Review of Samuel Johnson. Although a noble attempt,
    written out of the deepest sympathy and offering insights
    into Johnson's literary works, "a strong infusion of care-
    lessness, pedantry, and obtuseness spoils the book." Cites
    inaccuracies, generalizations, and misinterpretations as
    examples. Recommends a careful revision; in spite of all
    its defects, the biography has "extraordinary virtues."
    Excerpted: 1975.B31.

23 EVANS, MEDFORD. "De Libris." American Opinion, 18 (October),
    61-62.
        Review of Samuel Johnson. Wain's success with this
    book--in bringing Johnson to the moderns--"will be largely
    among those whose disillusionment with the arid skepticism
    of modernity has already led them to reconsider the claims
    of faith." Claims that a romantic age like ours cannot en-
    dure Johnson's piety, learning, and judicious charity.

24 FADIMAN, CLIFTON. Review of Samuel Johnson. Book-of-the-
    Month Club News (Spring), 1-3.
        Wain's admiration for Johnson "endows Johnson with a
    lovableness, a personal charm, that is lacking in more ob-
    jective studies." Wain places in perspective Johnson the
    writer and Johnson the thinker in "a fine, transparently
    readable interpretation (if a little over-sympathetic) of a
    great and heroic character." Summarizes the contents.

25 FERM, DEANE WILLIAMS. "Reviewers' Choice: Summertime Read-
    ing." Christian Century, 92 (30 April), 449.
        Brief mention of Samuel Johnson. This masterpiece is a
    "treasury of insights that incarnates both the man and his
    times."

26 FREEDMAN, RICHARD. "Era of Experimentation," in his The
    Novel. New York: Newsweek Books, p. 123.
        Brief mention of Wain and Amis, both of whom were re-
    sponsible for bringing back to the contemporary English
    social situation "the earthy, lower-middle-class comedy of
    Wells and Bennett."

1975

27   FULLER, EDMUND. "Man of Letters--and Much More." <u>Wall Street
      Journal</u>, 164 (24 February), 11.
         Review of <u>Samuel Johnson</u>. Wain's contribution is the
      "skillful ordering" of existing scholarship, "his warmth of
      perception, and the balance of his appraisals." He excels
      in his discussion of the works and in the evocation of
      Johnson's personality. He gives the reader the whole man.
      "You will find no more 'grown-up' book, no deeper compas-
      sion and wisdom, no more edifying and ageless portrait in
      any work of this or many a season." Excerpted: 1975.B15.

28   GLICKSBERG, CHARLES I. "Various Aspects of Modern Nihilism,"
      in his <u>The Literature of Nihilism</u>. London: Associate
      University Press, p. 265.
         Cites Wain's review of LeClezio's novel, <u>The Flood</u>.

29   GREEN, MARTIN. "Biography and Culture." <u>Commentary</u>, 60
      (August), 75-78.
         Review of <u>Samuel Johnson</u>. Wain's biography is written
      within the English tradition of the intelligent general
      reader, to which Orwell, Leavis, Raymond Williams and Hod-
      gart all belong; that is, they "press the claims of old
      achieved values, popular as well as literary." This tradi-
      tion has found expression in Wain's novels, particularly
      <u>A Winter in the Hills</u>. Argues with Wain's conservatism,
      saying that it offers nothing exploratory or challenging.
      In the long run, it may arouse "restlessness." Is also
      disturbed by Wain's over-attention to Johnson's size.
      Praises Wain's vivid, strong, and original sense of John-
      son, his geographical and social contexts, and his easy,
      unaffected writing, but is left with the feeling of sad-
      ness, "not for Wain but for England. This is what the
      country has come to."

30   HAMILTON, IAN. "Interviews with Philip Larkin and Christopher
      Middleton," in <u>Twentieth Century Poetry: Critical Essays
      and Documents</u>. Edited by Graham Martin and P. N. Furbank.
      London: The Open University, pp. 244, 248.
         Reprint of 1964.B15.

31 HARTLEY, LODWICK. "Current Books in Review: Samuel Johnson
     vs. the Great Cham." Sewanee Review, 83 (Fall), cxvii-cxxi.
        Review of Samuel Johnson. Wain's failure to recognize
     the fact that a thoroughly researched book is readable to
     both the scholar and layman is the major weakness here.
     His book is lengthy and filled with "digressive tendencies,
     frequent banalities, [and] factual errors." Surveys cur-
     rent reviews and finds that not one of them is "penetrat-
     ingly analytical." Excerpt of 1974.B14; 1974.B16; 1975.B22.

32 HICKS, JIM. "About John Wain." Book-of-the-Month Club News
     (Spring), 4.
        Biographical sketch, including facts about the writing
     of Samuel Johnson.

33 HILLES, FREDERICK W. "Old Wine in New Bottles." Yale Review,
     64 (Summer), 598, 602-606.
        Review of Samuel Johnson. Reviews Wain's interest in
     Johnson. Says his biography is better balanced than Bos-
     well's, for it brings the reader closer to the writer and
     succeeds in making him live for the reader. Recommends
     Chapter 23 as a sampling of Wain's admirable handling of
     Johnson.

34 HOMER, FRANK X. J. "A Spring Bookmark." America, 132
     (26 April), 318.
        Review of Samuel Johnson. Wain's admirable presentation
     conveys all of Johnson's energy and vitality. The reader
     is able to "sense the color of Johnson's age and especially
     of his beloved London of the mid-eighteenth century."

35 HOWES, VICTOR. "'Feng'--a Parable on Power." Christian
     Science Monitor, 68 (10 December), 35.
        Wain brings new ironies to a twice-told tale in Feng.
     Like Tom Stoppard's Rosencrantz and Guildenstern Are Dead,
     Feng singles out a minor figure to "refocus the tragedy
     that shook Elsinore."

36 MORRIS, JOHN W. "John Wain's Samuel Johnson." Hudson Review,
     28 (Summer), 279-84.
        Review of Samuel Johnson. The epigraphs and the text
     confirm that for Wain, Johnson is at once "more, and no
     more than we are; he is our master, instructor and exem-
     plar, and he is these things by right not only of his
     strength, to which his example encourages us to aspire, but
     of his weakness, upon which that strength practiced and in
     which we are joined with him." Wain modifies Boswell's
     picture of Johnson, and he offers him as "a focus of our

1975

moral sentiments." Moreover, Wain does three important
things well: (1) he dramatizes both the personal and professional Johnson; (2) he provides a "free-standing image"
apart from Boswell, with the best pages devoted to Hester
Thrale; and (3) he accounts for Johnson's writings and
sees them as episodes in his life. In all, he renders
Johnson "more actual" than other biographers.

37 MOSS, ROBERT F. "A New Boswell for the Doctor." Saturday
    Review, 2 (8 February), 25-26.
        Review of Samuel Johnson. Wain seeks to fill the need
    for a popular biography of Johnson; in doing so, he adopts
    a rather contemptuous attitude toward Boswell's Life. The
    weaknesses are a tendency toward "shoddy," fuzzy thinking
    and a mediocre style filled with clichés and sentimentali-
    ty. The strengths are a concise and convincing defense of
    Johnson's political attitudes, an honest appraisal of John-
    son's deficiencies, a successful dramatization of all
    stages of Johnson's life, and a confirmation of his place
    in English letters.

38 MUGGERIDGE, MALCOLM. "Books." Esquire, 83 (May), 16.
        Brief review of Samuel Johnson. Calls this a "well-
    written, affectionate, comprehensive book." Wain's atti-
    tudes are appealing in a time of confusion and torment.
    He offers an opportunity to compare the eighteenth-century
    literary scene to today's.

39 NICHOLLS, GRAHAM. "Smashing the Resilient Toby Jug." Times
    Higher Educational Supplement (10 January), p. 16.
        Review of Samuel Johnson. Wain's evocations of Lich-
    field, Oxford, and the world of London journalism shape the
    finest parts of the book. His love and enthusiasm for
    Johnson is "exhilarating and infectious." Occasionally the
    reader feels that Wain portrays Johnson as a "saintly so-
    cial democrat" who can do no wrong. Comments on a few
    textual errors.

40 NYE, ROBERT. "Samuel Johnson Biography: Roast Beef with
    Relish." Christian Science Monitor (29 January), p. 5.
        Review of Samuel Johnson. Notes that Wain's own writ-
    ings have some similarity to Johnson's, and perhaps this
    is the most important qualification for Wain to write a
    biography. Finds that Wain writes with sensitivity about
    that "odd mixture of normality and neurosis" in Johnson;
    although his writing is "more complex and interesting" than
    Boswell's, his style is disturbing, reminding one that Wain
    is Professor of Poetry.

41 OWEN, JOAN. "Biography: The Essential Fabric of a Special
    Life." Library Journal, 100 (15 February), 388.
        Brief review of Samuel Johnson. "Wain has a taste for
    the essential fabric and detail of this special life, which
    he tells richly, mingling dignity with compassion, humor,
    and a leavening of wry insight into our own sad times."

42 PADEL, RUTH. "Uncle to Amleth." Times Literary Supplement
    (26 September), p. 1080.
        Review of Feng. Wain rearranges Shakespeare's balance
    of "real and assumed madness" in this reinterpretation of
    Feng's love for the Ophelia figure. The main theme is "the
    sickness of the power-mad ruler." Says it is "pleasant to
    read, diffident, sad, sinister and thoughtful."

43 PICKETT, CALDER M. "Book Reviews." Journalism Quarterly, 52
    (Autumn), 564-65.
        Brief mention of Samuel Johnson. Although not a schol-
    arly book in documentation or tone, it is readable and
    succeeds in bringing Johnson, as a human being, closer to
    the nonspecialist.

44 QUENNELL, PETER. "Grub Street Sage." Washington Post Book
    World (23 February), pp. 1, 2.
        Review of Samuel Johnson. Disagrees with Wain that
    Johnson has been undervalued. Although Wain does not
    change previously held views of Johnson or increase admira-
    tion for his virtues, he does retell the story in "a thor-
    oughly readable and sympathetic style." His judgment is
    shrewd when he examines Johnson's personal problems and
    appraises his literary achievements. An uneven style is
    the chief defect. It is a style that "alternates between
    a decorative stateliness and an uncomfortable collo-
    quialism."

45 RICHARDSON, JACK. "A Rational Man." Harper's Magazine, 251
    (July), 87-90.
        Review of Samuel Johnson. Wain helps the reader to
    understand Johnson in the context of the eighteenth cen-
    tury. Wain increases the value of what Johnson achieved by
    stressing what he had to overcome--poverty, depression,
    lethargy. All of these barriers Wain understands as a fel-
    low writer. This is "a narrative of friendship." The
    reader feels the "human vitality" of the author and the
    goodness of the subject. Wain illustrates that the twen-
    tieth century suffers from a lack of Johnson's virtues, in-
    cluding common sense, moral courage, and intellectual self-
    respect.

1975

46   RICKS, CHRISTOPHER. "John Wain's Life of Samuel Johnson."
       New York Times Book Review (16 March), pp. 6-7.
           Review of Samuel Johnson. In this "noble story nobly
       told," Wain allows Johnson's words to speak for themselves.
       He does justice to the writer's range and depth. One of
       the book's strengths is the manner in which Wain takes
       well-known details from Johnson's life and sheds new light
       on them.

47   SAMPSON, ANTHONY. "Books of the Year." Observer (14 Decem-
       ber), p. 19.
           Cites Samuel Johnson as a "very stimulating, though
       often maddening" attempt to relate Johnson to contemporary
       problems.

48   SHORTER, ERIC. "Plays in Performance: Regions." Drama: The
       Quarterly Theatre Review, 119 (Winter), 65.
           Review of Wain's first play entitled Harry in the Night.
       Finds there is too much description and too little drama-
       tization in this work about "the middle-aged vexations of
       a provincial shopkeeper whose family life is getting on
       top of him." There is plenty of material here for a dozen
       plays. The play lacks dramatic coherence, and there is an
       "episodic monotony in its form." Concludes that Wain has
       a lot to learn about the differences between a novel and a
       play. "Let us hope he isn't easily discouraged. The best
       dramatists never are."

49   SMITH, ELTON EDWARD. "From Romantic Revolution to Welfare
       State," in his The Angry Young Men of the Thirties. Car-
       bondale: Southern Illinois University Press, pp. 146-48.
           Wain, Amis, Braine, and Osborne share "a vigorous and
       predominantly negative viewpoint that made them the most
       important literary phenomenon of the 1950's." Comments on
       Wain's life and the differences between the Angry Young Men
       of the 1950s and their predecessors.

50   STEINER, GEORGE. "Books: Bookmen." New Yorker, 51
       (28 April), 135.
           Review of Samuel Johnson. Wain emphasizes rightly both
       the "intrinsic quality" of Johnson's moral essays and po-
       etry and the role they have played in American and British
       style. Dislikes the few serious errors in details, the
       banalities, and the lopsided treatment of Johnson's life.
       Says the earlier years are developed in detail, but then
       Wain speeds by the latter portions of his life and only
       glances at "key relations." Moreover, Wain treats super-
       ficially Johnson's place in the "history of religious

feeling" and in the development of a "potentially neurotic
inwardness." Praises Wain's readable style, his "pride and
delight" in Johnson, his "acute touch for the graphic oddi-
ty," and his "alertness to continuity [which] is the psychological mainspring of the work."

51   TRACY, CLARENCE. "Reviews: Samuel Johnson." University of
       Toronto Quarterly, 44 (Spring), 260-61.
             Because of Wain's particular qualifications, this is the
       best modern general study of Johnson and his writings.
       Wain contributes not facts but understanding. He looks be-
       hind the facts for motives and feelings. Moreover, he sur-
       passes Boswell with his insights into Johnson's early years,
       and gives valuable new emphasis to Johnson's Journey to the
       Western Islands of Scotland. "He has presented Johnson to
       us not as a museum specimen but as a living voice well
       worth listening to even two centuries later."

52   WILLIAMSON, JR., CHILTON. "A Tory for Our Time." New Leader,
       58 (7 July), 21-22.
             Review of Samuel Johnson. Wain's purpose is to show
       Johnson's was a "humane Toryism," and to prove that his
       Toryism reflected his clarity of thought. Johnson's aim
       was to distinguish between the real and the unreal, the
       genuine and the imagined. Finds it pleasant to follow "an
       intelligent man as he descants on a genius who has contrib-
       uted to the art of his own thinking."

53   YODER, JR., EDWIN M. "Dr. Johnson's Luminosity." National
       Review, 27 (25 April), 461-62.
             Review of Samuel Johnson. Johnson is more believable to
       the twentieth century because Wain successfully portrays
       Johnson's strengths and weaknesses. Calls Wain "a curious-
       ly diffident biographer."

1976 A BOOKS - NONE

1976 B SHORTER WRITINGS

1   ANON. "Short List." London Sunday Times (11 April), p. 39.
           Review of Johnson on Johnson. Finds in this collection
       a wise introduction, illuminating commentary, and an adept
       selection. It reads almost as smoothly as a Johnson auto-
       biography. Comparable in editing and interpretation to
       Boswell's Life.

1976

2   ANON. "Briefly Noted: General." New Yorker, 52 (24 May), 154.
    Brief mention of Johnson on Johnson together with a summary of the contents. Especially impressive is one's realization of how well Johnson's prose has survived.

3   ANON. "Paperbacks: Nonfiction Reprints." Publishers' Weekly, 209 (7 June), 73.
    Review of the paperback edition of Samuel Johnson. Wain addresses himself to the intelligent general reader. He aims to portray the "essential Johnson" and to correct misconceptions of him.

4   BAIRD, A. J. "Doctored Prose." Times Educational Supplement (12 August), p. 23.
    Brief mention of A Visit at Tea-Time and Manhood. Says this is a simplified version of a difficult text.

5   BANERJEE, A. "The Pre-War Poetic Scene," in his Spirit Above Wars: A Study of the English Poetry of the Two World Wars. London and Basingstoke: The MacMillan Press, pp. 7-8.
    Wain and John Press assert that the Georgian poets are rebels against the poetry of the 1890s and the Imperialists.

6   CARNIE, R. H. "Book Reviews." Ariel, 7 (April), 81-83.
    Review of Johnson As Critic and Samuel Johnson. Wain's love for his subject is both the strength and the weakness of his biography. Some of the more disturbing elements in Johnson's personality are played down. Wain is at his best when he extols the finer sides of Johnson's moral thinking. However, he finds Boswell "more dramatic." Wain's criticism of Johnson as a writer shares qualities with Johnson's own criticism, for "it concentrates on essentials, it quotes and summarizes successfully, and is lucid and pleasant to read." Both books feature a "genuine modesty of the hidden scholarship."

7   GINDIN, JAMES. "John Wain," in Contemporary Novelists. Edited by James Vinson. London: St. James Press, pp. 1419-22.
    Reprint, with expanded comments on more recent works, of 1972.B14.

8   HALEY, WILLIAM. "Library for the Common Man." London Times (29 April), p. 13.
    Review of Johnson on Johnson. This collection reveals there was far more to Johnson than "bluntness and common sense." In this mosaic, the man emerges slowly but clearly.

It is not an egocentric book. Finds Wain's introduction
and linking passages "succinct and not obtrusive."

9   McVEIGH, TERRENCE A. "Biography." <u>Best Sellers</u>, 36 (August),
    160-61.
        Review of <u>Johnson on Johnson</u>. This is an unsuccessful
    attempt at creating a balanced picture of Johnson from his
    own writings, resulting in the reader concluding little
    about Johnson's attitudes. The selections introduce John-
    son as a warm human being, but Boswell and Wain in their
    respective biographies accomplish the same in "a more uni-
    fied, coherent, and satisfying manner."

10 OWEN, JOAN. "Literature." <u>Library Journal</u>, 101 (July), 1532.
        Brief mention of <u>Johnson on Johnson</u>. A delicately bal-
    anced selection enabling the reader to understand both the
    private and the public Johnson. Typical of Wain's "anti-
    pedantic approach to Johnson," the book suffers from lack
    of an index and bibliography.

11 PARTRIDGE, ERIC. "He's the Cham." <u>New Statesman</u>, 91
    (2 April), 440-41.
        Review of <u>Johnson on Johnson</u>. This selection is "at-
    tractive, erudite, appreciative and copious." Objects that
    Wain makes no reference to L. F. Powell in his recension of
    Birkbeck Hill's 1887 edition of Boswell's <u>Life</u>.

12 RABINOVITZ, RUBIN. "Iris Murdoch," in <u>Six Contemporary Brit-
    ish Novelists</u>. Edited by George Stade. New York: Colum-
    bia University Press, p. 282.
        Brief mention of Murdoch's affinity with Wain and Amis
    owing to their use of the picaresque tradition in their
    novels.

13 ROBERTS, JOHN J. "A Champion for the Cham." <u>Modern Age</u>, 20
    (Spring), 237-39.
        Review of <u>Samuel Johnson</u>. Unlike Boswell, Wain makes
    the reader intimate with Johnson. Although Wain's charac-
    terization of Johnson as benevolent is startling, the evi-
    dence is conclusive. Wain does much to restore those con-
    servative principles by which Johnson lived.

14 SAMBROOK, JAMES. "System within a System." <u>Times Higher Edu-
    cational Supplement</u> (28 May), p. 18.
        Review of <u>Johnson on Johnson</u>. This is a nice complement
    to Wain's <u>Samuel Johnson</u>. The introduction and linking
    commentary are "graceful, humane, sensible and unpreten-
    tious."

1976

15   STEVENSON, ANNE. "Claudius Speaks." <u>Listener</u>, 95 (15 Janu-
       ary), 60-61.
           Review of <u>Feng</u>. At its best, Wain's verse is powerful,
       particularly when Feng expresses a liking for animals.
       Finds a few "false notes" in the verse, and sometimes
       Wain's voice slips in, reminding the reader that Wain--and
       not Feng--is giving his impressions on sex or existential-
       ism.

<u>1977 A BOOKS - NONE</u>

<u>1977 B SHORTER WRITINGS</u>

1   ANON. "Poet and Prof." <u>Economist</u>, 265 (3 December), 149.
           Brief mention of <u>Professing Poetry</u>. Calls this "a curi-
       ous yet successful melange, a blending of seemingly incom-
       patible elements."

2   BERGONZI, BERNARD. "Poetry and Personality." <u>Observer Review</u>
       (20 November), p. 29.
           Review of <u>Professing Poetry</u>. Notes that it was an ad-
       miring essay on Empson, published in <u>Penguin New Writing</u> in
       1950, that started Wain on his career as a critic. In
       these essays, he ranges from "a deep love of poetry [to]
       energetic scholarship." His "bluff and breezy tone can
       sometimes seem insensitive, in ways that he certainly
       doesn't intend." At times his opinions become "hectoring
       and cantankerous."

3   BRADBURY, MALCOLM, ed. "Introduction," in <u>The Novel Today:</u>
       <u>Contemporary Writers on Modern Fiction</u>. Manchester: Man-
       chester University Press, p. 18.
           Says the tendency to associate together Wain, Amis,
       Braine, Storey, Wilson, and Murdoch as Angry Young Men--
       novelists of social realism--was far from accurate. This
       tendency totally confuses the significance of their subse-
       quent careers.

4   CONNELLY, JOHN L. "Softcover Selections for Seventy-Seven:
       History." <u>America</u>, 136 (29 January), 84.
           Review of <u>Samuel Johnson</u>. Wain locates "the sureness of
       [Johnson's] critical judgment" in overcoming enormous per-
       sonal problems. This is the "peculiar virtue" of the book.
       Paradoxically, Johnson turns out to be not only very sympa-
       thetic, but also "a very modern man."

5 HOMBERGER, ERIC. "The 1950s," in his <u>The Art of the Real:</u>
   <u>Poetry in England and America Since 1939</u>. London and
   Toronto: Dent, 246 pp., passim.
       Calls Wain, Larkin, Amis, Braine, Davie, and Osborne
   "sad hearts at the supermarket." Brief discussion of
   Wain's involvement with the Movement is included.

6 RABAN, JONATHAN. "Chaise Longue, Vita Brevis." <u>New States-</u>
   <u>man</u>, 94 (18 November), 693-94.
       Review of <u>Professing Poetry</u>. The lectures are as "inno-
   cent of purpose and direction as becalmed yachts in the
   Doldrums." For all his talk about maintaining standards,
   Wain is "a casual and sloppy critic."

7 RIES, LAWRENCE R. "John Wain: The Evasive Answer," in his
   <u>Wolf Masks: Violence in Contemporary Poetry</u>. New York,
   London: Kennikat Press, pp. 130-43.
       Wain, writing from the "neohumanistic conviction," seeks
   to rise above violence in the world, believing that "human
   goodness and love shall outlast violence and brutality."
   Wain believes the artist must not submit to the forces of
   destruction; if he does so, he is escaping from his artistic responsibilities. Rather, he must rise above the
   violence and "in this way withstand the onslaught of the
   darkness." Examines Wain's role as a spokesman for the
   neohumanistic position in his poetry and criticism, with
   emphasis on selected poems from <u>A Word Carved on the Sill</u>,
   <u>Wildtrack: A Poem</u>, <u>Weep Before God</u>, and <u>Letters to Five</u>
   <u>Artists</u>. Concludes that these poems are actually a means
   of escape rather than of confrontation. Wain does not try
   to come to an understanding of violence, and "it is this
   intellectual failure that precedes his poetic failure."
   Reprint, with additions, of 1971.B16.

8 WALKER, KEITH. "The Introspective Doctor." <u>Times Literary</u>
   <u>Supplement</u> (25 February), p. 218.
       Review and summary of <u>Johnson on Johnson</u>. Calls Wain's
   compilation of a life of Johnson mostly from Johnson's own
   works a "happy notion."

9 WILSON, EDMUND. "The Fifties: Edmund Wilson Interviews John
   Wain," in his <u>Letters on Literature and Politics: 1912-</u>
   <u>1972</u>. Edited by Elena Wilson. New York: Farrar, Straus
   and Giroux, p. 550.
       Lists a series of questions Wilson had typed out for
   Wain to answer prior to the interview. These questions
   cover the future of English literature, the question of a
   successor to John Masefield, the prestige of Eliot, the decline of Cyril Connolly's reputation, and the status of
   English culture.

INDEXES

Index to
Writings about John Braine

Index to
Writings about John Wain